The Gate City
A History of Omaha

The Gate City

A History of Omaha

ENLARGED EDITION

Lawrence H. Larsen

and

Barbara J. Cottrell

New conclusion by Harl A. Dalstrom

UNIVERSITY OF NEBRASKA PRESS

LINCOLN AND LONDON

⊜ The paper in this book meets the minimum requirements of American
National Standard for Information Sciences—Permanence of Paper for
Printed Library Materials, ANSI Z39.48-1984.

First printing: 1997
Most recent printing indicated by the last digit below:
10   9   8   7   6   5   4   3   2

Library of Congress Cataloging-in-Publication Data
Larsen, Lawrence Harold, 1931–
The gate city: a history of Omaha / Lawrence H. Larsen and Barbara J.
Cottrell; new conclusion by Harl A. Dalstrom.—Enl. ed.
p.   cm.
Originally published: Boulder, Colo.: Pruett Pub. Co., c1982.
Includes bibliographical references and index.
ISBN 0-8032-7967-1 (pa: alk. paper)
1. Omaha (Neb.)—History. I. Cottrell, Barbara J., 1936–   . II. Title.
F674.O557L37   1997
978.2′254—dc21
97-12743   CIP

Reprinted from the original 1982 edition by Pruett Publishing Company,
Boulder.

To James and Marian Cottrell

Contents

Illustrations

Preface

In 1854 promoters established Omaha at a ferry crossing in the then brand new Nebraska Territory. The city grew and prospered, overcoming periods of adversity, and by 1980 it was the heart of a metropolitan district of almost 570,000 persons. The rise of Omaha related to a number of regional and national developments: the construction of the first transcontinental railroad, the settlement of the Great Plains, the building of the meat packing industry, and the need for massive defense systems. Throughout Omaha's history, outside decisions have had a significant impact on the community. Local interests consistently welcomed outside public and private capital, while at the same time formulating policies designed to achieve economic independence and freedom of action. The successes and failures of Omahans in pursuit of these elusive goals are significant in the advance of the city to the status of a regional metropolis.

This book is an analytical urban biography. There are no lists of mayors or day-by-day chronological tables. Rather, we have written a synthesis designed to place the major events and decisions that shaped the city in historical perspective. Neither of us have ever lived in Omaha. It is not necessary to reside in a city to study it. We neither solicited nor received any monetary help from any source in Omaha. Our interest in the city is entirely professional.

It is important that a modern urban biography be written about Omaha. It is not a "great city"—a Paris, Rome, or London, which radiates the humanity that holds the flame of high civilization—but Omaha has long been a significant part of the American urban mosaic. The creation of cities has constituted a major part of the national experience. It transcends many concerns traditionally pursued by historians, such as studies of influential urban political and business leaders. In the total sweep of urbanization, they played only small roles.

Billions of decisions contributed to the building of Omaha. We agree with a distinguished historian of the Cornhusker State, James C. Olson, who wrote in the preface of the second edition of his *History of Nebraska* "No one can be more painfully aware than the author of the difficulties inherent in trying to encompass the history of one of our states within the cover of one brief volume. Necessarily, much of interest and value must be omitted, and it is easy to find fault with the author's judgement in this matter." In our case, the statement applies to Omaha rather than to Nebraska as a whole. A large body of secondary and primary literature exists on Omaha. Indeed, there is so much material that a primary task of a researcher is to decide what is important, rather than to find new information.

So many people gave encouragement and afforded assistance that all of them can not be acknowledged. Needless-to-say, we appreciated their efforts. Specifically, A. Theodore Brown, Lyle W. Dorsett, and Fredrick Spletstoser read the manuscript for content. James and Marian Cottrell saved us from many errors. James C. Olson — on a pleasant summer afternoon in Columbia, Missouri — provided valuable background information. So did Garneth Oldenkamp Peterson, Edward Longacre, Michael Kinzel, and Donald F. Danker. Niel M. Johnson contributed in many ways, giving us access to his files and photographs on Omaha in the 1970s. People at the Nebraska State Historical Society were universally helpful: James E. Potter, Donald Snoddy, Penelope Chatfield, Marvin Kivett, John C. Carter, Sherrill Daniels, and many others. Of special note was Anne Diffendal's aid in directing us to newspaper and manuscript materials. Patrick Brunet and Melvin M. Bohn of the University of Nebraska at Omaha Library lent valuable assistance. The same was true of archivists at the Kansas City Archives and Records Center: R. Reed Whitaker, Alan Perry, and Robert Knecht.

Harl Adams Dalstrom, who has written much and lectured widely about Omaha, generously furnished material, answered many specific questions, and lent support in a variety of positive ways. He is a leading student of the community's history. Several of his colleagues at the University of Nebraska at Omaha also contributed: William Petrowski, Richard Overfield, and William Pratt. Many people at the University of Missouri-Kansas City supported the project, including Stanley Parsons, Louis Potts, Kenneth LaBudde, William R. Brazelton, George Gale, William Jones, Richard McKinzie, Richard Elrod, and James Falls. Roger T. Johnson of *Milling & Baking News* fished with us and discussed agricultural economics. Dean Eldon Parizek of the UMKC College of Arts and Sciences nurtured a scholarly environment. We wish to thank Dean Herwig Zauchenberger of the UMKC School of Graduate Studies and the members of the Graduate Research Council for a faculty research grant. We also acknowledge the help of Burton and Eva Jay in Omaha, plus that of Donald and Virginia Marcussen in Lincoln. Among other people who helped were Charles N. Glaab, Jesse V. Clardy, Christopher Schnell, Robert W. Richmond, Larry Remele, William Reid, Richard Lowitt, David Boutros, and Patrick McLear. Barbara LoCascio, Claire Hildebrand, and Elizabeth McIntyre typed the manuscript.

Of course (though both custom and prudence demand it be said), we are responsible for errors of fact or interpretation.

Lawrence H. Larsen
Barbara J. Cottrell

The Gate City
A History of Omaha

Part One

Omaha

Looking North West fr

1850-1870

1867

15th and Douglas Sts.

1

The Signal Station at the Entrance of a Garden

The nine thoroughbreds in the sixth race thundered around the final turn, fighting for position. As they surged into and down the stretch, the spectators rose to their feet. They were anxious to see which horses had gained good inside positions and if any might come up from the outside. In a blaze of silks and colors, spurred on by the roar of the crowd, the jockeys' whips cracked as their mounts drove toward the finish line. Golden Observer, which left the starting gate at odds of 3 to 7 in favor to win, held a place on the inside throughout the race. He proved best at the end of a long drive, crossing the finish line two lengths ahead of the nearest challengers, Royal Pinjara and Prairie Music. Within seconds, statistics on the big electronic betting board in the infield indicated the unofficial order of finish — number two horse to win, number eight to show, and number six to place. A couple of minutes later, the board flashed "official" and posted the tabulated pari-mutuel results: $8.00 to win, $4.40 to place, and $3.20 to show. Persons holding winning tickets hastened to the lines at the payoff windows, others studied the initial odds for the seventh race and thumbed through racing forms, sports pages, and tout sheets. All were among the more than 30,000 onlookers at Ak-Sar-Ben Field in

1

Omaha, Nebraska, on the warm and sunny afternoon of May 19, 1979. The track, operated by a subsidiary of a local civic organization, the Knights of Ak-Sar-Ben, had the ninth highest handle in the United States. Except for a short ban on pari-mutuel betting in Nebraska during the Great Depression and a national injunction against horse racing in World War II, there had been annual meets since 1919. This continued a local tradition that stretched back to Civil War days. The track was one of Omaha's most visible and prestigious institutions.

Few of those who attended Ak-Sar-Ben, whether they came from the Flint Hills of Kansas, the suburbs of Kansas City, the farms of Iowa, the Platte River Valley of Nebraska, or the plains of South Dakota, gave much thought to past history. They were there to have a good time playing the horses. Almost all thought no further ahead than the next race. There was no reason for them to consider that the racing concourse was there as a result of another kind of gambling, one characteristic of American development: that of town building.

The Third Race at Ak-Sar-Ben, 4 July 1946

2

The odds had been against promoters who founded Omaha, as they were against the hopeful builders of any town in the nineteenth century. Yet the platting of potential metropolises became a mania as pioneers moved into the country west of the Appalachian Mountains. In the 1830s speculators platted dozens of "paper towns" along a narrow stretch of the Maumee River in Ohio. It was an era of imaginary villages. "We once saw a party of surveyors in midwinter laying out a village on the ice," a disillusioned investor reported. "The spot of ground, a marsh or swamp, with a small stream creeping lazily through it, was so low and wet that it could only be traversed by boats in summer." During the century, thousands of towns failed in the states created out of the old Northwest Territory. Many others achieved the status of names on a map: Rising Sun in Wisconsin, Zelma in Indiana, and Fostoria in Michigan. Missouri had over eight thousand unsuccessful town promotions, including the Missouri River city of Franklin, located on a low-lying island, which a spring flood washed away. By the late 1890s hundreds of the ghost towns dotted the upper Great Plains, dubious reminders of shattered hopes and aspirations. For every place that achieved a population of 10,000 or more, the generally accepted nineteenth century demarcation line between large and small cities, there were thousands of failures. The rewards of success were so great, however, as to encourage the throwing of good money after bad. Once in a while a long shot won, and there was no better example of such an unlikely triumph than that of Chicago, Illinois. Incorporated with a mere forty-two residents in 1834 at an unpromising swampy site on Lake Michigan, it became the fastest-growing place in the world. By 1890 over a million people called the Windy City home, despite initial odds of at least 1,000 to 1 against its ever being more than a squalid village.

Just as patrons at Ak-Sar-Ben tried to devise foolproof systems to bring them quick windfalls, including betting on certain jockeys or closely following track records, town promoters attempted to determine what locations were most conducive to urban development. Prior to the perfection of railroads in the 1850s, rivers served as major commercial arteries. As a result, "breaking points," such as the Falls of the Ohio at Louisville, Kentucky, commanded considerable attention. The transshipment of goods required the construction of a commercial emporium. "Great bends" of rivers, the curve of the Missouri River in the central United States serving as a prime example, attracted numerous investors. So did "river junctions" — the Kansas and Missouri at Kansas City, the Delaware and

Schuylkill at Philadelphia, and the Allegheny and Monongahela at Pittsburgh. Water power sites were important; few factories used steam engines. The first large textile mills in America were on the Merrimack and Connecticut rivers in New England; the Falls of St. Anthony provided the power that made Minneapolis a flour milling center. Furthermore, speculators studied migration trends, topography, and climatic factors. Such considerations became virtues or liabilities depending on the nature of the promotion. Industrial developers in Detroit, Michigan, stressed that manufacturing flourished best in a cool and invigorating climate; their counterparts in Montgomery, Alabama, made similar claims for warm weather.

The problem was that the urban mosaic often failed to follow predictable lines. There was nothing to prevent a town organizer from designating a site, no matter how remote or uninviting, as a "breaking point." Louisville flourished after the construction of a canal around the Falls of the Ohio. "Great bends" could be anywhere; investors at every point along the Missouri River from Rulo, Nebraska, to Jefferson City, Missouri, a distance of more than two hundred miles, claimed that their land lay on the river bend. Venture capital sunk into "river junction" sites frequently brought little or no return. Cairo, Illinois, at the confluence of the Ohio and Mississippi rivers, in the opinion of numerous observers the primary river juncture in North America, was a promotional disaster. Water powers were many times far removed from transportation systems, and they lost importance when industries converted to steam. Many places along major migration routes, the Ohio River or the Erie Canal and Great Lakes, failed. The owners of swamps and mountain tops conjured up visions of urban success; there was no proven connection between factories and climate. Given a combination of high odds and spurious advertising, it was no wonder that fortunes were lost and reputations destroyed in this great nineteenth century metropolitan land boom that was all too frequently little more than an overinflated bubble. Speculation in townsites helped cause the Panic of 1837 and the national depression that followed; articles in commercial publications warned readers against investing in cities prior to the settling of hinterlands. A contributor to the influential *Hunt's Merchants' Magazine and Commercial Review* for July 1840, commenting on how "thousands were defrauded" in Ohio projects, wrote: "The whole territory was regarded as a sort of lottery-office, to which individuals from all quarters might resort for the accumulation of wealth, and invoke the favors of the capricious and blind goddess. . . . The land swarmed with greedy speculators, who cut up the woods into paper villages, and constructed in imagination a chain of compact cities, from the head of the St. Clair to the rapids of the Maumee." Accounts of this sort had little impact—speculators continued with reckless abandon to pump money into all manner of potential town ventures.

The early line on Omaha would have been mixed. It enjoyed a reasonable chance of emerging as a prosperous village or even a small town, but prospects may have precluded achieving metropolitan status. The location was the problem. While it had few drawbacks, there was nothing particularly unique about it. A line of bluffs, none of which was over two hundred feet high, hardly qualified as what an early publicist described as "Temples fit for Jupiter Slator." First and second bottoms, one to two miles wide, undulated gently toward the bluffs directly above the site; at it and below the river bottom narrowed. Away from the bluffs, the topography was bold and rough for several miles, with numerous thickly-forested ravines and valleys, before dropping away into graceful prairie formations. The land, covered with a subsoil of loess between two and three feet deep, annually received about twenty-seven inches of rain. The climate, featuring harsh winters, hot summers, and unpredictable temperature fluctuations, was characteristic of that experience throughout the interior of large land masses in the northern middle latitudes. There were elements for successful city building, but the same could have been said for countless other sites on either side of the Missouri River, above or below, for several hundred miles. The Indians of Nebraska had never considered the Omaha area important, except for hunting, and it was uninhabited prior to the coming of the white man.

The region first attracted serious attention for its transportation and trading possibilities. The Missouri River was one of North America's important waterways; the Platte River stretched like a great slithering snake for four hundred miles across Nebraska, providing a natural highway through the plains. In the 1700s Spanish explorers and French voyageurs may have reached the area. The Lewis and Clark expedition arrived in 1804, marking the first official American penetration. William Clark noted in his journal that the bottom lands appeared a good place for a trading and military post. Manuel Lisa soon started a trading post, and other traders followed. In 1819 the United States Army established Fort Atkinson on the west bank of the river to protect the fur trade. Even though the army abandoned the fort in 1827, it had the effect of encouraging settlement. An Indian Agency for the Omahas, Otos, Missourias, and Pawnees at Bellevue, near the confluence of the Platte and Missouri rivers, attracted some traders and missionaries. Bellevue, a squalid collection of decrepit dwellings, became the terminal of a western highway. By 1842, when John C. Frémont led an exploring expedition through the Platte Valley, hundreds of persons had already taken the same route, following the two-thousand-mile-long Oregon Trail to the Pacific Northwest. There was still no organized settlement in Nebraska; three traders lived in the Omaha vicinity. However, the moving frontier line soon reached the Middle Border and significant changes were at hand.

A dramatic development occurred in 1846, in advance of the main vanguard of permanent settlement. Mormons under Brigham Young became the region's first city builders. Shortly after their unhappy expulsion from Nauvoo, Illinois, the Mormons negotiated agreements with federal authorities and local Indians to use a site a little above Council Bluffs on the Nebraska side of the Missouri River as a temporary residence. They constructed Winter Quarters, where three thousand Saints attempted to spend the winter far removed from conventional supply routes in log cabins, wagons, and caves. Over six hundred died, most buried in unmarked graves on barren hillsides. Winter Quarters survived as the administrative and processing center for the great Mormon migration to the Salt Lake Basin. Countless thousands of members of the "forces of Israel" passed through Winter Quarters before a controversy in 1848 over the cutting of timber on Indian land forced its abandonment. For several years after that the Mormons used the Iowa village of Council Bluffs (called first Miller's Hollow and then Kanesville, prior to acquiring its permanent name in 1853) as a way station. In 1856 the old Winter Quarters, renamed Florence, again became an important Mormon center. By then, Florence had no chance of success. The Mormon advent had important results—the establishment of a permanent settlement at Council Bluffs and the tracking of a well-defined trail through the Platte River Valley. Still, as happened earlier in the 1830s near Independence, Missouri, when armed mobs drove them out, town building activities by Mormons went for naught. Given their triumph at Salt Lake City, far removed from civilization, and their earlier fleeting success at Nauvoo, they might have done well in Nebraska. As it was, the job fell to others.

One William D. Brown, a former county sheriff and brickyard operator from southeastern Iowa, was the original Omaha pioneer. He had started west during the California gold rush, getting only as far as Council Bluffs. There, seeing the thousands of persons waiting to leave in the spring of 1850 for California, he decided that he could make more money by staying than by moving on. He started a Missouri River ferry, first near the old Winter Quarters and then a few miles further south. He called his operation the Lone Tree Ferry, naming it after some scattered trees on both sides of the river. Brown, whose ferry was an oar-propelled flat boat, soon became half owner of the Bluff House, a small hotel in Council Bluffs. He sought broader horizons and, in the summer of 1853, helped organize a steam ferry company, the Council Bluffs and Nebraska Ferry Company. Brown, with little money of his own, was not even the president of the enterprise. What he did have was vision. He wanted to found a town across from Council Bluffs. While the company did buy and operate a steam ferry, the *General Marion,* it remained interested in town promotion. Secrecy cloaked this purpose for obvious reasons; the Omaha Indians still owned the land.

In the fall of 1853 members of the ferry company undertook informal surveys of the site; in later years several of them took credit for staking the first claim. Three men crossed over from Council Bluffs in a leaky scow, after the ferry captain refused to go over through some ice floes. One pioneer bailed, one rowed, and one acted as helmsman. They waded ashore and spent a miserable night huddled by a flickering fire. Every waving tree appeared a band of tomahawk-wielding savages, and at first dawn the intrepid pioneers hastily undertook quick and rudimentary work. "With a hatchet," one wrote, "I blazed a corner tree near our camp, and stamped the initials of my name therein with a survey-making iron. . . . I claim that this was probably the first survey ever made in Douglas County." Shortly afterwards, he stumbled into a deep ravine, which he named Purgatory. Following such work, and after seeing an Indian some distance away on a bluff, the men pushed their boat through an ice-cold marsh and made an unpleasant and wet crossing, landing far downstream from their original starting point. Of such stuff were cities built. It was hardly a Roman triumph; even so, the men were the vanguard of settlement. All along the Middle Border speculators, land sharks, and settlers studied the bluffs across the wide Missouri. All were caught by a combination of greed, ambition, and idealism — the concept of

"Westward the Star of Empire." Here was a story of the American experience, one that went beyond the undertakings of under-financed Iowa frontier speculators, that would unfold with the rise of a midwestern metropolis.

The first organized activity in the history of Omaha occurred on a clear and hot Fourth of July in 1854. A group of men and women crossed over from Council Bluffs on the ferry to hold a picnic on newly-named Capitol Hill, high above the surrounding pastoral countryside. The owners of the town company wanted the celebration to have symbolic significance and to stimulate future real estate sales. All of those present felt part of great events. The United States was at a watershed. The month of May had seen the passage and signing of the Kansas-Nebraska Act. This controversial legislation reopened the slavery issue, split the Democratic party of President Franklin Pierce, tore the opposition Whig party apart, and led to the formation of the Republican party, which opposed the extension of slavery.

The measure was part of a political power play engineered by Senator Stephen A. Douglas of Illinois, a railroad advocate and a Democratic presidential hopeful whom his supporters praised as the choice of "Young America," shorthand for the West. Douglas, in what opponents claimed was a ploy to quickly people the central Great Plains so that a federally subsidized transcontinental railroad benefited Chicago rather than a southern terminal, had introduced a bill in 1853 to create a gigantic new territory opposite Missouri and Iowa. When the measure failed, he returned the next session with a compromise that held out to the South the prospect of a new slave state in exchange for a northern transcontinental. His new plan called for the creation of two new territories, Kansas and Nebraska. It necessitated the repeal of the 36°30′ line that since the Compromise of 1820 had kept slavery, except in Missouri, out of the northern parts of the Louisiana Purchase. Voters in the two new territories would decide whether they wanted freedom or slavery. The phrase coined by the politicians was "Popular Sovereignty," which sounded good, but left fundamental questions unresolved. A basic assumption was that persons from the slave state of Missouri would furnish the bulk of Kansas residents, while Nebraska would be settled by Iowa free staters. Kansas colonization, because of alleged outside interference by pro and antislavery forces, was a catastrophe. President Pierce had to send federal troops into "Bleeding Kansas" to restore order. Meanwhile few, except those directly involved, paid much attention to Nebraska.

8

There were no reporters present to record the excursionists' activities on Capitol Hill. If there had been, they might have caught the optimism, warranted or otherwise, so much a part of the American frontier experience.

A presidential proclamation of June 24, 1854, enhanced Omaha's chances. It announced the ratification of a treaty with the Omaha Indians that extinguished area tribal claims. The promoters, disregarding the niceties of federal land laws, quickly hired a surveying party. Carrying chains and driving stakes, the surveyors platted 320 blocks, each 264 feet square, plus streets of 100 to 120 feet in width. The name of the new town may or may not have had Indian origins. One version claimed that Omaha meant, "Above all others upon the stream!" Another account contended that the speculators thought Omaha sounded pretty. Whatever the source of the name, the people at the Fourth of July picnic tried to think in larger terms. They had lunch, started to build a log cabin, and listened to a toast: "Nebraska–May her gentle zephyrs and rolling prairies invite pioneers from beyond the muddy Missouri river to happy homes within her borders, and may her lands ever be dedicated to free soil, free labor, and free men." Afterwards, a politician started a speech. Suddenly, Indians appeared and frightened the audience. Everyone climbed on the wagon that had brought provisions across, returned to the ferry, and went back to Council Bluffs. Over thirty years later, an old settler, addressing the Nebraska State Historical Society, recalled, "I remember that some resolutions were adopted and a few speeches made. The stand on which the speakers stood was a common wagon owned by my old friend Harrison Johnson, who, with some of the members of his family, constituted a portion of the party." Yet the picnic had accomplished a significant purpose. It provided Omaha with an official founding date.

Exuberant visions of urban destiny often accompanied city building in the American West. Jeffersonian ideas, which envisioned an agrarian society, were only of importance to urban promoters so far as farms might result in prosperous hinterlands to exploit. Predictions of material success – great moneyed operations and gargantuan transportation systems – sustained settlers, created a sense of pride, and provided a framework for defining aspirations.

Omaha had a booster before it had a street map. He was J. W. Pattison, a lawyer, business agent, and coeditor of the first newspaper published under an Omaha dateline. He had come west as a correspondent for the New York *Herald.* His paper, the *Arrow,* published in Council Bluffs, appeared on June 28, 1854. While the masthead proclaimed it "a family newspaper devoted to the arts, sciences, general literature, agriculture, and politics," the *Arrow* was strictly a promotional sheet. In his first editorial, "A Night in Our Sanctum," Pattison discussed the possibility of Omaha becoming a commercial metropolis. He claimed that he had dreamed of a great future for the new city as he lay beneath buffalo robes on Nebraska soil, listening to the howl of wolves and knowing that not far away glimmered the crackling campfires of the Pawnees and Omahas.

Pattison said that after he went to sleep the busy hum of industrial and commercial activities reached his ears and the ears of those around him, all of whom had spent a hard day cutting logs for cabin claims.

> The incessant rattle of innumerable drays over the paved streets, the steady tramp of ten thousand of an animated, enterprising population, the hoarse orders fast issued from the crowd of steamers upon the levee loading with the rich products of the state of Nebraska and unloading the fruits, species and products of other climes and soils greeted our ears. Far away from toward the setting sun came telegraphic dispatches of improvements, progress and moral advancement upon the Pacific coast. Cars full freighted with teas, silks, etc., were arriving from thence and passing across the stationary channel of the Missouri river with lightning speed hurrying on to the Atlantic seaboard. The third express train on the Council Bluffs and Galveston R. R. came thundering close by us with a shrill whistle that brought us to our feet with knife in hand. We rubbed our eyes, looked into the darkness beyond to see the flying train. They had vanished and the shrill second neigh of our lariated horses gave indication of the danger near. The hum of business, in and around the city, and the same rude camp-fires were before us.

Many images had more substance in flickering fires than in the cold light of dawn. Pattison must have thought so. The *Arrow* suspended publication in November of 1854, after only twelve intermittent issues, and he left for Missouri. He never returned to Omaha to see his dream come true.

The first objective of the members of the Council Bluffs and Nebraska Ferry Company was to obtain the territorial capital. They wanted to fix or at the very least influence the race for urban power in Nebraska before it started. Otherwise, many distinctive duly chronicled events — first religious service, first actual settlers, first forge, first white child, and first hotel — would probably mean nothing. In September 1854 a map appeared that showed Omaha the location of a territorial meeting place. To buttress the claim, the diagram called the place "Omaha City." It was an attempt to convince potential investors of its supposed significant urban dimensions, but the ploy failed and "City" was soon dropped from the name.

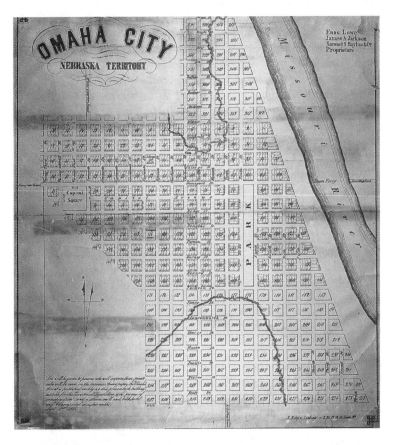

1854 Map of Omaha City

Omaha was only one of several "paper towns" on the Nebraska side of the Missouri River. Excitement ran high above and below Omaha in Fontanelle, Florence, Bellevue, Plattsmouth, Nebraska City, and Brownsville, at least during daylight hours, when entrepreneurs crossed over from Iowa to improve their property. Omaha and Bellevue had the best chances. Both had the backing of different combinations of Iowa Democratic politicians. The bill establishing Nebraska Territory specified that the territorial governor would designate the initial meeting site. President Pierce appointed Francis Burt, an obscure South Carolina politician. The forty-seven-year-old Burt, who held a patronage job in the Department of Treasury at the time of his selection, had previously been a state legislator for almost twenty years. The son of a slaveholder, he was a former newspaper editor. As a delegate at the 1832 South Carolina nullification convention, he had supported an ordinance that opposed a federally enacted tariff. He hardly seemed the right choice to launch a free state, and he never had the opportunity. On October 7, 1854, he reached Bellevue, suffering from an undiagnosed illness. Hospitalized at the local Presbyterian mission, his condition steadily worsened and he died on October 16, two days after taking the oath of office. Various town delegations had visited his sickbed, pressing their claims. He may have favored Bellevue as the first territorial meeting place, but he never issued an official proclamation. His death placed the decision in the hands of the Territorial Secretary, Thomas B. Cuming, who became acting governor.

Cuming, a rising young Iowa Democratic politician, was a short and swarthy man with raven-black hair and eyes set deep in bushy eyebrows. He claimed to have been born in New York in 1828, but he was probably older. After graduating from the University of Michigan, he had worked as a geologist and had served in the Army during the Mexican War. Following hostilities he had moved to Keokuk, Iowa, where he became first a telegrapher and then a newspaper editor. He wanted to further his political ambitions in western Iowa by helping Council Bluffs, and he had landholdings in Omaha. According to opponents, he demanded and received bribes from the Council Bluffs and Nebraska Ferry Company.

Cuming moved swiftly to establish civil government, and to advance Omaha's fortunes. He divided Nebraska Territory into eight counties, with an equal number north and south of the Platte River. The wide, shallow, and sandy Platte, which was very difficult to ford and had few ferry sites, acted as a natural division, cutting the territory in half and promoting competing political interests. He placed Omaha and Bellevue in Douglas County, and appointed Omahans to county offices. Although a census showed more people to the south than north of the Platte, he apportioned the territorial legislature in favor of the north bank. Then, in December 1854, after an election held posthaste, Cuming announced that the first legislative session would convene in Omaha. His critics, just about everyone in Nebraska outside of Omaha, assumed a fix. Mass meetings denounced him and a convention in Nebraska City, fifty miles south of Omaha, approved a resolution that called him an "unprincipled knave." The participants in these assemblies had been in Nebraska Territory only a short time. J. Sterling Morton, the author of the Nebraska City resolution, had arrived a month earlier from Michigan. The whole controversy was typical of the frontier. Crucial decisions were made with no knowledge of the land.

The first Nebraska territorial legislature assembled in Omaha on January 16, 1855, in a meeting house provided for "public purposes" by the Council Bluffs and Nebraska Ferry Company. The thirty by forty-five foot two-story structure stood out from the surrounding twenty or so shacks, houses, saloons, and stores; it was the only brick building in town. The editor of the Bellevue *Palladium* claimed that it was too small: "We were struck with the singularity of taste displayed in the curtain furniture of the different rooms, which consisted of two folds of plain calico, the one green and the other red, which we took to be symbolic of jealousy and war — which monsters we fear, will make their appearance before right is enthroned and peace established." During the initial meeting the delegates from Bellevue and from south of the Platte wore red blankets to indicate their "savage" intentions toward Cuming. Few of the members had spent more than a night in their districts. After each day's business, they took the ferry to Council Bluffs. A saloon, adjacent to the assembly chamber, set the tone for riotous proceedings. Members, some moving back and forth from their seats to the bar, gave impassioned speeches. There were numerous hot verbal exchanges and threats of physical violence. The acrimonious session had a major accomplishment: the new territorial governor, Mark W. Izard of Arkansas, arrived in time to persuade the body to establish a framework of government by adopting *in toto* the laws of Iowa. That took half an hour.

Much of the time featured public debates and private manipulations over the location of the territorial capital. Omaha promoters took precautionary measures, bribing members—induce was the word used—with money, land, and promises. Some received "sugar," while others got "salt" in what sarcastic observers called "Scrip Town," a half mile wide stretch of property on Omaha's north and west sides. A joint resolution of February 22, 1855, placed the capitol building in Omaha. The representative from Florence switched his support to Omaha at the last minute after receiving sixty lots, which he soon sold for sixty dollars each. Two Glenwood, Iowa, residents all committed to Plattsmouth voted for Omaha. One had to move to Council Bluffs to escape a lynching; the other barely avoided a public beating. A Glenwood mass meeting denounced them for misrepresentation in "the Nebraska legislature." The question of whether the territorial government should remain in Omaha occupied every Nebraska territorial assembly, inflamed by the indignation of people outside the city and prolonged by the precedent of rewards for votes. Once, a rump group attempted to move the body to Florence. Another time, opposing forces brandished knives and guns at each other. By hook or crook, the territorial government remained in Omaha until statehood.

During the bitterest moments of the capital fight, Acting Governor Cuming had struck a responsive chord among even his most vehement legislative foes by calling upon them to petition Congress to build a Pacific railroad through Nebraska.

> Many reasons lead to the conclusion that such a memorial from you will be of practical efficacy in contributing to the speedy consummation of such an enterprise—an enterprise of such absolute necessity as a means of inter-communication between the Atlantic and Pacific states, and as a purveyor of a lucrative commerce with India, China and the Pacific islands. Among these are the facts that the valley of the Platte is on the nearest and most direct continuous line from the commercial metropolis of the east, by railroad and the great lakes, through the most practical mountain passes, to the metropolis of the west; that it is fitted by nature for an easy grade; and that it is central and convenient to a great majority of grain-growing states.

Almost everyone in Nebraska agreed who heard or read his address. After all, that was why they had come to the territory—to take advantage of its potential as a highway across the upper Plains to the Rocky Mountains and the Pacific Slope.

The Transcontinental, after two decades of research and development, appeared on the verge of realization. In the middle of

14

the 1850s a survey of five possible routes by the United States Corps of Topographical Engineers indicated that a railroad could be built over a "Central Route" from Council Bluffs to California. However, the estimated cost of $131 million was prohibitive and the maps produced too general for construction purposes. Survey parties representing Chicago lines and headed by Grenville Dodge, one of the nation's first railroad engineers, started detailed studies of a route through Nebraska. Dodge wanted to apply a "commercial point of view" to the federal reports and to find the lowest grades and least curvatures, never previously investigated or reported. He later wrote: "Private enterprise explored and developed that line along the forty-second parallel of latitude. This route was made by the buffalo, next used by the Indians, then by the fur traders, next by the Mormons, and then by the overland immigration to California and Oregon. It is known as the 'Great Platte River Route.' " If either public or private interests built a railroad through the valley, its Missouri River terminal would be of crucial importance; the technology did not exist to bridge the stream. So, all concerned with urban developments in Nebraska concentrated on obtaining communication connections; the capital fight only gave Omaha an initial advantage, at least in the rationales concocted by its pursuers. Entrepreneurial decisions, rather than theories of urban dominance or political intrigues, would determine the winner. Or was that the case? Had Omaha's political ties given it an overwhelming advantage, predetermining the victor, no matter what other places did? This was the claim of critics in rival communities.

During the steamboat era, Omaha had trouble competing with other river towns. One of the first steamboats on the Missouri, the *Western Engineer*, had run up to the region in 1819 carrying federal troops and explorer Stephen H. Long. During the 1830s the American Fur Company had used steamboats on the upper Missouri as effective means of building a fur trading monopoly. In the late 1840s a few boats carried Mormons and California gold seekers to Winter Quarters and Council Bluffs. By 1854 Council Bluffs had regular service, soon extended to the settlements in Nebraska. Omaha's steamboat connections developed gradually, reaching a peak during the Colorado gold rush, when 268 boats arrived between March and November of 1859. A few sidewheelers ran over a thousand miles above Omaha to Fort Benton in Montana. There were tri-weekly runs between Omaha and St. Joseph, Missouri, the western terminal of the Hannibal and St. Joseph Railroad. A passenger line operated on regular schedules from St. Louis to Omaha.

The steamboats used on the lower Missouri were as elegant as any on the Mississippi. The largest were 250 feet long, carried four hundred passengers, and had a freight capacity of seven hundred tons. Arrivals in Omaha were major community events. One traveler reported fifteen hundred persons at the landing to welcome his boat. Captains frequently allowed visitors aboard for a formal dance in the grand salon. The great white steamboats with their enormous side and paddle wheels, and tall black stacks—the *Spread Eagle,* the *Florilda,* the *Alonzo Child,* and the *Platte Valley* —signaled community progress in the America of their day. With two to seven arrivals weekly, Omaha surpassed Council Bluffs and Florence as a steamboat port. The editor of the Omaha *Nebraskian* crowed, "Of all the would-be towns in Nebraska, Florence has received the most puffing and blowing. . . . So blow away ye Florenceites, despite the vast sums you have expanded for wind, your town is but a sickly 'Infant mewing and pucking in its nurse's arms.' " What the journalist failed to mention was that Nebraska City eclipsed Omaha as a steamboat and trading center.

Omaha interests emphasized the virtues of a 180-mile-long trail, called either the North Platte Trail or the Mormon Trail. It ran from the city to Fort Kearny. "Mormons, like buffalo and Indians, always choose the shortest and best routes," the editor of the Omaha *Times* claimed. The trail, improved between 1856 and 1858 by the federal government, had good and bad points. For the first twenty-five miles out of Omaha it passed through fairly settled areas; users had little trouble obtaining provisions and usually made steady progress. Beyond that point came muddy sloughs, expensive ferries, and hazardous crossings, especially over the Loup Fork and Platte rivers. The Platte sometimes took several days to cross, usually at considerable risk to wagons and supplies. Guide books issued in Omaha claimed the route was seventy-five miles shorter than the one along the south side of the Platte from Nebraska City. This was untrue. In 1857, when the Leavenworth freighting firm of Russell, Majors and Waddell, which handled most of the Army's freighting business in the West, established an up-river head-quarters, it never seriously considered Omaha, deciding instead on Nebraska City. The concern bought 138 town lots and spent $300,000 on facilities. It also built a new road that short-ened the distance between Nebraska City and Fort Kearny. Russell, Majors and Waddell turned Nebraska City into a roaring

Steamboats Unloading Supplies, 1865

camp. Every month thousands of wagons rolled through the streets, as bullwhackers cracked whips over the plodding teams of oxen. River boats lined the waterfront. Other western freighting concerns moved to the town, which soon became the second most important settlement in the territory. It easily eclipsed Brownville and Plattsmouth, and threatened Omaha. By the end of the 1850s there were sixty-four freighters in Nebraska City and twenty-four in Omaha. And, to make matters worse for Omaha, none of its firms were comparable to Russell, Majors and Waddell.

Freighters operating out of Omaha traded in Colorado, Utah, and California. Early ties built up with Mormon interests and gold seekers paid handsome dividends. Local merchants handled the buffalo hide business, a colorful but relatively insignificant activity. More materially, the freighters' wagons carried a wide variety of items, from food stuffs to mining machinery, essential to western development. Some concerns had only a wagon, capable of hauling three to five tons of freight, and six to twelve yoke of oxen. Large operations, which relied on government contracts and bulk shipments, frequently had hundreds of wagons and thousands of oxen. Profits and risks were high.

Omaha freighting firms incurred serious losses in the doldrums that followed the Panic of 1857. "Wild Cat" banks, which issued their own paper currency with dubious backing, failed. The bottom dropped out of the real estate market; $50,000 in scrip issued by the city to help pay for a capitol building lost all value, and jobs were scarce. An 1858 arrival in the settlement, which then had approximately two thousand inhabitants, wrote, "And, as I soon learned, not one in twenty of these had any visible means of support, any faith in the country, or any expectation whatever, other than to leave as soon as he could sell his lot in town, or his pre-emption in the country, which, quite likely he had acquired, not by an investment of hard-earned money, but by certain circumlocutory processes—the inventions of speculators of inventive genius." This was a dark hour for Omaha. After a successful start, it appeared on the verge of oblivion, relegated to a ferry station opposite Council Bluffs, overshadowed on the Missouri's west bank by Nebraska City. Then came the 1859 Pike's Peak gold rush. It happened so suddenly, and at such a fortuitous moment, that some conspiracy-minded observers charged that reports of gold came in advance of actual discovery. In any event, Omahans could hardly believe their good fortune; the city went from bust to boom within a few months.

Omaha was in an ideal position to serve Colorado gold seekers. Nebraska City was a freighting center geared to supporting military posts. It had no way of dealing with the needs of thousands of emigrants, nor did any of Omaha's other rivals. Bellevue had no facilities; Florence had such poor accommodations that travelers were diverted to Omaha. The steamboats that operated from St. Louis and St. Joseph to Omaha took on new significance, as did the steam ferry between Council Bluffs and Omaha, along with previously minor express, mail, and stage routes. The Western Stage Line ran through Omaha from the end of the track in eastern Iowa to Fort Kearny and other points. Omaha merchants quickly recouped their losses. In 1859 it cost a person over $500 for outfitting and travel from Omaha to Colorado. Adventurers crowded the new four-story Herndon House, which boasted over one hundred rooms. White-topped wagons, handcarts, and men on foot filled the streets. Outfitters made tremendous profits; freighters received or initiated large orders. One small carrier transported apples to the gold fields and another a load of domestic cats. The return of prosperity bolstered the spirits of Omaha's entrepreneurs, several of whom were Council Bluffs merchants who opened branches in the village. By the spring of 1859, grocery and hardware stores had daily sales over $3,000. Without exaggeration, a writer in the Omaha *Nebraskian and Times* wrote, "No one can fail to note the rapid increase of business in our city, and each succeeding day adds to our commercial operations, in an arithmetical ratio."

The sudden prosperity did not immediately lead to the formation of a cohesive business community. The city was very new and it had experienced enough serious problems to deter some investors. The Council Bluffs and Nebraska Ferry Company lost importance after selling off most of its lots. Ferry operator Brown, eventually killed in a street brawl, was never a town leader; former Acting Governor Cuming died suddenly in 1858. Some early investors moved on in the wake of the Panic of 1857, seeking places with better prospects. It was a common practice on the frontier. The emerging leaders in Omaha were men who arrived during the first few years of settlement, and who had enough faith to stay during the short period of financial adversity. While they engaged in a wide variety of business pursuits, everything from banking to lumbering, they all had freighting and outfitting connections.

The most visible combinations were members of the Kountze and Creighton families. Both groups, made up of Ohio natives, started

Omaha, ca. 1860

their Omaha operations in 1856. The four Kountze brothers, Augustus, Charles, Herman, and Luther, were the sons of a German immigrant from Saxony. After making money carrying freight for the federal government, they founded the Kountze Brothers Bank, one of Omaha's first successful banks. Luther moved to Denver, where he established a financial institution, giving the family an impressive regional base. Charles soon followed. Augustus and Herman remained in Omaha to consolidate and coordinate activities. The Kountzes called themselves "Bankers and Collectors," dealing in "Gold Dust and Land Warrants." They reorganized their bank in 1863 as the First National Bank of Omaha. Later they broadened their holdings still more by establishing a bank in New York City and by buying property in Texas and Chicago.

The three Creighton brothers, Edward, John, and Joseph, plus a cousin, James, were among the first suppliers of Colorado miners. Edward Creighton, born in 1820, was the most important member of the family. He started out in Omaha as the owner of a lumber yard, a business he soon abandoned. It was far removed from his area of specialization, that of building telegraph lines, the "singing wires" that had an electrifying effect on nineteenth century communication. In the late 1850s he supervised the construction of a line from Jefferson City, Missouri, to Fort Smith, Arkansas. He met in Cleveland, Ohio, with powerful Western Union capitalists and became the company's general agent. After Western Union persuaded the last Congress prior to the Civil War to award a $40,000 annual subsidy for ten years to the builder of a system from the Missouri border to California, Creighton completed the Missouri and Western line from St. Louis to Omaha in the early fall of 1860, pushing on before winter to Fort Kearny. He then undertook a hazardous survey trip to California, stopping for several days in Salt Lake City to cultivate a friendship with Brigham Young. Following negotiations in San Francisco, in which Creighton arranged for telegraph connections to be built east from California, he returned east by ocean steamer. Despite the Civil War, he hurried west to direct construction. Overcoming logistical problems through a series of brilliant decisions, among them dividing his construction parties into eastern and western units, he linked up with the California line at Salt Lake City on October 20, 1862, many months ahead of schedule. Stock issues enabled Creighton to make several hundred thousand dollars, which he parlayed into a considerable fortune. He invested in a wide variety of

Edward Creighton

enterprises, and joined with the Kountze interests in establishing the First National Bank of Omaha. One of the richest men in Nebraska at the time of his death from a stroke in 1874, Creighton gave Omaha needed direction, pointing it on a course of destiny as a communications center.

The key to the future of Omaha was the Pacific Railroad Act approved by President Abraham Lincoln on July 1, 1862, which provided for construction with federal help of a transcontinental railroad. Under the act the Central Pacific Railroad received federal help to build east from Sacremento, California. In addition, the measure chartered a new corporation, the Union Pacific Railroad. It was authorized to construct a single line west from an "initial point" 247 miles west of Omaha. Surveyors were to fix the exact location on the one-hundredth meridian, between the southern edge of the Republican River Valley and the north margin of the Platte River Valley. With southern interests out of Congress, a road over a northern route became a foregone conclusion. Four branch lines would radiate eastward from the "initial point" to Omaha, Sioux City, Kansas City, and Atchison. Of special importance was the "Iowa Branch" running through Nebraska from the "initial point" to the Missouri River. It was to become part of the Union Pacific's main line, connecting with eastern roads at a point on the western boundary determined by the President of the United States. The Sioux City and Atchison spurs, included to satisfy parochial interests and to cloak actual intentions, were of no real importance. The "Kansas City Branch" was to run no further than the one-hundredth meridian. On the surface, the legislation seemed to favor Omaha.

Chicago railroad interests, in league with powerful eastern capitalists and Iowa promoters, were instrumental in helping to secure passage. The plan, sold in part as a war measure, although there was no concerted Confederate threat in the West, tied in with Chicago's emerging railroad strategy. It ignored two St. Louis-controlled roads, the Hannibal and St. Joseph Railroad and the Missouri Pacific Railroad, which had a railhead in Sedalia, Missouri, two-thirds of the way across the state. Three Chicago lines that had already penetrated eastern Iowa planned to build on to Council Bluffs as soon as hostilities ended. Indeed, most of the survey work had already been completed. Omaha leaders were jubilant. "We have an abiding faith that if our people prove true to themselves, there is a prosperous future for Omaha," the editor of the Omaha *Nebraska Republican* wrote on March 11, 1863. "The prospect that the Pacific Rail Road is to have its eastern terminus here–the fact that the Iowa system of Railroads is to terminate in Council Bluffs, or rather on the river's edge, opposite this city–the certainty that the Platte River and the Loup Fork are to be speedily bridged–our rapidly growing trade with the Western Mines–all point to such a consummation."

The original leaders of the Union Pacific were not satisfied with the act, because they thought it failed to provide large enough government subsidies. This was particularly true of the road's first promoter, Thomas C. Durant, a physician turned financier, who had a reputation for "sharp" dealings. Stock subscriptions went slowly, although Omahans subscribed $12,000. In the spring of 1863 Lincoln summoned Grenville Dodge, who had left surveying work to become a major general in the Union army, from the battlefields of northern Mississippi to Washington. The President, despite the war — the summer would see his soldiers triumph at Gettysburg and Vicksburg — was anxious for the Union Pacific to start construction. He understood the complicated nature of the whole Pacific railroad strategy. During the 1850s he had worked as a lawyer for Chicago lines, most notably the Rock Island and Illinois Central railroads. When Lincoln asked Dodge about the problem, he replied that he thought the project of such great magnitude that it should be undertaken entirely by the federal government. "He objected to this," Dodge recalled, "saying the Government would give the project all possible aid and support, but could not build the road; that it had all it could handle in the conflict now going on. But the Government would make any change in the law or give any reasonable aid to insure the building of the road by private enterprise." That was what Dodge had wanted to hear. Before returning to the field, he went to New York City to convey the news to Durant. The railroad leader, who had decided that his railroad interests were too important to allow him to take the time to participate in the war effort, knew what to do. He went back to Congress, spending money lavishly in the right places. He received the aid of powerful Massachusetts Republican Congressman Oakes Ames, who along with his brother Oliver Ames, would later enter the Union Pacific management group. As a result of Durant's manipulations, an amendment to the original act became law in the summer of 1864. The measure, which among other things doubled the size of the land grant, pleased the owners and encouraged them to quickly go ahead with plans to sell bonds and start construction.

Meanwhile, Lincoln had designated the eastern terminal. John

P. Usher, the Secretary of the Interior, related a conversation that he said took place between Durant and the President. "Now the natural place for this terminal point is at the mouth of the Platte River," Durant explained, "but Omaha is the principal town in Nebraska . . . the best thing is to start it from Omaha." Lincoln, after studying a map of the region, replied, "I have got a quarter section of land right across there, and if I fix it there they will say that I have done it to benefit my land. But, I will fix it there, anyhow." Prior to his presidency, Lincoln had acquired residential property in Council Bluffs. He issued an ambiguous executive order in November of 1863 designating the terminal at Council Bluffs.

Durant arbitrarily decided that Lincoln meant for the Union Pacific to start from Omaha. To dramatize the occasion and to impress investors with the company's determination, Durant orchestrated a gala celebration in Omaha. On December 2, 1863, he flashed the word of the presidential order in a telegram from his New York headquarters, directing the Union Pacific engineer in Omaha to "break ground." In the middle of the afternoon, a thousand persons assembled near the north end of the levee, a short distance from where the Pacific Telegraph crossed the Missouri River. Some of the spectators from Iowa had walked across the ice. While a large American flag flapped in the breeze, and following an invocation that invoked the blessings of Divine Providence, officials turned the first shovels of earth. The crowd cheered and politicians made speeches.

The orators stressed the importance of the Union Pacific in saving the Union, binding the nation's wounds, and altering false geographical notions. Mayor B. E. B. Kennedy of Omaha, after talking about "those iron bands wherewith we hope to gird the continent," claimed, "The act of Congress establishing this great enterprise, should have been entitled 'an act to promote the preservation of the Union to prevent national dissolution, to bind together the Atlantic and Pacific coasts by an indissoluble covenant, to resist and repel Foreign aggression.' " Territorial Governor Alvin Saunders contended that the railroad would become the "Nation's Great Highway," forming a grand thoroughfare to carry the manufactured articles of New England, the agricultural staples of the Mississippi Valley, and the gold and silver of the Far West. Another leader proclaimed: "The region of the Rocky Mountains and the great plains beyond, once regarded by geographers, and geologists as a wild waste of volcanic desolation has unbosomed unknown wealth, of which this road is now to be the outlet. . . . Nebraska, the great American desert, as it was then called, will, under the influence of this road, be revealed to the world as the great American garden."

After closing remarks, ceremonial guns boomed on both sides of the river. On the same day, federal troops fought and died in the South. While one speaker had talked of Ulysses S. Grant hurling "victorious sons" against the "very vitals of the so-called confederacy," the theme of the day, on a wintery mud flat far removed from the fighting, was peace, progress, and prosperity. Perhaps this was not inappropriate. Those present were also a long way from the board rooms of greedy New York speculators or the congressional haunts of grasping politicians. Almost all of those assembled felt that they bore witness to the start of a great enterprise and a watershed that ushered in a new industrial era in America, one that would totally change the country after the Civil War. That was the result desired by the organizer of the affair, George Francis Train, the chief publicist for the Union Pacific Railroad. Things went about as planned.

Train came and left just as fast. The five-foot-ten-inch tall Train had a corpulent build, blue eyes, a prominent nose, and dark curly hair streaked with grey. He said he was born in Boston in 1829 and that he earned $95,000 at age twenty-one, while running a shipping firm in Melbourne, Australia. He traveled extensively throughout the world, and wrote a number of books, including *An American Merchant in Europe, Asia, and Australia* and *Young America in Wall Street*. Shortly before the Civil War, he promoted street railroads in the United Kingdom and the Atlantic and Great Western Railroad in Ohio. An accomplished lecturer on his own activities and an inspirational speaker, his stirring speeches on behalf of the Union cause and his experience in railroad work attracted the interest of Union Pacific leaders. He seemed an excellent choice to head their advertising campaign, despite an 1862 arrest in Boston for disrupting a public meeting. He was an accomplished salesman. People who came in close contact with Train thought his ideas "extravagant," at the same time finding him likable; he did not seem to take life all that seriously and he liked practical jokes.

A friend called him:

A locomotive that has run off the track, turned upside down with its cowcatcher buried in a stump and the wheels making a thousand revolutions in a minute—a kite in the air which has lost its tail—a human novel without a hero—a man who climbs a tree for a bird's nest out on a limb, and in order to get it saws the limb off between himself and the tree — a ship without a rudder — a clock without hands — a sermon that is all text — a pantomime of words — an arrow shot into the air — the apotheosis of talk — the incarnation of gab. Handsome, vivacious, versatile, muscular, as neat as a cat, clean to the marrow, a judge of the effect of clothes, frugal in food and regular only in habits. A noonday mystery, a solved conundrum — a practical joke in earnest — a cipher wanting a figure to pass for something; with the brains of twenty men in his head all pulling in different ways; not bad as to heart, but a man who has shaken hands with reverence.

Train asserted that Omaha was at the starting point of the grandest undertaking God ever witnessed in the history of the world. He said that when called upon to speak at the end of the Union Pacific ground breaking ceremony. At first, he had demurred, pleading that the effects of three nights in a stage across Iowa had "done him up." But, when the crowd refused to leave, he mounted a buggy, took off his overcoat, rolled up his sleeves, and launched into an address. Speaking rapidly and without notes, he demonstrated why he had a reputation as a spellbinder. An observer said that Train "took the crowd" through a combination of telling points and clever witticisms. Applause greeted Train's assertions about Omaha's future role in America: "The *Great Pacific Railway is convened.* . . . The President has shown his good judgment in locating the road where the Almighty has placed the signal station at the entrance of a garden seven hundred miles in length and twenty broad. Look at the face of nature here — study the map, and point out, if you can, another place for the central station of the *World's Highway.* The enterprise is national — 'tis the *People's* road." That night he was the center of attention at a railroad banquet; he had become an instant community hero.

Train founded Credit Foncier of America to build and develop communities along the Union Pacific route. "One of my plans," he recorded, "was the creation of a chain of great towns across the continent, connecting Boston with San Francisco by a magnificent highway of cities." He bought five thousand lots in Omaha, helped erect the $40,000 Cozzen's House Hotel, and purchased ten other buildings. His holdings in other places were equally impressive — seven thousand lots and a hotel in Columbus, Nebraska, plus one thousand lots in Council Bluffs. He was eased out as an important Union Pacific official after a number of congressmen contended he was mentally unbalanced and proof that the Union Pacific would never be completed. Train's town promotions went sour; he failed to recoup by making heavy investments in Denver. Going into politics, he supported the Fenian cause and went to France to work with communists. He continued to enjoy a good press in Omaha. In 1872, when he ran unsuccessfully for president on a third party ticket, an Omahan called him a "Man of Destiny and the People's Candidate." After that, Train's career took erratic turns; he served time in prison for circulating obscene literature and was declared legally insane. His Omaha fortunes waned and the original owners foreclosed on his property. The Omaha *Bee* editor commented: "His name was George Francis Train and he signed his presence in our midst by a spread eagle, Chinese wall, maid of Gizeh, oration at the breaking of grounds on the sandy banks of the Missouri near what are now known as the telegraph poles." Train, who always said he owned $30 million in Omaha land, drifted on to new promotions and controversies before his death in 1904. In his final days, he talked only to children, and called himself the "Champion Crank." Many years earlier, he was an Omaha prophet of destiny. Train made another contribution, if it can be called that: he was responsible for naming what became one of the most controversial American corporations of the nineteenth century—Credit Mobilier of America, the construction company set up by the owners of the Union Pacific to build the railroad.

The initial activities of Credit Mobilier had caused anxiety in Omaha. Except for preliminary work, very little happened until after the war. For a time it appeared that Omaha might lose the terminal. To keep its charter, the Union Pacific had to finish much of the stretch between the Missouri River and the "initial point" by June 27, 1866. In addition, to earn the right to build on west it had to beat any other road to the one hundredth meridian.

After spending $100,000 on an unsatisfactory due west course, Durant ordered new surveys, one to the north at Florence and the other to the south at Bellevue. He selected the so-called "ox-bow" route, which dipped south from Omaha for a distance of nine miles, before turning west at the northern environs of Bellevue. Leaders in Omaha, which had not considered Bellevue a rival since the capital fight, were, to say the least, very upset. They feared that the Union Pacific would build a bridge and shops at Bellevue, making their city on an insignificant spur. They did not trust Durant, with reason. In February of 1865 he issued a statement. "The line," he said, "has been changed to avoid heavy grades, not with the intention of interfering with the terminus." Soon afterwards, however, he secretly wired his engineers: "Make surveys immediately from river at Bellevue to the nearest point on the line and report probable cost of right of way. Also best location for shops at Bellevue or Fremont."

After threats and counterthreats, the Union Pacific built over the "ox-bow" route, but the terminal stayed in Omaha. Durant owned 4,360 acres in Omaha and 951 acres in Council Bluffs. He was afraid that a blatant change might upset delicate political relationships, complicated by Lincoln's assassination. The new Reconstruction president, Andrew Johnson, was unenthusiastic about government participation in a transcontinental out of Omaha. Anyway, Durant, whose critics implied his only purpose was to shake down Omaha interests for more money, acted in character. He ordered the maps used for subsidy payments adjusted so that the Omaha terminal would start two miles north of the station.

The Union Pacific had to overcome major difficulties. Stock issues did badly, despite fanfare. Durant had a bad commercial reputation, and businessmen considered the Union Pacific a premature enterprise thrust into empty country. Under the circumstances, the subsidies—the greatest ever granted a railroad—were unattractive. In 1866 the adding of New England investors headed by the Ames brothers improved confidence and guaranteed a major construction effort. The new group planned to take advantage of the company's role as its own chief contractor through Credit Mobilier. Using railroad construction companies to ensure profits from high risk lines was a common business device. However, there had never before been so much federal money involved, and Oakes Ames had no scruples about using his congressional position to ensure success. When questions rose about the inflated size of construction contracts, he gave Credit Mobilier stock to prominent politicians. Apparently, Ames saw nothing wrong with his activities. Insiders knew how to conduct business in Congress. The public morality of the "Gilded Age" was fast and loose, and, after all, he was not handing out flat cash payments as the Union Pacific-Eastern Division Railroad did to get a charter to build across Kansas beyond the "initial point." In 1872 New York *Sun* reporters exposed Ames, then a member of the Union Pacific executive committee, calling him "The King of Frauds," and detailing his Credit Mobilier stock transactions. Censured in 1873 by the House of Representatives, he died a few months later, leaving an estate of several million dollars.

Congressional hearings showed that Credit Mobilier charged $92 million for a road that cost $40 million to build. Those connected with the enterprise argued that the profit margin was reasonable under the circumstances. Few agreed. Credit Mobilier—a nineteenth century Teapot Dome and Watergate—ultimately cast a pall over the whole Pacific Railroad project, causing long-run problems for both the Union Pacific and Omaha. These difficulties lay ahead when the Union Pacific mounted a gigantic construction effort out of Omaha in the spring of 1866.

It was important that the Union Pacific build through the Platte Valley, reaching the one hundredth meridian and beyond as quickly as possible. What became the Union Pacific-Eastern Division Railroad, which had no business connections with the Union Pacific, had already started building toward central Kansas. The Pacific Railroad Act of 1866 authorized the Central Pacific to continue eastward from Nevada, where the road was originally to stop. Durant came to Omaha to deal with mounting problems. The tall, thin, and sharp-featured financier dressed in the style of a frontier dandy, wearing a costly slouch hat, velvet sack coat and vest, corduroy breeches, and high top boots. "Durant was of a nervous temperament—all nerve-quick in motion and speech, and decisive in character, sometimes rather imperious," an Omahan remembered. Durant, accompanied by a beautiful blond woman, took up residence for six months in a Lutheran parsonage; rumors spread that he had bought his traveling companion a $25,000 gown. His presence had little impact on railroad affairs, and things did not get moving until Grenville Dodge returned from the Army on May 6, 1866 to assume duties as the Union Pacific's chief engineer. Wounded three times in action, he left service a hero. Dodge, small in stature, had what a friend called a "modest demeanor" and an even disposition. He quickly organized survey, construction, and supply operations along military lines, and hired two brothers, John and Daniel Casement, to lay track and keep discipline in the work force.

Building proceeded rapidly, saving the charter by reaching the one hundredth meridian on October 6, 1866, well ahead of the opposition. Over the next three years, Union Pacific rails drove west, overcoming Indians, rivers, financial problems, and internal bickering. The Casemonts kept one thousand men employed at the head of the track. Thousands of others worked on other aspects of the tremendous undertaking. It required forty carloads of material and supplies to lay one mile of track, all of which had to be transported from the Missouri River. Every mile the railroad moved westward vastly complicated supply considerations.

Omaha reaped rewards beyond expectations from the building of the great railroad. The Union Pacific made the city its base of operations, leasing the Herndon House as a headquarters. Crews laid out a large yard and erected massive shops. The company employed six Missouri River steamboats. Hundreds of teams and wagons operated between Iowa railheads and Omaha. Oliver Ames bought $5,000 in shares in an Omaha bank; other railroad officials poured in money, hoping to capitalize on a boom that they had initiated. Speculators arrived from across the country, and several businesses in Council Bluffs and rival Nebraska communities relocated in Omaha. The city became a roaring camp that handled every conceivable need of the Union Pacific. Thousands of workers came through town. So did gamblers, prostitutes, thieves, and bunco artists. They were interested in a share of the action at the Hell-on-Wheels, the colorful tent city gambling and recreational center that moved west with the tracks. In Omaha gigantic piles of tracks and stacks of ties awaited shipment from the waterfront to distant plains and mountains. Merchants and jobbers received railroad orders, and business further increased as the first small towns sprang up along the line.

Conditions were so good that in 1867 Omaha interests acquiesced at the time of Nebraska statehood to the moving of the government to Lincoln, sixty miles to the southwest. What had been considered a prize fifteen years earlier no longer seemed worth bothering about. The state government's importance hardly compared with the fulfillment of railroad destiny. Early in the same year, on a cold seventeenth of January, the first Chicago and North Western train from the east had chugged into Omaha on a temporary pole bridge over the Missouri. The same residents who ten years earlier had despaired for the future now saw unlimited glory. On May 10, 1869, the last spike welded the Union Pacific and Central Pacific together at Promontory Point in western Utah. The word "Done," transmitted to Omaha over a thousand miles of wire, touched off a prearranged celebration. A thousand-gun salute boomed out, bells rang, whistles blew, and fire wagons paraded through the streets. A leader said, "Westward the Star of Empire Has Found Its Way," closing the first chapter in the history of Omaha.

The city proved a better bet than some of the horses that ran over a hundred years later at Ak-Sar-Ben. In retrospect, observers claimed Omaha's success was easily explained. They cited a number of geographic factors, such as "river lines" and "breaking points," as proof of the inevitability of Omaha's role as the Gate City. By applying the theories commonly used by nineteenth century urban developers, a tremendously complex chain of events became predestined. This reduced to little consequence the hopes and aspirations of the participants in the Omaha story: William D. Brown and his hope of a town at the western terminal of his ferry, J. W. Pattison and his dream of greatness in the *Arrow*, Thomas B. Cuming and his stake in selecting a territorial capital, Augustus Kountze and his plan for regional banking, Edward Creighton and his knowledge of telegraphy, Grenville Dodge and his surveys of railroad routes, Abraham Lincoln and his strategy for making a national state, Thomas Durant and his design of a railroad empire, George Francis Train and his extravagant plans, and Oakes Ames and his desire to build a gigantic fortune. These and others made the decisions that helped Omaha grow. They formulated the programs and marshaled the resources. It remained to see what lay ahead. Would Omaha go on to other triumphs, becoming a regional metropolis? Or would it become just another provincial city of medium stature? The answer depended on new considerations, not the least the fortunes of the Union Pacific and the future of Nebraska.

2

A Little Pioneer Town

On a warm afternoon in August 1859 Abraham Lincoln, standing on an Iowa bluff, looked across the Missouri River at Omaha. Lincoln, an unannounced candidate for the 1860 Republican presidential nomination, was in the midst of a business, political, and pleasure trip. He had made public appearances in Kansas before taking a steamboat from St. Joseph to Council Bluffs. Whenever Lincoln went on deck a crowd surrounded him, charmed by his interesting comments and distinctive manner of speech. In Council Bluffs he checked into the Pacific House. His presence attracted a delegation of civic leaders who persuaded him to give a speech at the Concert Hall. The next day he transacted private business. He carefully studied ten acres on the west side of Council Bluffs that he had received as collateral for a defaulted $3,500 loan. After determining the land was worth at least that much, he decided to take it as payment in full. He returned to the Pacific House, where he met Grenville Dodge, then an unknown surveyor passing through Council Bluffs. Dodge said that Lincoln's "kindly ways" soon drew from him all he knew about the western country. "As the saying is," Dodge recalled, "he completely 'shelled my woods,' getting all the secrets that were later to go to my employers." The next day, Lincoln went east by stage. Lincoln had not considered it worth the

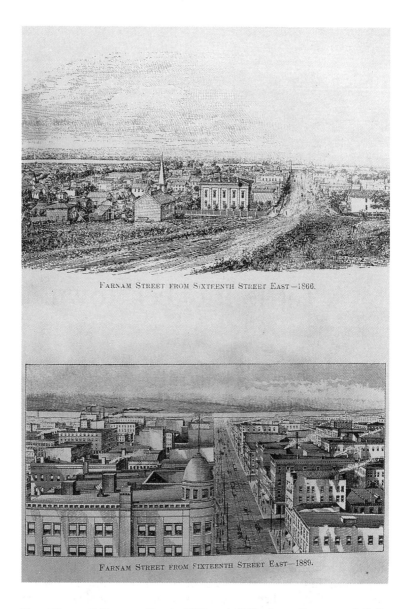

FARNAM STREET FROM SIXTEENTH STREET EAST—1866.

FARNAM STREET FROM SIXTEENTH STREET EAST—1889.

Two Views of Farnam Street, 1866 and 1889, from Savage and Bell, *History of Omaha*

time to cross over and visit Omaha. To him the village was just another frontier town, of the kind he had been familiar with throughout his career.

Early Omaha was an ugly and unpleasant place. The original plat was a conventional grid. Farnam, the main street, ran west from near the river. For a couple of blocks, saloons, hotels, banks, mercantile houses, and other commercial establishments lined the thoroughfare. Behind it were other buildings, scattered across the landscape in no particular order. The first permanent structure in town was a sixteen by sixteen foot square log cabin that the Council Bluffs and Omaha Ferry Company erected to house employees. Identified as the St. Nicholas Hotel on promotional maps, it was better known locally as "The Claim House." Omaha pioneers lived in log cabins, dugouts, and sod houses. One settler resided in a thatched hut of "luxuriant" slough grass. The first baby was born in a squatter's log cabin called "Pork Wild." A large sod house, the Big 6, was a combination grocery and saloon. Throughout the village, tallow candles provided illumination; fireplaces were used for cooking fires and heat. Territorial Governor Mark W. Izard shivered noticeably in a cold room at an executive ball in his honor. Water for domestic purposes came from wells lined with brick, stone, or wood, except during droughts when most went dry. Then, people depended upon muddy Missouri River water. Debris of all kinds piled up in yards, and during the summer tall weeds were everywhere. Neighbors laughed at a Michigan man who planted some ornamental shrubs on his property. As long as Omaha was a frontier camp, few persons, despite the promoters' lavish claims for the future, were willing to invest money in long-range projects. They wanted to wait and see whether Omaha would last and grow. This was in the tradition of town building in America.

Observers viewed Omaha from different perspectives. The Reverend Joseph Barker, an English immigrant who arrived with his family on April 2, 1856, found little that impressed him. "At that time the city consisted of a few huts, two or three decent houses, a bank, the State House, a saw mill, and a few stores," he recalled. "The population would be about three or four hundred. The country round was one vast wild. The prairie fires had passed over it, as far as your eye could reach. The surface was black as coal. To us it had a somewhat hideous appearance. It looked anything but inviting to the eye." A few days earlier, on March 26, the editor of the Omaha *Nebraskian* had described the scene more positively: "Every thing about our city, gives promise of unparalleled improvement and prosperity. Settlers are constantly arriving and sales in real estate are going as briskly as ever. Persons are much more eager to purchase than to sell. Several new frames have already been put up and enclosed this season." It was a familiar story on the frontier and was repeated time and time again as settlement progressed across the continent. There was a wide difference between what boosters claimed and what settlers found.

In Omaha as all along the Middle Border, everyone, no matter what their goals or impressions, wanted to believe in the inevitability of success. J. Sterling Morton, a Nebraska City promoter and politician, caught the spirit of town building. He admitted, "We all felt, as they used to print in large letters on every new town plat, that we were 'located adjacent to the very finest groves of timber, surrounded by a very rich agricultural country, in prospective, abundantly supplied with building rock of finest description, beautifully watered, and possessing very fine indications of lead, iron, coal, and salt in great abundance.' In my opinion we felt richer, better and more millionarish than any poor deluded ever did on the same amount of moonshine and pluck."

Frontier communities attracted a wide variety of people, and Omaha was no exception. The village was a transfer point and jumping off place for thousands of emigrants—Mormons, fur traders, freighters, soldiers, gold seekers, and adventurers. There was no civilization for countless thousands of square miles to the west. Over six thousand western pilgrims, most of whom were bound for Colorado, passed through during the spring and early summer of 1859. Emigrants, frequently dressed in the style favored by veteran mountaineers—red shirts, high-topped boots, and slouched hats—roamed the streets, affecting a rollicking, independent air. During the Pike's Peak rush, the town's stores and saloons operated around the clock. Bull-whackers could be heard at all hours cursing and cracking whips. Plainsmen from the West frequently remained a few days to "rest up" from their sojourns in the trackless wilderness. According to a local expression, they made "Rome howl." An early wholesaler explained, "After having thoroughly 'rested,' the freighters would put in an appearance, and then all would be rush and bustle, to get their trains in order, and they generally wanted this done on Sunday, the day of rest."

A large floating population remained a characteristic of Omaha; the construction of the Union Pacific Railroad in the 1860s brought more wayfarers through town than the mineral rushes of the 1850s.

Although of crucial importance in building an economy, voyagers did not form the nucleus of a permanent citizenry. All promotional tub thumping to the contrary, few looked around and decided they wanted to remain. If anything, most carried away negative impressions, believing that storekeepers had overcharged them. Reactions to Omaha were typical of attitudes held toward other towns along the eastern edge of the Great Plains. In western Missouri, for example, emigrants could hardly wait to leave Independence and Kansas City. The travelers ignored exhortations that they were in the "Centropolis" of North America and should go no further. Settlers had to come from other sources.

Many of Omaha's pioneers were from right across the river in Council Bluffs, although a few came from farther away. There were the officials of the founding land company, plus the usual quota of land sharks and unsavory characters drawn to any highly touted new community. A large number claimed they were lawyers. All hoped to make quick fortunes or gain political advantages. A couple of merchants and physicians drifted in, as did some skilled and unskilled workers. Few families came; the early Omahans included many ambitious young men. In the beginning, not as many settlers arrived as the promoters had hoped. Confident accounts in the Omaha *Arrow* about tremendous progress were not substantiated by statistics. By June of 1855, a little less than a year after initial settlement, there were only between 250 and 300 inhabitants. The population increased slowly and then spurted in 1856 during a premature boom. Between June and October of that year, the number of Omahans climbed from eight hundred to fifteen hundred. This rise, hardly comparable to San Francisco swelling from one hundred to ten thousand people in one year during the 1849 gold rush, caused an Omaha newspaper editor to proclaim: "The growth of Omaha astonishes — is a fact few can comprehend." After that many people left, their spirits crushed by the adversity that followed the Panic of 1857.

At the start of the Civil War, Omaha had fewer than two thousand residents, but thousands more had passed through the town on the way to more promising destinations. William N. Byers, born in Ohio in 1831, was one of many settlers who made an imprint on early Omaha and then moved on. The town company hired him as a surveyor and he produced the first map of the city. After serving in the first territorial legislature and the first Omaha city council, he struck out for Denver in 1859 taking a printing press with him. In the Queen City he founded the *Rocky Mountain*

News and made a fortune in Colorado real estate promotion and other schemes. William Clancy was another member of the first territorial legislature who migrated to Colorado. The owner of the Big 6, he became embittered when authorities cracked down on his business. In retaliation he made himself unpopular by supporting a "manifesto" to remove the capital to Florence. When he pulled up stakes, he left behind few friends and many enemies. A native West Virginian, Fleming Davidson, arrived in Omaha in October of 1854 in time to serve in the first legislature. He ran an ice business in Omaha until 1861 when he pushed on to California. Another man who came in the founding year and who was in the first assembly, Thomas Davis, was a Welsh immigrant. He owned a sawmill for many years and was active in local politics before returning east in 1870 to Indianapolis, Indiana. Robert B. Whitted, an early territorial and city politician, left for Texas in 1857. Such men were not unusual in mid-nineteenth century America. They were but one part of a vast reservoir of restless people who went to the frontier to seek a better life. The superintendent of the 1850 census had discussed the "roving tendency" of the nation's people, a conclusion that described Omahans of the 1850s.

Some other pioneers remained despite the community's inauspicious beginnings. They came for a variety of reasons and stayed because they eventually did well. George R. Armstrong, born in Maryland in 1819, was a printer in Ohio when he decided to "go west and grow up with the country." Following visits to several localities, he settled in Omaha in 1854. He made money as a construction contractor and he enjoyed a successful career as a local and territorial politician. Elected mayor in 1862, he resigned to lead the Second Nebraska Cavalry against the Indians. After that venture he returned to Omaha where for many years he worked for the Union Pacific Railroad and ran an agricultural implement business. Charles W. Hamilton, a New York native, reached Omaha in 1856. He worked for a time as a hotel clerk, but soon went into banking. He became a prominent citizen and served in many religious, civic, and fraternal offices prior to his death in 1906. A Pennsylvania man, John A. Horbach, was twenty-five years old in 1856 when he accepted a position in Omaha as a clerk in the federal land office. During the 1860s he was an express and travel agent, and in following decades he prospered in railroading, banking, and ranching. A physician turned politician, Enos Lowe, was an organizer of the Council Bluffs and Nebraska Ferry Company. Lowe, born in 1804 in North Carolina, had served as president of the second Iowa constitutional convention. He expected to make money in Omaha and he did. He built a gas works, engaged in railroad speculation, incorporated a bank, and invested in a hotel. In 1866 he helped establish the Old Settlers Association, composed of "Builders of Omaha" who had arrived before 1858.

No one saw anything wrong with creating a society to honor the founding fathers of a community only twelve years old. The frontiersmen of Omaha were well aware that the town had succeeded, and they were proud of their own accomplishments. They thought it important to record that O. B. Seldon fired the first forge, that William Snowden conducted the first auction, and that John Withnell laid the first brick. A list of settlers had another effect; it placed everyone on the same level, in a small way acknowledging the contributions and lending a degree of human dignity to those who did not achieve positions of high responsibility—Joseph Miller, John Davis, Edwin Patrick, H. A. Koster, and others.

Many of the pioneers had experienced hard times. One young German immigrant, Vincent Burkley, who had anglicized his name, came to Omaha with his wife and children. He started a small clothing store that failed in 1857 and for a while hewed out a meager living selling vegetables from his garden door-to-door. He went to Colorado to make a quick fortune in the gold fields but returned empty handed. For the next year he husked corn in the fall, cut and sold hardwood in the winter, and operated his small produce business in the spring and summer. Although he had little money, his family had plenty to eat. His few cows and chickens assured a ready supply of milk, cheese, butter, and eggs. He bought, slaughtered, and dressed an occasional pig or calf. A nephew in St. Joseph, Missouri, sent apples every year from his orchard. "Mother's cellar would be considered comfortably stocked in the fall," Burkley's son wrote, "when she had a hundred pounds of lard, three or four hams and shoulders, a half barrel of sauerkraut, a large crock of mince meat, and the safe or cupboard well filled with pickles, preserves, cheese, etc., also a liberal quantity of sausage meat cut fine and seasoned to our own taste which certainly went well with homemade buckwheat cakes on a cold wintry morning. Besides these we had wild gooseberries, currants, grapes, strawberries, raspberries, plums, haws, elderberries, chokecherries, and quantities of hazel nuts, walnuts and hickory nuts which we would gather in the fall." After business conditions improved, Vincent Burkley worked as a clerk in a general store. He renewed ties with his old suppliers in the East, many of whom were reluctant until a general wartime prosperity to resume wholesale operations on the frontier. Early in the Civil War he again opened his own store and went on to a successful career, first in business and then in journalism. His experience of frequently shifting occupations was characteristic of the frontier. Few persons enjoyed immediate success.

An early problem that confronted the Omaha founders involved federal land laws that they considered unfair and unenforceable. Critics—meaning the vast majority of people in the West—argued that the government's policy of selling land impeded rather than promoted progress. They ignored the fact that land sales represented a major source of federal revenue. Rather they believed sinister elements responsible. Some imagined a plot by southern planters to curtail free homesteading; others thought industrialists in the Northeast wanted to hold up settlement to prevent drains on populations in the older states. Almost all thought that the land policy favored wealthy speculators. There was a growing conviction that the government should give land away to encourage western settlement. The Free Soil party of Martin Van Buren, which ran third in the 1848 presidential election, advocated such a course. The clamor increased the next year, when the Illinois Central Railroad received a gigantic land grant. Free land became a tenet of the Republican party, culminating in the passage of the Homestead Act of 1862, under which an individual could obtain 160 acres for a small price. Arrangements were different in 1854 before the change in policy. Land office clerks continued to take in money and to go through the motions of pretending to enforce an unpopular system that had severe operational defects.

On paper the first Omahans could obtain land under the Pre-emption Act of 1841. An individual marked out a claim to a 160-acre quarter section, made certain improvements, waited for the official survey, and obtained a clear title by paying $1.25 an acre on the date that the government put the property up for sale. Payment could either be in cash or military land warrants. Special provisions covered some potentially serious problems. Survey crews had the responsibility of making minor adjustments in property lines to ensure equity; titles could be conveyed by quitclaim deeds. Another piece of legislation, the Federal Townsite Act, allowed a town company to stake out 320 acres. The proprietors, acting on their own, had the right to claim their 160-acre tracts to which the Pre-emption Act entitled them from adjoining land.

These were the general ground rules. The problem was that what looked clear on paper failed to work in practice. The land office did not officially begin survey work around Omaha until 1856, two years after the ending of Indian claims and the start of settlement. An office, authorized for Omaha in 1854, opened three years later. The land sale, scheduled for 1857 but held up for political and economic reasons, finally occurred in July 1859, five years after settlement. With the prospect of homestead legislation, settlers throughout Nebraska fought to put the sale date off as long as possible.

The Omaha investors, almost all members of the Council Bluffs and Nebraska Ferry Company, acted on their own and on the side of what a local historian and early resident, Alfred Sorenson, claimed was human greed. He said they "accordingly undertook to secure the lion's share of the plunder." First, they took more land than they were entitled to by the law. The ferry company grabbed at least six sections. Members of the enterprise, along with other favored persons, each claimed an additional quarter section. This effectively tied up roughly sixty square miles of the public domain. The participants saw nothing wrong with their actions. They had no respect for the federal land laws, and at the very least they hoped to use proceeds from sale of the added acres to pay for entitled holdings. All involved took a calculated risk. If the project failed, as did most town speculations, the legal essentials lost meaning. At any rate, they wanted to protect their interests. So they turned to a common frontier extra-legal device, a claim association. Indeed, rival town promotions in Nebraska all formed similar organizations.

On July 22, 1854, persons who "got in on the ground floor" crossed the river from Council Bluffs and founded what became the Omaha Township Claim Association. Assembled under the "lone tree," the company quickly ratified claim laws characteristic of those used as the frontier moved westward through the Northwest Territory to the Middle Border. The rules provided for the protection of all holdings up to 320 acres, with the understanding that no member could own more than eighty acres of timber. There were a number of detailed provisions, including one requiring a claimant to erect a house within thirty days. This was cynical to say the least; the moving of a mobile dwelling from place to place satisfied the requirement. More importantly, the organizers made provisions for enforcement. Elected officers included a "judge" and a "sheriff." Serving under their jurisdiction were "regulators" from the ranks of association members. The motto was the same as elsewhere: "An injury to one is the concern of all." To remain in good standing, members were required to spend $50 annually to improve their claims.

At first, the Omaha club functioned much like others along the eastern border of Nebraska. It dissuaded land sharks and other unsavory elements from taking advantage of the drifting nature of a weak central government by intruding on what should have been an orderly procedure. However, "regulators" chased away some legitimate settlers in full compliance with federal law, setting precedents for later actions. On one occasion a hundred armed men destroyed a shack. They scattered the lumber to the four winds, before allowing a terrified owner to flee back to Iowa. In another episode, a member of the organization got in trouble for a casual remark that United States laws allowed a man to enter 160 acres of land. The first territorial legislature, oblivious to the Constitution, passed a bill recognizing the activities of claim clubs. This was only natural. Most members belonged to one, as did the signer of the measure, Acting Governor Thomas Cuming.

Sporadic violence occurred in the Omaha area in 1856 and 1857 when regulators dealt harshly with suspected or actual claim jumpers. That was at the height of the first Omaha land boom, when choice river lots sold for as much as $2,500. At a mass meeting of the Omaha club, a member who recently had been acquitted of murder made a choking noise and thrust his hand in the air, yelling: "Instead of letting them prove up we'll send them up." His colleagues, while having no intention of going that far, were ready to intimidate people. Regulators burned the premises of Jacob S. Schull, forcing him to leave the territory. An Irishman accused of signing a false name at the land office underwent systematic torture. After being knocked down, tied, hung twice by the neck for short periods, locked up, and starved, he agreed to sign a quit claim before being run out of town.

A most highly publicized incident concerned a man named Callahan. In the winter of 1857, he claimed a piece of land on Omaha's west side. Officers from the Omaha Township Claim Association, arraigned him and forced him to stand at a mock trial. The verdict was that he renounce the claim or face drowning. Given thirty minutes to decide, he refused to relinquish his holdings. Led onto the Missouri River ice, he remained obstinate as regulators chopped a hole, big enough for a man. He held out through three lengthy dunkings before capitulating, convinced that his tormentors intended to let go the next time they pushed him under. He was nearly frozen stiff. Following a cursory medical examination, Callahan, wrapped in heavy blankets and fortified with three doses of whisky, signed a document of relinquishment. That affair convinced most other potential claim jumpers to stay away. In the few cases where the association lost, challengers defended claims by brandishing rifles and shotguns, touching off feuds and generating ill-will that lasted for years. On the whole, however, the claim association, according to one of its members, functioned as an omnipotent force.

The Omaha Township Claim Association disbanded following the official government land sale. There was no further need for the body. Almost all claimants who filed for additional land gained permanent titles through false entries. The original speculators succeeded in protecting their holdings. In a later decision, the United States Supreme Court refused to overrule the actions of frontier claim associations. The Omaha club contributed stability to a chaotic process. The club's main function had been to preserve what members saw as legitimate rights of property. It had the usual contradictions of frontier voluntary societies. They protected members from illegal actions, at the same time guarding their acquisition of more land than allowed by law. As it was, claim associations were only a part of an intricate structure of informal control mechanisms.

Vigilante committees, disorderly throngs, and extra-legal tribunals meted out punishment for criminal acts. This approach to law and order related directly to the inability of the federal government to develop machinery to protect citizens from criminal elements—horse thieves, rapists, murderers, and robbers—common to the frontier. Incompetence, delays, and technicalities made it easy for law violators to go free without standing trial. Federal judges concentrated on civil cases. It made little difference that the first territorial legislature in Nebraska had adopted the criminal laws of Iowa; there were not enough officials to run a system. As late as 1857, the only regular judicial authority in Omaha was the mayor sitting as a police judge. The Nebraska federal marshals were not of the same stripe as those who later tamed the Kansas cattletowns. There were no Wyatt Earps or "Wild Bill" Hickocks. Rather, they were nondescript political appointees. United States Marshal B. P. Rankin, ordered by the chief justice of the territorial court to disperse a mob, delivered the command in a stage whisper, knowing full well that no one would pay attention. Nor was the federal attorney of any help in prosecuting offenders. He concentrated on personal pursuits. In essence there was no federal legal presence in Nebraska Territory. To make matters worse, the mess in Kansas occupied officials in Washington. Nebraska had a low priority and seemed far away from the thoughts of embattled national politicians trying to contain the explosive issue of slavery in the territories. Against the backdrop of "Bleeding Kansas," the thirteen slaves reported in the first Nebraska territorial census virtually assured a policy of statutory neglect; slaveholders and abolitionists knew what side would win. The first wave of Nebraska settlers took advantage of the opportunity to take the law into their own hands.

Frontier Nebraska was probably not as violent as several previous pioneer settlements. Back in the 1790s a spirit of lawlessness had prevailed in Tennessee, far removed from organized government. The threat of Indian uprisings and the rough-and-ready character of the frontiersman contributed to the problem. So did government officials. The federal district attorney in what was then the Western District of North Carolina was Andrew Jackson, a hot-tempered young lawyer and land speculator, who engaged in many duels. In the Northwest Territory, the federal court records for the Additional Circuit Court for Michigan Territory, which in the 1820s and 1830s had jurisdiction over the future states of Wisconsin, Minnesota, and Iowa, indicated a high incidence of violence among lead miners and fur traders, attributed directly to the heavy use of hard liquor. Ax murders and brawls happened frequently. Few criminal actions ever went to trial. The court left the punishment up to local citizens, concentrating instead on civil land and personal property suits. During the 1849 gold rush, when there was no legal structure in California, law and order broke down completely. Only a quick institution of harsh vigilante justice stopped the outrages. Over 50,000 persons had swarmed into California from all across the country. The situation in Nebraska was much different. A few thousand settlers arrived in the first couple of years, and almost all lived along an eighty-mile stretch of the Missouri River. An organized judicial system existed directly across the river in Iowa, which had already passed through the territorial stage. So, the persons from the Hawkeye State who crossed over to Nebraska were already accustomed to an established legal process. Moreover, while freebooters did go to the new territory, more went to Kansas, attracted by the possibility of quick plunder under the guise of serving the causes of slavery or freedom. Naturally, the criminals in Nebraska caused serious concern. In Omaha, citizens attempted to stop nefarious practices, moving from informal mob action to sophisticated vigilante activities. The progression illustrated an aspect of community building, showing how Omaha passed through an important part of the frontier experience.

In 1856 two bungling offenders were the first to feel the brunt of Omaha frontier justice. They stole two horses in Omaha, selling them to nearby Pawnee Indians, who traditionally had good relations with whites. The horses escaped and galloped home. The Indians followed, learned they had been duped, and promised to provide what help they could. Not long afterwards, the thieves appeared at the Pawnee village trying to sell two mules. The Indians grabbed the men and took them to Omaha. The surprised residents could hardly believe their good fortune; horse thieves, unless captured at the scene of the crime, almost always escaped punishment. Omaha did not have a jail, and a mob gathered around the hapless prisoners. Following a discussion, a consensus developed; the prisoners would have their heads shaved and given thirty-nine lashes. After a barber shaved the right side of one man's head and the left of the other, they were led to a "liberty pole" across from the Apex Saloon. Members of the mob tied the first thief to the pole. Next, there was a slight delay. No one volunteered to apply a rawhide horse whip. After a discussion, those assembled decided that the Indians should do the work, on the grounds that they were the main victims. They readily assented, but when one of their number applied the lash with killing strokes, the mob decided that something else would have to be done. The job fell to the owners of the horses, who carried out the punishment. One man seemed to enjoy the work. He counted each lash and after the last stroke shouted, "That's all." The Indians whooped and yelled. Many whites watched in a solemn mood, feeling the affair necessary but regrettable. The only person opposed to the punishment, the chief justice of the territorial court, had to watch helplessly. When it was over, escorts took the two victims to the steam ferry and ushered them out of the territory. They were never seen again in Omaha. That ended the incident, and the chastened criminals may have considered themselves lucky to have escaped with a whipping. Nebraska Territory's criminal code provided for jail terms for convicted horse thieves. The penalty for armed robbery was ten to twenty years, and for other robbery two to ten years. The usual punishment handed out by a frontier mob was lynching.

The Omahans had acted with restraint. The next time would be much different.

In March 1858 a posse chased and apprehended two Iowans, Harvey Braden and John Daley, accused of stealing horses near Florence. Both men, known desperadoes, had the horses in their possession. In Omaha, Braden and Daley had a preliminary hearing before a magistrate. In default of bail, he committed them for trial. Early in the evening a few days later, a small group appeared at the jail. The sheriff was away and there were no pedestrians in the streets. Only the sheriff's wife was in the building, and she offered no resistance as men took the key, opened the cell, led Braden and Daley outside, tied them up, dumped them on a wagon, and drove away. The vigilantes, followed by a large crowd of onlookers, took their captives north of town. The procession stopped by a stout oak tree with a large protruding branch. Men threw a single rope over the limb, tying one end around Braden's neck and the other Daley's, as they stood huddled together on the wagon. A whip cracked and the vehicle moved away, leaving the horse thieves, back-to-back, dangling in the air. The mob quickly dispersed; the two men swung freely through the night. The next day, authorities transported the bodies back to Omaha. Prior to burial, a rat pack mutilated the remains. A coroner's jury examined twenty to thirty hostile witnesses. They admitted being present, contending they had not participated and were unable to identify any of the perpetrators. The jury brought four bills, but no one was ever convicted. The cases, tried in another county after a change of venue, ended in acquittal. Hauling two men out of jail and hanging them with a single rope before an enthusiastic crowd was an indictment against the community. Still, apologists argued that cruel as the act was, there was a process involved. Out of barbarity, Omaha supposedly moved closer to the standards that prevailed in civilized places.

A brutal incident marked the final series of actions that moved Omaha in the direction of law and order. George Taylor, a construction engineer, and his wife lived ten miles out of Omaha on the military road. Taylor was away on business in the spring of 1861 when two men, James Bouve and John S. Ilher, appeared at his isolated homestead. They tied his wife to the bed, assaulted her, and absconded with valuables, including the silverware. Ilher had to restrain his accomplice, Bouve, when he threatened Mrs. Taylor with a gun and said he wanted to burn her alive in her own bed. The two men fled to Omaha, where they buried their loot on the river front and went to a saloon. There, they drank, played cards, and attracted attention by freely spending money. They expected no trouble; rape was a crime that usually went unreported. Furthermore, itinerant big spenders were frequent in Omaha. They reckoned without George Taylor. He returned home, heard his wife out, went to Omaha, and swore out a robbery complaint. Ilher and Bouve, arrested on suspicion, loudly protested their innocence, claiming they had just come in from the west to seek employment as laborers. Released for lack of evidence, they returned to the saloon, playing innocent. They claimed to expect money from friends and swore to "make the town ring." Not realizing they were under surveillance, the two eventually left the tavern. At that point, the city marshal placed them under arrest.

The victim identified the two men at a hastily held arraignment. Described as a tall, slim, and stately woman, she answered a judge's question about her assailants by screaming, "Yes, I could tell them among ten thousand people!" Some of those in the room thought her attitude overly tragic and that she had seen her better days, speculating on what she had done for a living prior to her marriage. She picked both men out of an identification line. Stopping before Bouve, she exclaimed, "You are the man. I know you even if you have shaved off your whiskers, for I never can forget those eyes!" Walking a few steps further, she halted before Ilher, stating, "And you are the other man; you saved my life. It was you who said, 'Jim, don't shoot the old woman!' " That night, after intensive questioning, Ilher confessed and led authorities to the bottoms, where, with the aid of lanterns, they found the loot from the Taylor cottage. The next day, five hundred men assembled, selected a "jury," appointed managers, and tried the two men in a kangaroo court. Two lawyers represented them, arguing that the law should be allowed to take its course. The "jury" brought in a verdict of guilty, recommended clemency for Ilher, and left the crowd to decide whether or not to turn the two over to the vigilance committee for a "neck-tie sociable." Following pro and con speeches, the throng, voting by walking across a line, turned the affair over to the vigilantes. At midnight, a mob appeared at the jail and overpowered the marshal. Ilher was set free and allowed to run off into the darkness as revolvers cracked, whistling bullets past his ears. Bouve, a professional gambler and criminal reported to have killed many men in Colorado, suffered a different fate. He died, strung up on a hall beam in the jail, the tip of his toes touching the floor.

A coroner's jury, possibly consisting of some of the killers, attributed his death to hanging by persons unknown.

The vigilantes did other things designed to bring law and order. They staged mock hangings of two men, a counterfeiter and a jewel thief. Amid laughter, they strung up one young man and then cut him loose, dropping him into fifteen feet of snow. Gamblers also incurred wrath. A campaign against them had dramatic results. Some received late night visitations. Masked vigilantes with dim lanterns and cocked pistols broke into their rooms, giving them twenty-four hours to leave town. They heeded the advice, as did others who found a skull and crossbones painted on their doors.

Frightening suspected thieves and chasing away gamblers failed to end crime in Omaha. There were several sensational murders in the sixties. In 1863 Cyrus Tator, a former member of the Kansas territorial legislature, went to the gallows for killing a business associate. There was a difference between his case and others. He received a trial before a legally constituted jury that declared him guilty, and a higher court denied his appeal. On April 23, 1863, after he gave an hour-long speech stating his innocence, officials tied a rope around his neck, drew a black cap over his head, and dropped him into eternity. That concluded the first legal execution in Nebraska, and with it the activities of the Omaha vigilantes. There was no longer a need for such an order. A lawful hanging — hardly an event that a community wanted to commemorate — signified a fundamental change in standards. The city had crossed an invisible line. The administration of justice in Omaha had passed out of the frontier period. This and other signs seemed to indicate a new era.

The settlement slowly evolved into an established community. This was a goal of all western town promoters. As quickly as possible they wanted to recreate the institutions associated with civilization in the eastern portions of the United States. What they wanted was hardly unique, but merely an extension of the experiences of city builders in the Northeast and Midwest. The decisions of individual entrepreneurs, who had little vision beyond their immediate past experiences, was crucial in determining urban contours. During the first years environmental factors, so important after a place started to show significant growth, had little if any impact. No one in early Omaha worried about industrial pollution or grasshopper infestations; it was a case of one thing at a time. Omaha's promoters were aware that most town sites never had the opportunity to grow. Cut off in infancy, they at best were relegated

Bird's Eye View of Omaha, 1868

to the role of country crossings, marked only by a roadhouse and a few houses. Moreover, a large population by western standards did not always result in the creation of an established social order. Many mining camps, which at the height of their glory had several thousand inhabitants, never had schools or churches. Conversely, carefully planned small Puritan communities in colonial New England quickly acquired religious and educational institutions. In the middle of the nineteenth century this pattern held in frontier Wisconsin. Galesville and Whitehall in predominantly rural Trempealeau County soon acquired the social and political forms of participatory democracy. In contrast to this was Iowa County in the heart of Wisconsin's lead mining region, where the considerably larger towns of Mineral Point and Dodgeville had few settled institutions, many bars, and much original sin.

Creating a city that mirrored eastern norms was somewhat like constructing a house. There was already a generally understood blueprint. Yet much needed to be done from the laying of the foundations to final completion. Sometimes building went forward at a rapid rate; at others there were long delays. Certain activities might move ahead with dispatch, such as putting on siding. At the same time, window framing could lag from a want of materials. The speed of the accomplishment depended upon the mix, the ingredients that went into the initial years of organization. Omaha was never a pastoral village or a mining camp. It was a speculation and a communications point, helped at its inception by corrupt politics. The territorial government had little positive influence on the cultural scene. If anything, considering the antics of members of the territorial legislature — they frequently adjourned so that the proceedings would not affect their alcoholic consumption, brawls occurred with regularity on the floor, and debates had juvenile attributes — their presence retarded the establishment of conventional practices. The work fell to a few dedicated individuals who felt it important to bring stability to the Nebraska frontier.

In 1857 a group of businessmen and lawyers founded the Omaha Library Association. Motives varied, but they included the education of future generations, the desire to promote adult education, the wish to copy eastern practices, the aim to further reform, and the plan to sell Omaha as a cultural center. The organizers rented a room, charged a nominal fee to join, and soon acquired over a hundred different publications, including many current newspapers and periodicals. The Nebraska delegate to Congress sent the *Congressional Globe* and various printed compilations of federal documents. The regents of the State University of New York donated eight books. Within short order, the Omaha association decided to hold a lecture series, a widely used device in other parts of the country to cultivate the arts. There was no way to obtain top talent from the East; Omaha was too far off the beaten path for such luminaries as Henry David Thoreau and Ralph Waldo Emerson. Instead, the Omaha association relied on area residents. Speakers gave formal talks on "Our Constitution and the Laws," "Progress," "Emigration," "Free Thought," and "Labor." While the lecturers were admonished to avoid religion and politics, Amelia Bloomer, a Council Bluffs feminist, gave a controversial presentation, claiming women were intellectual equals of men. Between 250 and 400 persons, close to a third of the population, attended at least one session during the 1857 season, encouraging organizers to offer programs the next year. The editor of the Omaha *Times* gave extensive coverage, claiming the lectures afforded "positive evidence" that there were people on the frontier "capable of delivering good lectures." Contradictions existed between the goals of the association and reality. The claim association continued to drive off land claimants; the vigilantes were at the apex of their power. Some of the same individuals probably belonged to all three groups. Be that as it may, a few Omahans saw the value of bringing intellectual pursuits to the village. Their contribution loomed large in creating a community. Without articulating a viewpoint, they realized that there was more to forming a city than protecting property and taking a harsh position on law and order.

There was a gradual building up of religious institutions. In August 1854 a Methodist, Peter Cooper, an English immigrant and quarry operator, gave the first sermon in Omaha in a private home. The sixteen worshippers entered through a kitchen shed. The service was symbolic; at that time almost all the Omaha pioneers lived in Iowa. Next spring, the Methodists sent a circuit rider. He conducted services in the territorial capitol and started a six-member congregation, hardly an auspicious beginning. The town company donated two lots to the new organization, which sold them for $1,500, using the proceeds to erect a church. Baptists, Presbyterians, Congregationalists, Episcopalians, and Roman Catholics followed, enjoying various degrees of success. The Roman Catholics dedicated St. Philomena's Cathedral in 1856, a plain structure that within three years became the seat of the Nebraska See. The wife of Edward Creighton strongly supported the Catholic Church, which grew into one of the most affluent religious bodies in the

THE FIRST CHURCH IN OMAHA

First Roman Catholic Church in Omaha, 1856

region. The Episcopalians in Omaha counted many local leaders among their membership. Baptists, Congregationalists, and Presbyterians had trouble getting established; a pioneer Baptist preacher commented that religion "met only a left-handed favor." A succession of study groups, store front churches, and itinerate ministers failed before the creation of permanent bodies.

Those who strove without success to found churches agreed with a threadbare Omaha Methodist cleric who told his small flock on Thanksgiving in 1859 that he could not think of anything those present had to be thankful for. Ministers in Omaha worked at sectarian positions during the week and shared sanctuaries on Sunday. Omaha's potentialities sustained one early pastor. "My father thought Omaha an excellent place for the establishment of a United Presbyterian church," one of his daughters recalled, "as well as a good place for investing some of the money his father had left him." By the late 1860s religious institutions appeared on the way to solid establishment. While Omaha was hardly a city of churches, and attendance was not as good as leaders desired, steeples that rose toward the heavens were further indications that Omaha neared the end of the frontier experience.

Education gained a footing. In the earliest days there was more interest in promoting higher than primary or secondary schools. Omaha merely copied earlier urban experiences in the older sections. The desire to first stress higher learning characterized early American settlements from colonial times onward. The Council Bluffs and Nebraska Ferry Company persuaded the territorial legislature to charter a "paper university" and claimed to set aside a thousand acres to further development. The institution acquired a name, Simpson University, and a governing board. Announcements proclaimed the start of classes, but none were ever held and the school died stillborn. It was simply a promotional device, as were several other colleges founded in Nebraska during the fifties. The first schools in Omaha were "subscription schools," where patrons paid set student fees directly to teachers. Again, this was a common part of the nation's educational experience. There was no public system until 1859. The curriculum emphasized the three Rs, "Readin', Ritin', and 'Rithmetic." Discipline was harsh. Teachers generally accepted the adage, "No lickin', no larnin'," and kept switches on prominent display. The board of education, beset with financial problems, established a tuition structure based on matriculation levels for individual courses; arithmetic cost one dollar per quarter and algebra three dollars. Even though almost five hundred students enrolled, exigencies forced the schools to close for two years during the Civil War. Private schools filled the void. S. D. Beals started what he called a high school, which soon had almost three hundred pupils. For a time, the institution aroused suspicion and hostility; supposedly it instilled "highfalutin" elitist concepts. Despite criticism, a realization dawned that Omaha needed good primary and secondary schools; it was part of the coming of civilization. The public schools reopened. The board erected three frame primary buildings and made a commitment to run a high school. In 1871 the state legislature created a consolidated school board in Omaha. Although a great deal remained to be done, public education, nonexistent in the community's formative years, had become a reality.

In 1857 the third Nebraska territorial legislature granted Omaha a city charter, providing for a mayor and council. This was the standard form of local government used in the United States. The legislature kept certain powers over financial matters and the police. Imprecise wording over technical issues and partisan politics resulted in long and drawn-out controversies. There were several charters before one in 1873 increased the role of the mayor and allowed a measure of home rule. The original charter had left the mayor without a veto power and made him just another member of the city council. While the charter provided the machinery for the first election, it gave no guidance on council procedures. The new government had to meet daily for a couple of months to determine routine business practices. The city recorder obtained copies of the ordinances for Iowa City, Iowa, which became the basis for those subsequently written for Omaha.

The elected officials had little previous experience in government. Proceedings were very informal, with the tone set by the first mayor, Jesse Lowe, a forty-three-year-old former North Carolinian and a first settler. He was a combination Indian trader, banker, and real estate man, with a colorful and sinister past. "He was a strange man," an Omaha minister said. "I suppose in his younger days he was Captain of a robber band in Texas where he made a great deal of money. . . . They say he was a very dangerous man. His body, I suppose, has numerous cuts & scars & gunshot wounds, and a Bowie knife was once pushed through his body, but escaped killing him. They say he has four wives living." Lowe presided over a council that local residents called the "city circus." As the territorial legislature demonstrated, parliamentary procedure and

Ice Bridge over Missouri River

decorum were not strong points of the governmental process in Nebraska Territory.

The territorial city government hired officials, established departments, passed ordinances, and strongly supported spending money on projects designed to help Omaha. The first city councils appointed a number of municipal officers; a collector, a treasurer, a marshal, a clerk, and a few others, such as election judges, on a temporary basis. A major item of concern was fire protection. The first council rejected a plan to buy a $1,500 engine. Instead, they purchased hooks and ladders. In 1860, after an insurance company contributed seventy-five dollars toward the formation of "Pioneer Hook and Ladder Co. No. 1," the council purchased a fire engine. From then on, expenditures increased in relation to growth; in 1865, at the organization of "Fire King Engine Co. No. 1," the aldermen authorized another engine, plus 1,500 feet of hose.

Ordinances covered everything from animal control to the regulation of bowling alleys. One statute encouraged citizens to plant shade trees; another allowed the stacking of hay on designated streets. In early actions, the council committed the city to spending $50,000 to finish the territorial capitol and extended aid for the construction of the Herndon House. The hotel owners received land originally set aside for park purposes. The council's attempt to finance the capitol with $50,000 in scrip ended disastrously in the wake of the Panic of 1857, contributing to a city debt in 1858 of $60,000. This brought a sense of false economy. The city printer presented a bill for $110 and received $70, and the election clerks had $3 bills cut in half. In 1868, after threats from Union Pacific leaders, the council floated a $200,000 bond issue to help the railroad build a Missouri River bridge at Omaha. A decade later, city debts totaled close to $288,000; only $28,000 of the Union Pacific bonds had been redeemed and canceled. The first political leaders, all of whom had close business ties, took such a policy for granted. Like their counterparts in rival towns along the Missouri, they accepted the need to use public indebtedness and tax revenues as a means of promoting growth.

Omaha advanced in many ways through its first two decades. There was no longer a need for a claim association; the vigilante committee had outlived its usefulness. The Omaha Library Association signified a move in the direction of a developed society. By the 1870s Omaha had taken on the physical attributes of eastern cities in which buildings were jammed together, business streets

Omaha in 1870

were crowded, and a smoky haze rose from hundreds of chimneys. Still, it remained a frontier community. Josie McCague McCulloch remembered:

> Omaha at this time of course was a little pioneer town, with streets deep in mud or dust. Tiny cottages of frame were the rule, with occasional two-story houses and a very few brick ones. The Kountze home a block south of us seemed palatial. It was surrounded by a few acres of ground and had a fence and gate around it. But this was exceptional, and young men brought their brides out here from comfortable homes back East furnished with every convenience. In Omaha the young wives found two- or three-room houses scattered here and there on the prairie, without water, light or heat, except from cisterns or wells, kerosene lamps, and wood stoves.

On the edge of the plains, along one of the great rivers of North America, the raising up of Omaha had just begun. Those who followed the pioneers had an opportunity to build upon what a local historian called, "A record of settlement, organization, progress and achievement."

Part Two

COPYRIGHT, 1898 — RINEHART, OMAHA. PHOTO —

HORTICULTURE BLD

1870-1900

LILY POND

Nº679

3

Omaha Was Born with Her Fighting Garments

Between 1870 and 1900 Omaha grew from a frontier railroad center into a regional metropolis, despite recurring economic troubles. The Panic of 1873 and the national depression that followed brought to a halt several years of prosperity. Hard times set in and recovery failed to come until near the decade's end. There followed tremendous progress in the eighties. Transportation, commerce, and industry flourished. Rapid settlement of the upper Great Plains created the opportunity for vast hinterlands. Omaha developed a clearly defined business community. During the nineties, drought conditions in Nebraska and the Panic of 1893 once more brought severe adversity. Thousands of persons left Omaha during the economic decline before it, along with the rest of the country, regained a solid financial footing. By the turn of the century, prosperity had returned and Omahans believed their community on the threshold of a golden age. "Few, if any, were idle, and the busy hum of industry was heard and could be seen on every hand," a local leader remembered. "Immigration was fast pouring into our state, wholesale houses were being established here, parks and boulevards were improved or constructed—all giving evidence of our city's future greatness, permanency, and stability. In short, not a cloud appeared upon the horizon without its silver lining." Omaha had secured a place in the American urban mosaic, but questions remained. Had it done as well as hoped? Had opportunities been lost? Would different leadership and goals have allowed Omaha to become one of North America's great centers? Could it yet do so? There were no easy answers.

Omaha had to operate within the context of an emerging urban system. The large outfitting trade in the 1850s and the location of the Union Pacific Railroad ensured survival and dominance in Nebraska. Freighters in Nebraska City could not compete, and the town's prospects fell accordingly. Success, though, brought new obligations and problems. As it tried to move ahead, Omaha had to challenge other new western cities. When the frontier drew to a close, several places had already hewed out regional empires that affected Omaha's aspirations. San Francisco, created in the frenzy of a great gold rush, was among the top cities in the nation. In 1882 an expert recorded, "Its growth was rapid; its enterprises were magnificent; its hotels were the grandest, its ventures the most daring, and its speculations the wildest, in modern commercial history." The aggressive businessmen of the boisterous city on the bay had extended their interests far beyond the boundaries of California, throughout the gold fields of Nevada and Colorado, challenging Omaha interests. Salt Lake City, a unique community, its policy determined by Mormon leaders before the arrival of overland railroads or gold discoveries, had a firm grasp over the economy in the Salt Lake Basin. The best Omahans could hope for was to improve upon established relations. The same was true in regard to Denver. The Queen City had created the "Rocky Mountain Empire" and had excellent ties with Omaha.

How firm these links were would depend upon what happened with the opening of areas of potential competition in Wyoming and Montana. Portland posed another potential source of friction. Its bankers transacted the chief commercial business of Oregon and Washington Territory. If the Union Pacific should decide to build into Oregon, Omaha would automatically become a rival of Portland. As it was, other cities and economic combinations felt that the conservative policies of Portland's Scottish and New England bankers left the Northwest ripe for the picking. This proved a correct assessment, but it was Seattle that eclipsed Portland in the 1890s, not Omaha.

Closer to home, Omaha had to contend with other regional forces. Less than two hundred miles to the south, Kansas City had achieved part of the promise predicted by earlier experts. It out-distanced several neighboring towns. Then, in the competition to win regional prominence it contested successfully with Leaven-worth, Atchison, and St. Joseph for the first railroad bridge over the Missouri River. The span opened on July 3, 1869, and Kansas City quickly gained connections into the southwest. In addition, the old Union Pacific-Eastern Division Railroad, renamed the Kansas Pacific Railroad, joined the Union Pacific at Cheyenne, providing a transcontinental route. Kansas City capitalists wanted to extend their interests into Nebraska, competing directly with their Omaha counterparts. Members of the Kansas City Board of Trade hoped to make their town the country's prime livestock and packing center, building on a profitable and growing agricultural base in Kansas. On the northern plains, another city threatened Omaha. At the Falls of St. Anthony in Minnesota the old lumber town of Minneapolis, helped by a massive influx of outside capi-tal, moved ahead in the first years following the Civil War to corner the flour milling industry. The mill owners, operating in concert, plotted to control sources of supply. Their strategy in-volved dominating grain supplies in the Dakotas, which Omaha merchants had taken for granted as part of their natural marketing area. There were other places that needed consideration. Sioux City enjoyed a short-lived promotional boom. Some economic analysts had believed that Fargo and Bismarck properties represented good investments. Rapid City and Sioux Falls experienced a flurry of economic activity during the Black Hills gold rush. Omaha had nothing to fear from those towns; despite attractive geographical features, they never had metropolitan dimensions. Of more real danger to Omaha was another place, one that had played a part in its rise—Chicago.

The Lake Michigan city of Chicago prospered initially because of a canal, but its leaders soon formulated a successful railroad strategy based on the assumption that "natural channels" had had their day. The first Chicago line, the Galena and Chicago Union Railroad, garnered an impressive amount of upper Mississippi River trade and paid large dividends. As a result, northeastern cap-italists eagerly invested the millions of dollars that Chicago rail-roaders needed to construct massive systems. In the fifties several new railroads helped the Windy City take trade away from its major challenger in the Midwest, the Mississippi River city of St. Louis. First overconfidence and then a recognition that it had no way of countering Chicago's railroad strategy ended the hopes of

St. Louis. Enriched by the fruits of Midwest commerce and industry, Chicago surged to hegemony over a vast section of the upper Mississippi River Valley. An important aspect of Chicago's drive had involved, in addition to a Pacific Railroad out of Omaha, the building of railroads across Iowa to Council Bluffs. Held up by the Civil War at obscure railheads, the three main routes had resumed construction after the end of hostilities. In early 1867 the Chicago and North Western Railroad reached Council Bluffs; two other Chicago roads arrived in 1869, the Chicago and Rock Island Railroad and the Chicago, Burlington and Quincy Railroad. These ribbons of steel, thrust across the Hawkeye State, provided positive evidence of Chicago's plans to extend its commercial interests into Nebraska and other points outside the Midwest.

None of the Omaha business leaders had a grand railroad strategy. They left matters up to the Union Pacific Railroad. Until the Union Pacific, Omahans had shown little interest in railroads. In the fifties, when pioneer Chicago railroad builders plotted lines of economic conquest and when Kansas City promoters made the "Iron Horse" a symbol of community aspirations, the best Omahans could do was to chart a couple of "paper railroads" over trackless prairies. They thought in terms of outfitting and freighting. The construction of the Pacific telegraph failed to generate a railroad frenzy. There were no local railroad programs at the time of the decision to build the Union Pacific out of Omaha. The city could not even boast a railroad messiah until George Francis Train proclaimed: "The Pacific railroad is the nation and the nation is the Pacific railway." Omahans welcomed the Union Pacific with open arms, extended favors, and went on the company payroll. It ended there. The Omaha capitalists had no way of controlling the broad contours of their own destiny. They lost that opportunity with the driving of the first Union Pacific spike. Of course, there was no reason to assume they would have been able to build a great city if they had unlimited funds and decision-making powers. They were mainly men of small vision. Anyway, the great capitalists who started the Union Pacific had no intention of letting Omaha entrepreneurs have a major say in affairs. Telegraph executive Edward Creighton fell out with railroad officials; banker Augustus Kountze served as window dressing on the board of directors. At the dawn of the Gilded Age the future of Omaha was in the hands of the railroad's executive group, which included some of the most buccaneering capitalists in all of American business history.

What should have been a minor and unimportant controversy concerning the first Union Pacific bridge across the Missouri River accentuated the subservient position of the Omaha interests. After Omaha and Council Bluffs officials disagreed over the bridge's location, the Union Pacific proposed a site that would have entirely avoided Omaha. The Omaha business community responded by sending a delegation, which included the governor of Nebraska, to New York to negotiate with Thomas C. Durant and other Union Pacific leaders. At first a solution favorable to Omaha had appeared impossible. The delegation received a cool reception; the members had to sit for a day in the railroad's offices before Union Pacific leaders would receive them. Eventually, a "compromise" provided for an Omaha bridge. On March 26, 1868, the delegation's chairman sent a telegram home that contained news of the agreement: "The bridge is located at Train table. Omaha pledges the depot grounds and $250,000; Council Bluffs pledges $200,000; ground and right of way will be condemned." The message started a spontaneous community celebration, and people set bonfires in the streets. The delegates returned in triumph.

The whole affair may have been an elaborate charade arranged by the company. Jay Gould, a rising Wall Street financier and a new member of the Union Pacific ownership group, had sided with the Omahans. He told them that he had persuaded his fellow entrepreneurs with great difficulty to change their minds. Was that the case? The "High Bridge," a twenty-seven hundred foot long structure, officially opened to traffic in 1872 and the Union Pacific reacted resolutely when the Council Bluffs city government brought suit in federal court to force the terminal to be moved there from Omaha. Because Iowa law prevented the three railroads that stopped in Council Bluffs from crossing the river, the Union Pacific established a subsidiary railroad company to operate the bridge. It transferred freight cars and ran a "Dummy Train" for through passengers. In 1876 the Supreme Court ruled against the Union Pacific, and the railroad had to terminate trains in Council Bluffs. This came too late, so the city's leaders gave up hopes of greatness and concentrated on securing markets in the rural districts of western Iowa. The Union Pacific, because of large investments, was probably committed all along to Omaha. However, local leaders had no way of being sure; there was always an element of chance even in the most honorable of business dealings. So they had gone to the Union Pacific promoters, giving them what they wanted and leaving Omaha deeply in debt.

Union Pacific Bridge, 1872

The completion of the Union Pacific left open the possibility that the city would stagnate as a division point. Despite grim predictions, however, the local economy flourished in the early seventies. Migration into Nebraska generated new business. The whole decade saw considerable construction in Omaha; the erection of several large structures lent a more cosmopolitan flavor to Farnam Street and its environs in the downtown district. Union Pacific shops employed over six hundred workers. James E. Boyd started a successful pork packing business; he slaughtered forty-five hundred pigs in the 1872-73 season. Hotels reported good and improving business. The work of building a hinterland went ahead. At least fifty-six commercial travelers operated out of Omaha. Then came the Panic of 1873 which ushered in a national depression that lasted several years. By early 1874 Omaha's economy had taken a sharp downturn. Conditions were so bad that the local press felt compelled to take note. On January 17, 1874, the Omaha

Bee obliquely acknowledged, "Several business failures have occurred in this city within the past few days but not as many as were expected by the knowing ones." The downturn continued during the next four years. Agriculture prices dropped for Nebraska products; grasshoppers ravaged crops. As if all this was not bad enough, disastrous events affected the Union Pacific. The startling exposures of corruption discredited the original management; Gould took over as president and followed unsound policies. He built branch lines into unsettled territory. Some ran through barren wilderness directly parallel to the Kansas Pacific Railroad, which he then bought, compounding his problems. Instead of one idle railroad he had two. When business finally began to improve, there was a growing belief that Omaha needed to establish economic independence. The Union Pacific connection had not worked out as hoped.

Union Pacific Headquarters, ca. 1870s

Edward Rosewater

On May 8, 1874, Edward Rosewater, a rising figure in Omaha life and the editor of the *Bee*, took local businessmen to task for following what he considered a policy of complacency. He accused them of sitting around, "like so many opium eating Turks, enveloped in the illusive but enchanting cloud land, where magic air castles are built and precious gifts abound." Meanwhile, he said, "wide-awake and energetic rivals, without natural advantages" had industriously applied artificial resources in building up profitable commerce, using the profits to develop home manufacturing. He said that Omaha had allowed Kansas City, St. Joseph, and Sioux City to garner Nebraska trade. Instead of fighting, he claimed, Omaha capitalists had invested their money and time in "wildcat speculations" in Texas, Utah, and Colorado, inaugurating "a system of public stagnation on the do-nothing plan." Rosewater contended that it was "no wonder" that retail trade had stagnated and unemployment increased. He called upon the city to shake off the "blightening role of old foggies," and to renew its advance. "She cannot afford to remain contented with mere transfer pickings, and roads from nowhere to nowhere," he concluded. "We must have railroad outlets to the northern and southern borders, and we must open an outlet to the vast granaries in Central Nebraska." Implicit in Rosewater's criticism was that Omaha leaders should concentrate on building profitable markets in Nebraska, finding ways to encourage the rapid settlement of the state's vast prairies.

Omaha had powerful allies in exhorting settlers to come to Nebraska. The Union Pacific wanted people along its line. Land companies, some under railroad ownership, wanted to sell real estate. Early in statehood, Nebraska established an immigration board. Pamphlets were a favorite promotional device. In 1878, L. D. Burch, the western correspondent for a Chicago newspaper, wrote *Nebraska as it is: A Comprehensive Summary of the Resources, Advantages and Drawbacks of the Great Prairie State*. In his introduction, Burch thanked state agencies, land company owners, railroad executives, political leaders, and Omaha businessmen. As might have been expected, Burch found the region had few drawbacks. He attacked "grumblers" and "nomads" interested in "howling" about droughts, hot winds, Indians, and grasshoppers. He condemned "lazy, thriftless, shiftless, improvident fellows who never struck a sturdy blow," whose incompetence in dealing with what should have been a minor problem gave the state a bad name during the 1874 grasshopper infestation. He ridiculed men with a "passion for farm machinery," who wasted money on all kinds of unneeded implements. Conversely, Burch found much to praise in what he called "an empire, almost as fair as the fabled Eden, and as rich in productive resource as the historic valleys of the older lands."

Burch called Nebraska "THE GARDEN LAND," where a farmer, rarely "driven with his work," could easily grow anything from peanuts to wheat without even having to use fertilizer. He declared:

> The cultivator has few foul weeds or foul grasses to encounter and there are no roots, stumps, or stones, or other barriers to impede the progress of the joyous plowman. . . . It is no uncommon thing for one man and a medium team to plow, plant and cultivate one hundred acres of land, and gather, thresh and market 2,000 and 3,000 bushels of the staple grains therefrom, hiring only for harvesting and threshing. The whole South Platte country, from the slopes of Cass and Otoe counties, westward to the plains of Juniata is veritably a farmers' paradise, whose valleys are wanting only in the enchantment of distance and glamour of history to give them the fame of the Arno. So too, I might say of the North Platte country — the land of valleys. The proud Roman could hardly blame his Cincinnatus for following the plow along the valleys of the Blue and Nemeha, or the matchless plain between Crete and Juniata."

That was the siren call of the plains.

Of more interest than the lay of the land to potential migrants was the problem of rain. Burch, stressing that Nebraska in Indian dialect signified "wide flowing water," argued that scientific meteorological studies conducted by University of Nebraska professors indicated that rainfall in the state increased between 1867 and 1877. "A gradual change," he claimed, "had come over the State, which is still going on, and this change is indicated by an increasing moisture of the atmosphere and rainfall. . . . From the increasing rainfall of the State, it is also evident that at no distant day the whole State as far as its western limits, will have an abundant rainfall for all the needs of the agriculturist." Burch did not explain the reasons for the startling change, but several self-proclaimed experts presented what they considered plausible reasons. A favored theory held that rain followed the plow. Supposedly, moisture that fell on broken ground recirculated into the atmosphere, automatically increasing the rain supply. Another idea was that rainfall rose in direct proportion to settlement. Other postulates emphasized the influence of modern technology in bringing rain. Humming telegraph wires created an electric quality in the sky, causing electric storms. Heavy railroad trains rumbled along, shaking rain from the heavens. Smoke from belching locomotives made rain clouds. If all else failed, the setting off of explosive charges and the firing of artillery pieces brought rain. In one form or another, the message was loud and clear; irrigation was unnecessary in even the most sub-humid parts of Nebraska. Farmers could succeed by using the same methods used back east. As Burch said, "The same labor the farmer of Wisconsin, Michigan, Ohio, Pennsylvania, New York or New England, bestows upon thirty acres of land, will cultivate one hundred acres of average Nebraska soil, and do it well."

In the eighties Nebraska enjoyed spectacular growth. The state shared in the movement of hundreds of thousands of people to the arid sections of the plains. Settlers, lured by easy land and lavish promotional claims, flocked to "banana belts" and "silk growing regions." During the decade enough rain to grow grain fell just about every year, even on the western edges of the plains, lending substance to claims of gradually increasing rainfall. The pioneers came from many places—the steppes of Russia, the lowlands of Denmark, the fjords of Norway, the green fields of England, the hills of Germany, and the fruited plains of America. According to official statistics, Nebraska had 452,402 inhabitants at the start of the 1880s and 1,058,910 at the end, an increase of more than 600,000. This represented a growth rate of 134.06 percent, far above the national average. Previously remote areas, far off the path of civilization, registered substantial gains. Custer County, in the rolling treeless hills of central Nebraska, jumped from 2,211 people in 1880 to 21,677 in 1890. The newcomers were home-steaders who arrived after a Union Pacific branch line reached the county seat of Broken Bow in the mid-1880s. Sheridan County in the Sand Hills of western Nebraska, one of twenty-six counties organized in the eighties, had 8,687 residents in 1890. Several farming counties experienced growth rates in excess of 1,000 percent. Even though some observers later questioned the validity of the census totals, there was no doubt of significant progress. Nebraska became a major cattle and grain producing state. The sod houses on the "Farmers' Last Frontier" had tremendous significance for Omaha. Almost overnight, the city gained an agricultural hinterland.

Stockyards were the cornerstone of a new economic policy for Omaha. Agitation for one had started back in the 1870s, with insignificant results. There were few cattle herds on the upper plains, and the main goal of local business interest had been to ride out the depression. A leader had set the tone in a rousing 1876 July the Fourth oration, when he said, "As the fabled Minerva came full-fledged from the brain of Jupiter, so was Omaha born with her fighting garments upon her. . . . If she seems weary with her duties to-day, she goes forth to-morrow to encounter and overcome new and greater obstacles with the strength of inspiration."

In 1876 John A. Smiley organized the Union Stock Yards Company. He planned to erect facilities on an eighty-acre tract just north of the Omaha city limits, but he soon abandoned the project. The following year a livestock committee appointed by the new Omaha Board of Trade investigated the possibilities of a stockyard and interviewed Union Pacific officials. During 1878 three groups organized stockyards. One never opened. Another, the Union Stock Yards Company, a small "transfer yard" tied in with certain ranch properties in western Nebraska and Wyoming, moved to Council Bluffs. The other yard, the Omaha Stock Yards Company, had trouble from the start. The Union Pacific refused to give it shipping advantages and levied a heavy toll on cattle crossing the bridge. Cries of the existence of a "Bridge Moloch" had no effect on the railroad. In 1880, after the Union Pacific started a small stockyard in Omaha and threatened to construct a major facility in Spoon Lake, Iowa, the Omaha Stock Yards Company sold out to the Union Pacific — at a sixty percent loss. The lesson was clear. No stockyards could succeed in Omaha without the cooperation and participation of the Union Pacific Railroad. That meant doing business with Jay Gould. As it turned out, there was an Omaha capitalist ready and willing to do just that. His name was William A. Paxton.

Paxton was a classic rugged individualist of the Horatio Alger mold. Born on a Kentucky farm in 1837, he grew up in Missouri. He first came to Omaha in 1857 to build bridges along the military road that extended from the city to Fort Kearny. After that he drifted back and forth between Missouri and Nebraska, working on construction projects. He married a Missouri woman and made Omaha his home. In 1860 he worked as a foreman for Edward Creighton on the Pacific telegraph. Next, Paxton ran a livery stable in Omaha, earning twenty dollars a month. Dissatisfied with that position, he became a mule skinner and started a small freighting business. He carried freight between Omaha and Denver, and for the then under construction Union Pacific. He quickly put to good use $14,500 that he made on Union Pacific contracts. During 1869 he went to Abilene, Kansas, where he bought cattle from

Texas, brought them to Omaha, and sold them on the hoof for a $12,000 profit. After that he engaged in new speculations. He bought stock in the local Omaha & Northwestern Railroad and directed construction of the first twenty miles of the line. More importantly, he became a partner in a firm that won a lucrative government contract to supply the beef allotment for Indian agencies, furnishing from 25,000 to 75,000 head of cattle annually.

By the middle of 1870s, Paxton was a major plunger. Taking advantage of rock bottom depression prices he invested heavily in Omaha real estate, branching out into other activities. He bought stock in local banks, started a wholesale grocery, and acquired an interest in the Council Bluffs stockyard. Paxton proceeded quietly and his activities went relatively unnoticed, hardly receiving the publicity of Andrew J. Poppleton, real estate man, politician, and lawyer for the Union Pacific; John Creighton, philanthropist and administrator of his late brother Edward Creighton's vast holdings; and Andrew Hanscom, land speculator and traction line operator. Many thought Paxton another mule skinner who had made some money. He soon acquired a much different image.

Paxton, as a successful speculator must do, anticipated a trend: the coming of fundamental changes in the range cattle industry. By the Civil War, an estimated four million longhorn cattle roamed the Texas plains. Worth a dollar a head in their native habitat, they had the potential to bring as much as forty dollars each on the eastern market. The problem was how to get them there; no through railroads ran into Texas. The end of the war saw the initiation of the famous long drives, first to Sedalia in Missouri and then to a series of Kansas cattle towns. Paxton was among those who saw a way around the expensive drives and long rail trips, once lines were built into Texas. The solution was relatively simple; stock upper plains ranges with beef cattle.

In 1873 Paxton started a cattle ranch some three hundred miles west of Omaha near Ogallala, Nebraska, a division point on the Union Pacific main line. He was extremely successful, receiving more than the forty percent annual return customary in the greatest days of the range cattle industry. In one complex transaction, he made a quick $675,000 by selling 22,000 head of cattle to the Ogallala Land and Cattle Company. This was a firm that he had helped to found and in which he owned $125,000 in stock. As he rose to power, Paxton, a hulking man, seldom seen without a pipe between his clenched teeth, became increasingly ruthless. Speaking about a competitor who sought an accommodation, Paxton loudly proclaimed, "Who in the hell wants to go into partnership with a fool, the best way is to freeze out the son-of-a-bitch."

In 1883 Paxton was a prime mover in making Omaha a livestock center. He helped organize two concerns—the Union Stock Yards Company of Omaha (Limited), and the South Omaha Land Company. Both were controlled by a "Syndicate" that established the Ogallala Land and Cattle Company. The "Syndicate" consisted of Paxton, several Omaha businessmen, and Alexander Swan, a powerful Wyoming "Cattle King." Swan later took credit for organizing the Omaha stockyards. While he may have thought it his idea, because others involved enthusiastically went along with his initial proposals, there had been much prior agitation. He was never more than a minority stockholder in any of the "Syndicate's" three companies. Of more importance was the role of the Union Pacific. Gould, desperate for traffic to solve his railroad's increasingly serious financial difficulties, made an arrangement with the "Syndicate." In doing so he abandoned plans to put the railroad into the stockyard business in a big way. The "Syndicate" received favorable shipping rates, assuring a corner on all livestock trade handled by the Union Pacific. Some of the "Syndicate" members worked for the Union Pacific and the first stockyard went up on land purchased from the railroad by the South Omaha Land Company. It was a convenient arrangement for all concerned.

The Union Stock Yards Company of Omaha (Limited) had an initial capital of $1 million. A total of $700,000 was subscribed at the time of establishment. Paxton, who held four hundred shares with an opening book value of $40,000, became president. In an early order of business, the firm bought his holdings in the small Council Bluffs "transfer yard" for $100,000. Next, the Union Stock Yards Company of Omaha (Limited), bought 156.5 acres of land from its companion South Omaha Land Company and started construction. The yard opened in August 1884. The first shipment handled consisted of 531 longhorns from Medicine Bow, Wyoming. The cattle, after feeding and watering, were transshipped east within twenty-four hours to Chicago packing plants. Receipts of livestock for 1885, the first full year of operations, totaled 117,000 head of cattle, 153,000 hogs, 19,000 sheep, and 2,000 horses and mules. "It was slow work at first; the market did not build in a day, and for a considerable time the yards remained merely a feeding station for stock en route to the eastern markets," an official contended. "Being located on the natural route from the West to the East, the beaten trail so to speak, of the stockmen going to and from market, Omaha's natural advantages were easily advertised, and as the volume of stock which stopped at the Union Stock Yards, for rest and feed, increased, it at length began to draw buyers and dealers as honey draws bees." It also helped to have a monopoly. In 1890 the yards handled 615,000 head of cattle, 1,700,000 hogs, 154,000 sheep, and 5,000 horses and mules. The stockyards, by then worth over $4 million, paid handsome dividends to the investors. The yards, capable of handling over 10,000 cattle alone daily, had within a few years become the heart of a gigantic livestock producing complex.

A whole new town, South Omaha, developed in the vicinity of the stockyards on property originally owned by the South Omaha Land Company. It was a fantastic success story, made possible by the policies of the "Syndicate" and far-reaching changes in meat packing. The perfection of refrigerated boxcars, the creation of fast through freight service, and hauling agreements favorable to packers eliminated the need to process meat in distribution centers. In the 1870s Chicago houses had established Kansas City plants that handled southwestern livestock for the national market. The spreading of cattle to the northern plains, coupled with the dramatic increase in Nebraska livestock production, made similar plants economically feasible possibilities for the Omaha area. Even so, the great Chicago packers had no intention of coming to Omaha on their own volition; they demanded inducements and the laying of the necessary groundwork. It was not enough for the South Omaha Land Company to build packing houses and to lease them at very liberal terms. Those considerations persuaded Geo. H. Hammond & Co., of Detroit to open a slaughterhouse in South Omaha in 1885. Other actions, typical of the morality of the Gilded Age, needed to be undertaken.

John A. McShane, a major stockholder in the three "Syndicate" companies, had the task of carrying on negotiations. At first, he faced problems from Chicago railroads that operated in Iowa. When the Chicago and North Western placed an embargo on livestock shipments to Omaha, McShane went to the railroad's main office. He threatened to have a bill passed by the Nebraska legislature prohibiting the shipping of livestock from the state to Chicago. When a railroad executive asked him in a matter of fact way if he could do it, McShane replied, "I know I can do it." Two weeks later the railroad lifted the embargo. It was just a routine shakedown that had failed because of counterthreats.

Dealing with the giants in the packing industry was another matter for McShane. They were not about to be intimidated by the possibility of action by the Nebraska state government. More tangible and lucrative inducements attracted them. Gustavus F. Swift decided to open a plant after a visit to Omaha. "We handed him $100,000 in cash and $100,000 in stock," McShane admitted. Another packer, Robert Fowler, established a plant in Omaha in exchange for an offer similar to the one Swift took, plus a rent free house for five years and $25,000 in South Omaha Land Company stock.

Negotiations with other prospects proceeded in kind. Sir Thomas Lipton, the English tea merchant and yachtsman, promised to open a hog slaughterhouse in exchange for a free five year lease. After the completion of the building, he pulled out of the deal because he could not obtain the kind of "light hogs" he desired. McShane used the facility as part of an offer to lure the Armours and Cudahys. Philip Armour, at first rejecting overtures, telegraphed McShane to come to Chicago for an interview. McShane recounted:

> He referred to his former statement that he had declined to consider any Omaha project owing to the fact that he had all the business he desired, and he then said that he had a boy in his employ to whom he was paying a salary of $25,000 a year, and was willing to pay him $50,000 if he could stay with him. But the boy wanted an interest in the Armour business. "I can't give him that as I want the business to go to my sons," said Armour, "but I stand ready to finance this boy — Ed Cudahy — to any extent necessary to establish a packing house in Omaha." I then suggested that he buy the Lipton equipment, and he acted almost at once on the proposition. Terms were soon arranged. We gave Armour the Lipton house and $350,000 of stock in the stockyards company, and the contract was signed by myself. Within less than eighty days Michael Cudahy had the beef house completed and was killing cattle and sheep.

The results of what McShane called "promoting the stockyard enterprise," satisfactory to all parties directly involved, represented a triumph for Omaha. It was on a par with obtaining the Union Pacific Railroad; Omaha assured itself of becoming the dominant city in an emerging region. In a single stroke, its capitalists enriched themselves, lessened the domination of the Union Pacific, garnered millions of dollars in packing plants, assured a large working population, and created a strong friend out of a potential enemy. No longer did Omaha interests need to respond to threats to move bridge or stockyard locations. They could now start to think in different terms. The Chicago packers were components of great regional combinations, involved in a wide variety of activities, including railroading and banking. They had gained a foothold in Nebraska and the West with what they considered advantageous terms. In effect, the move into Omaha increased the size of Chicago's midwestern empire, ultimately leading to the incorporation of Nebraska into the new region.

The only loser was the Union Pacific. Gould left in 1884 and Charles Francis Adams, Jr., started an ill-starred reform administration; lines ran to nowhere. The "Iowa Pool" of Chicago lines refused to give shipping breaks on the light traffic over the main tracks, and the decades of corruption destroyed financial confidence. Adams, a member of one of America's most distinguished families, was an expert on regional urban railroad strategy. Two decades earlier, he had written, "The material destiny of Chicago is now fixed. . . . Thus the young city of the West has instinctively appreciated the position and necessity of the country and the age; she has flung herself, heart, soul, and body, into the movement of her time; she has bound her whole existence up in the great power of modern times." In the late 1880s, beset with a host of vexing problems, he had no choice except to stand aside as Chicago interests moved into his terminal. They added insult to injury by constructing massive plants on what a few years earlier was Union Pacific land. Adams, unable to turn the Union Pacific around, resigned. Gould returned, and the railroad went into receivership.

South Omaha developed into what its promoters called the "Magic City." By 1890 it had over 10,000 inhabitants, and under Nebraska law was a city of the second class. The new community claimed to have 327 businesses, among them 3 banks and 37 cattle companies. The cornerstones were the packing plants of the "Big Four"—Swift & Co.; Geo. H. Hammond & Co.; the Cudahy Packing Company; and the Omaha Packing Company. They all had their killing areas, fertilizing departments, bone yards, "arctic" rooms, and gut departments. Worth millions of dollars, they employed thousands of men who yearly slaughtered and dressed millions of animals. The only other large packing centers in the United States were Kansas City and Chicago; the plants in those cities and South Omaha were part of a single monopolistic system. Actually, South Omaha was not a true suburban area. To get there, all one had to do was to cross a railroad track; there was no open ground. What incorporation did was to provide the founders of the "Syndicate" with their own private town. Anyway, there was no

Cudahy Packing Co., 21 January 1896

way to ignore the contribution of William Paxton. "Omaha is indebted to him probably more than any other man for its present prosperity," Alfred Sorenson wrote in 1889. "He was one of the original and principal promoters of the South Omaha enterprise, which is conceded to be the backbone of Omaha." Paxton was not content to rest on his reputation as a town builder. He became an official of the Union Stock Yards Bank, and along with his other holdings, continued to make money in South Omaha.

During the 1880s manufacturing moved ahead in Omaha as part of the original boom. A Missouri River flood that inundated the industrial districts in 1881 caused only short term disruptions. The $2.5 million Union Pacific machine and car shops was the biggest concern. It covered fifty acres and employed sixteen hundred men, many of whom were skilled mechanics and engineers. In an average year, the facility repaired or rebuilt seven thousand cars and two hundred locomotives. Another large company, the Omaha and Grant Smelting and Refining Works, which had six hundred workers, processed a significant amount of the lead, gold, and silver produced by western mines. In 1890 it smelted over 65,000 tons of ore valued at $14 million. The firm, in which Union Pacific officials had large holdings, was worth $3 million. No other Omaha factory had a capitalization approaching $1 million. There were a wide variety of different lines, including basket manufacturers, foundries, carriage works, and syrup refiners, among the more than 150 ventures. Most were small scale operations. Metz Brothers' Brewery employed forty men; the Woodman Linseed Oil Works an average of seventy-five. Despite promotional claims, Omaha was not a major industrial center.

In a more immediate sense, Omaha experienced a great boost in trade and commerce. By the end of the 1880s, there were more than five thousand miles of railroad tracks in Nebraska. The Union Pacific main line was the spine of a gigantic network that covered the center of the state from east to west. The Chicago, Burlington and Quincy Railroad, which entered Omaha in 1871 by buying a short line, then crossed the Platte south of the city, built through Lincoln, and on to Kearney, where it joined the Union Pacific. Other roads, among them the Missouri Pacific Railraod; the Chicago, St. Paul, Minneapolis and Omaha Railroad; and the Fremont, Elkhorn and Missouri Valley Railroad, added further luster to Omaha's railroad web.

The city's jobbing trade grew correspondingly. An 1890 credit report listed 207 retail and jobbing firms with aggregate sales of

$50.2 million. They dealt in just about every conceivable product: groceries and provisions, dry goods, toys, drugs, millinery, lumber, oysters and fish, notions, twines and cordage, books and stationery, and illuminating oils. A considerable warehouse district developed. Department stores, notably one owned by Jonas L. Brandeis, did a flourishing business. The New York Life Insurance Co. and other eastern businesses established regional headquarters in Omaha. The seven national, seven private, and four savings banks underwent healthy expansions. The private banks were very important in cementing hinterland ties. They bought and sold land, made farm loans, wrote insurance, and dealt in grain and livestock. Over six hundred commercial travelers scoured Nebraska and neighboring states for new business. Omaha was in motion. Tens of thousands of new residents arrived every year. The city received national attention; some observers predicted it would be the next Chicago, a true "Wonder City of the West." Then came the fall. Omaha's commercial economy collapsed like a house of cards.

It all started with a bad crop year. In 1890 Nebraska received seventeen inches of rain or less, the lowest since 1864. This had an immediate impact on Omaha. "The short crops in 1890 caused a heavy falling off in business during the first half of the year," the Board of Trade's fiscal 1891 report admitted. "The retail dealers found it difficult to meet obligations, men were forced to sell goods on long credit. The money stringency further complicated the matter producing a feeling of insecurity."

The adverse conditions touched off a political explosion in Nebraska. Railroads were special targets of collective wrath. Just about every farmer in the state accused the railroad leaders of taking up the best soil under their land grants, bribing all levels of government by giving out free passes, charging excessive rates, engaging in monopolistic business policies, fixing prices, and luring settlers with false claims. The practices of the Union Pacific added fuel to the fire. It openly falsified prices. A general freight agent in Omaha, when asked by a reporter about rates, replied: "Certainly, which side do you want to prove? I can give you figures for either." Other aspects of Nebraska life rankled the agrarians almost as much. Farm machinery cost so much that they sensed a conspiracy. Produce prices seemed exorbitantly low, reflecting collusion. Town dwellers appeared eager to gouge farmers at every turn. Mortgage rates rose so sharply that debtors believed bankers parasites who wanted to live off honest labor. As a bleak year drew to a close, an Omaha businessman had cheerily prophesied, "To truly present the possibilities in store for Nebraska, one would need the pen of inspiration. . . . There is yet room for millions more upon our vast prairies and fertile fields. . . . It is the favored country, the modern Eden." Few people on the sod house frontier agreed.

Nebraska farmers turned to politics. While the revolt against the established order seemed sudden, agrarian discontent had roots that extended back into the early days of statehood. The Patrons of Husbandry, commonly called the Grange, gained control of several Midwest legislatures in the 1870s. Its platform called for state regulation of railroads and an end to alleged exploitation of farmers by middlemen and manufacturers. In Nebraska, the Grange enrolled an estimated 20,000 members. The fraternal body, never strong enough to take over the statehouse, did start cooperatives and two farm implement factories. When these enterprises failed, the Nebraska Grange went into decline. The organization left a twin legacy: a provision in a new state constitution requiring railroad regulation and a precedent for political action by farmers.

During the 1880s another midwestern protest movement, the Farmers' Alliance, gained a foothold in Nebraska. Its leaders called for laws designed to enforce the constitutional provision on railroads and for a general war against the excesses of capitalists. There was little interest until the end of the decade; as late as 1889 a state meeting of the Alliance attracted only a hundred delegates from fourteen counties. The next year was different; the bad crop conditions brought thousands to the Alliance's banner. Former Republicans sang rousing songs; "Goodbye, Old Party, Goodbye," and "A Mortgage Has Taken the Farm, Mary." In the fall, the Alliance gained control of both houses of the legislature, almost beat the Republican nominee for governor, and elected a young Democrat from Lincoln, William Jennings Bryan, to Congress. The Alliance triumphed in other parts of the country. Its candidates, running under a variety of labels, won offices at all levels throughout the northern plains. In the South men favorable to the Alliance principles captured many Democratic primaries, assuring victory in the general election. Alliance candidates did so well that there was soon a call for a national party.

In early July 1892 over 10,000 persons assembled in Omaha to nominate the People's party first candidate for president of the United States. They selected an aging former northern Civil War general from Iowa, James B. Weaver, whose choice seemed incidental to the proceedings; he had changed sides so frequently that friend and foe alike called him "Jumping Jim." But the convention did call attention to agrarian demands. Colorful and extravagant oratory dominated the proceedings. "And now for the first time the classes in these United States are marshaling their armies for the greatest struggle the world ever saw," a speaker proclaimed. "A mortal combat is on, and the ballot will be the weapon of the war. And here in Omaha, a new city in a new state, a state which had no existence when first the clamor of war was heard in the land, a portion of the people of the great republic, the representatives of the industrial classes of every home and type and from every state in this union are assembled in august convention."

Ignatius Donnelly of Minnesota, Paul Vanderford of Nebraska, Mary Lease of Kansas, and other orators flayed the nation's financiers and called upon producers to rise. An hour demonstration followed Mrs. Lease's speech. "It had the appearance of pandemonium turned loose," an alternate delegate claimed, "a parade that will pale into insignificance any ever witnessed in Omaha — banners waved, drums beat, flutes and fifes without number played." The Populist party platform called for nationalization of railroads, government ownership of communication systems, reform of the monetary system, change in election practices, establishment of postal savings banks, and the end of subsidies to private corporations. Critics denounced the goals as socialistic, although many Populists were small capitalists. What they wanted to do was to improve their position in the system by socializing enemies. This was not exactly what the Omaha businessmen had in mind when they had constructed the huge arena to attract conventions. They much preferred the patronage of the General Methodist Episcopal Conference or the Human Freedom League. Yet the great Populist meeting, held in the midst of another year of drought as a hot July sun streamed through the windows of the auditorium, was but a portent of things to come for Omaha. Grim events lay ahead.

In the spring of 1893 a great depression swept across the United States. The economic misfortune wrought havoc upon Nebraska farmers, already hard pressed by low rainfalls, rising costs, and falling prices. The state received 16.24 inches of rain in 1893 and 13.54 the next year, far from enough to successfully raise crops. The state's Populist party became involved in partisan political controversies that clouded the original aims. The old parties embraced Populist positions and fusion became a common device. Democrats and Republicans combined to denounce "Popocrats" as "hogs in the parlor" and "political thugs." Even though the Populists elected a governor in 1892, it was never the same as two years earlier. The original reform aims submerged in bitter political acrimony. Then, too, countless thousands of people had no choice except to give up the struggle to hew out a living on the arid plains of western Nebraska.

Empty homesteads and the wagons of discouraged settlers moving toward other parts attested to the agony. Drummers found no markets; sales plummeted for all categories of goods. Hog prices were so low that some producers shot their pigs rather than pay shipping costs. Boosters argued that the conditions had a salutary effect, driving out malcontents and those seeking an easy berth. "The time has come," the president of the Improved Stock-Breeders Association said, "when the farmer must mix brains with his soil or fall on his rear." This tough talk, delivered in 1895 in an address, "The Lessons of the Drouth," had no influence. Migration out of Nebraska continued. A Sherman County farmer summed up the feelings of colleagues in a sign that stated: "Good-bye, old homestead, I bid you fair adieu; Some day I may go to hell, but I'll never return to you."

Omaha's economy was nearly paralyzed. Factories and stores closed. The city, which had gained an estimated 60,000 residents in the late 1880s, lost over 30,000 in the 1890s. For many of those remaining, soup kitchens and charity houses seemed the only flourishing establishments. Construction stopped; over five thousand homes stood empty. There was no money available. The Union Pacific was bankrupt and the Nebraska hinterland prostrate.

Edward Morearty, an Omaha lawyer and politician, thought his fellow citizens in "anguish and despair" during 1895, the worst year of the depression. He declared:

> Times were growing harder and men and women were out of employment, with no ray of hope in sight. Raids by the depositors were made on many of our strongest financial institutions, some of whom were fortunate enough to meet the demands made on them, thereby restoring confidence to the depositors, who in most cases re-deposited. Others were not so able to weather the storm and were forced to close their doors. . . . Those failures worked additional hardship and suffering on the public and the depositors, many of whom were forced to wait for years the report of the receivers, then receiving but a few cents on the dollar. That year gold was discovered at Cripple Creek, Colorado, and many Omaha men left for the new Eldorado, I being one of them, remaining there at intervals for the great part of that year. On one of my return trips I brought with me five $100 bills, which I had realized through a mining investment. Going into an Omaha

department store and making a purchase, I offered one to be changed. To my surprise and humiliation I had every important attache of the place eyeing me with suspicion due only a bank robber—this was but an instance of the scarcity of money at the time.

The hard times continued into 1896. In that year, the Democratic party nominated Bryan for president. He embraced Populist doctrines, and the party with no real alternatives available, made him their candidate as well. During the canvass, most Populist groups were absorbed into the Democratic party. At the Democratic National Convention, Bryan gave his famous "Cross of Gold" speech, claiming that the nation would prosper only if agriculture prospered. His panacea for recovery was the creation of an inflation through a pat formula: the free coinage of silver at a ratio of sixteen ounces to one ounce of gold, taking the United States off the gold standard. In Omaha advocates of "16 to 1" harangued the unemployed, claiming that adoption of the policy would pay off the entire national debt within a year. On election day, Bryan lost Omaha by 1,000 out of 18,000 votes cast. He carried Nebraska, most of the rest of the plains, and the silver producing states of the West. He suffered defeat after defeat in the remainder of the country, running poorly in eastern urban centers. William McKinley, the Republican victor, represented conservative eastern interests of the same type that had long dominated Omaha. Still, the election settled vexing national monetary questions.

Business, which had started to recover shortly before the election, continued to register gains following McKinley's inauguration. Industries reopened and the real estate market improved. Charitable organizations closed. And, rain fell again on Nebraska. The farmers who had survived knew much more about plains agriculture than before the debacle, particularly the folly of planting crops on grazing land. The claims of early propagandists only had substance in that they applied to good cycles; inevitably, farmers would have to plan for prolonged dry periods, taking them as a matter of course. In addition to such fluctuations, they had to reconcile themselves to varying prices and monopolistic practices. Few people pondered those kinds of basic considerations for very long; they enjoyed the return of prosperity. Old Populists welcomed the improvements. Morearty, active in the movement, exclaimed, "In 1898 the joy bells began to ring, not in gay Malehide, but in Omaha; nature seemed to have removed that staring,

Grand Court, Trans-Mississippi Exhibition, 1898

dejected and melancholy look from the faces of the people, and in its stead left a look of joy, hope, confidence and contentment. A smile like unto that which spread upon the faces of the children of Israel when led out of the land of Egypt and the house of bondage."

The symbol of Omaha's rebirth was the Trans-Mississippi and International Exposition of 1898. Conceived as a means of promoting the city, it had the strong backing of all major civic groups, including the Omaha Business Men's Association and the Knights of Ak-Sar-Ben. The former was an umbrella organization through which the Board of Trade, the Commercial Club, the Chamber of Commerce, and other assemblies engaged in joint actions. The latter, patterned after similar societies in New Orleans, St. Louis, and Kansas City, sought to unite business leaders into a fraternal order that would carry out various activities aimed at helping Omaha and improving its image. Omaha obtained the exposition after complex negotiations with members of the Trans-Mississippi Commercial Congress. Central to success was the active participation in 1895 of Bryan, at the time a newspaper editor in Omaha. He gave a rousing presentation, claiming that Omaha was an ideal place to display the products of the West. It was the center of a region with 16.5 million persons who had an aggregate wealth of $20 billion. Bryan's blatant urban boosterism, far different from his position toward cities in his unsuccessful presidential campaign, demonstrated the importance placed upon the exposition by Omahans.

The driving force in making the exposition a success was Gurdon W. Wattles, president of the corporation established to operate the extravaganza. Wattles was a relative newcomer to the Omaha scene. He had arrived in town in 1892, at age thirty-six. Born in New York, he grew up in Iowa, attended college, and taught school. Making considerable money in small town banking in Iowa, he had sought new horizons, coming to Omaha as the vice president of the Union National Bank. Wattles appeared almost a stereotypical village banker. Yet he was more than that. He was an intelligent and calculating man with a driving ambition, underscored by an ability to develop a successful and calculated plan to rise rapidly in Omaha business. The Panic of 1893 helped him to achieve his goals; it created opportunities for new men. Wattles joined all the right clubs. He said in his memoirs that he "sought every available means to make new acquaintances and friends and to serve the people of my new home." Undertaking the task of running the Trans-Mississippi and International Exposition was a risk on Wattle's part. If he failed, he could be discredited; and at first, his prospects did not appear bright. "It quickly became evident," he recalled, "that we had undertaken a Herculean task at a time when it seemed absolutely impossible to secure the money for its completion." Of course he had immense faith, not misplaced, in his own ability and a belief that the economy would improve.

Wattles did an excellent job of raising money from a wide variety of public and private sources. He accomplished his objectives by adroit lobbying, the use of delegations of businessmen, and appeals to self-interest. The Nebraska legislature contributed $100,000; other states and territories gave $138,000 for buildings and exhibits. Congress appropriated $250,000, on the condition of matching funds. Omaha business interests made generous contributions. In all, Wattles raised a total of $600,000. To ensure a favorable press, he dispensed liberal printing contracts to Omaha newspapers. His gamble was an outstanding success. Between the spring and fall of 1898, despite the Spanish-American War, over 2.6 million persons attended the fair. Visitors included President McKinley. He used the occasion to call the war a "wonderful experience from the standpoint of patriotism and achievement." Wattles took justifiable pride in the Trans-Mississippi Exhibition. He saw it as the start of an era. In opening day ceremonies, he proclaimed, "This exposition . . . opens new fields to the investor, inspires the ambition of genius, incites the emulation of states and stands the crowning glory in the history of the West."

The Omaha exhibition had no relationship to the sod houses of western Nebraska or the modest houses of South Omaha packing house workers. Inspired in part by the Chicago World's Columbian Exposition of 1893-94, the Omaha exposition represented an attempt to be as up-to-date as the Illinois metropolis. At the center of the Omaha showcase for the West was a Venetian lagoon, complete with small craft and gondoliers. The eclectic plaster of Paris structures around the Grand Court were, according to an observer, "freely inspired by the classical and the renaissance." The Fine Arts Building had a statue of a young girl surrounded by cupids; semi-naked nymphs adorned the grounds. A huge plaster of Paris warrior, "Omaha," drawn in a chariot pulled by four lions occupied a conspicuous place. Behind the main buildings was a wide Midway where the main attraction, until forced to change their act, was a group of dancing girls who performed in the "Streets of Cairo" concession. Off to one side was an Indian pow wow grounds, where several hundred aborigines displayed wares, danced, and lost mock battles to whites. To many Omahans, the exhibition represented a release from a long period of black nights.

The fair raised hope and lifted up hearts even before the first visitor passed through the gates. "After so many years of financial depression, it was a joy to the heart and souls of us all to hear the pleasing sound of hundreds of hammers and saws and the presentment of so many beautiful buildings in course of construction," an old resident recalled. "The new white city seemed magic, rising Phoenix-like from clay—nay, like reading a chapter from Arabian Nights." And so, after a decade of shattered ambitions, Omaha and its people moved confidently into the twentieth century. Few doubted that untold triumps lay ahead. The Omaha story was just beginning.

4

The City Has Grown
Too Fast

The Trans-Mississippi Exposition celebrated the march of American civilization. "Within the memory of men now living almost every foot of the great trans-Mississippi country was the habitat of Indian tribes," Albert Shaw wrote in an 1898 article in a national magazine. "The Omaha Exposition signalizes the triumph of the Anglo-Saxon pioneers, first over the aborigines, and second, over the forces of nature." According to the director of the 1890 census the frontier was over. In 1893 historian Frederick Jackson Turner had analyzed the meaning of the change. He said that America's democratic institutions owed much to the frontier, and that its closing had ended the first chapter in the nation's history. Omaha was no longer a city in the wilderness. While an occasional Indian and many cattlemen continued to appear on the streets, the community had completed a civilizing process. At some point after 1870 it had entered a new era. It had acquired the settled characteristics of places in the eastern United States. Social and political institutions had matured and stabilized. Visions of metropolis that helped sustain the early builders of Omaha had taken on substance. Many of the pioneers were active participants in the transformation, and took satisfaction in contributing to the construction of a great regional center.

A major consideration had involved overcoming Omaha's image as a wild and wide-open town. Its role as a transfer terminal automatically attracted numerous undesirable elements. The First Ward was the center of vice. The tenderloin district, in the vicinity of Ninth and Douglas streets, a short distance from the Union Pacific station, operated around the clock. There was a great deal of truth in the poem, "Hast Ever Been In Omaha," which appeared in an 1869 issue of *Harper's Magazine:*

> Hast ever been in Omaha,
>> Where rolls the dark Missouri down,
> And four strong horses scarce can draw
>> An empty wagon through the town?
>
> Where sand is blown from every mound
>> To fill your eyes and ears and throat—
> Where all the steamers are aground
>> And all the shanties are afloat?
>
> Where whiskey shops the livelong night
>> Are vending out their poison juice;
> Where men are often *very* tight
>> And women deemed a trifle loose?
>
> Where taverns have an anxious guest
>> For every corner, shelf and crack;
> With half the people going west,
>> And *all* the others going back?
>
> Where theaters are all the run,
>> And bloody scalpers come to trade;
> Where everything is overdone
>> And everybody underpaid?
>
> If not, take heed to what I say:
>> You'll find it just as I have found it;
> And if it lies upon your way,
>> For God's sake, reader, *go around it!*

The author was probably Frank Streamer, an itinerant newspaper-man, who worked in various capacities for local papers. Said to have had a severe drinking problem, he had first-hand knowledge of the dives of Omaha. After a few years he drifted on to the Pacific Coast to try his luck somewhere else.

Rotten politics was the rule in Omaha. During the 1870s and 1880s the First Ward frequently decided the outcome of local elections. An often heard expression was, "As goes the First Ward, so goes the city." There was no corrupt practices act. Votes, in a day before the Australian ballot, sold for one dollar; election judges, all in league with criminal elements, did not challenge the many "repeaters" escorted to cast votes by their handlers from one polling station to another. Saloon keepers represented the First Ward on the council. An Omaha editor who regularly attended meetings called the body a haven for rogues. Champion S. Chase, the mayor of Omaha in the late 1870s, ran a free and easy city. He was impeached following disclosures that his appointee as city marshal had pocketed fines collected from inmates of houses of prostitution. There was an unofficial license system that avoided police court coffers. A designated city official received ten dollars a month from madams and five dollars from inmates, which supposedly went to the city treasury.

Police judges were part of the corruption system. Judge Patrick O. Hawes, a genial man, who always wore a silk vest and a white stiff-bosom shirt, carried on business in a casual manner making a living from court costs. "It was no unusual thing for him," an acquaintance recalled, "to fine a prisoner while sitting at a beer table, on the statement of a friend who related the facts to him, sticking the fine in one pocket and the costs in the other." After a police raid resulted in the arrest of several men and netted a large "haul," another police judge, hastily summoned at midnight, fixed bail at five dollars. He then adjourned with the accused men and the city marshal to the notorious Crystal Saloon to negotiate the fines. It was no wonder that prostitution, gambling, and saloons flourished, with all their attendant violence and social evils.

It was easy to get a drink throughout the town and at any time of the day or night. All the grocery stores, including those patronized by the town's leading citizens, kept a keg of whiskey on tap as a regular service. Customers imbibed while shopping, charging the costs of shots on their pass books just the same as sugar or potatoes. Saloons had no closing times; some of the busier establishments never locked their front doors. Between 130 and 140 saloons operated in Omaha, roughly one for every 110 men, women, and children. The Crystal Saloon, a haunt of gamblers and politicians, was one of the more luxurious places. On New Year's eve in 1875 the owner held a formal masquerade ball for the sporting crowd. All the leading madams and their prettiest and most sought-after charges attended, dressed in evening gowns and wearing expensive jewelry. Less ornate but well-patronized was the large Central Beer Garden, located by the railroad station. Professional gamblers owned the garden, using it as a front for their activities. A saloon run by "Fatty Flynn," a 425-pound former circus clown and fat man, catered to "visiting sports" interested in a quick game of cards

Beer Saloon, 1886

Waiting Room, Union Pacific Depot, from *Leslie's Illustrated Newspaper*

for high stakes between trains. Of less repute were a series of "colored dens," notorious gambling houses presided over by black managers and owned by white criminals. Near the Fort Omaha barracks, a small military post north of town, a dozen unsavory dives, few of which bothered to pay license fees, only stayed open until the soldiers had spent their monthly pay. These rough places palled when compared with a First Ward dance hall, the St. Elmo Theatre. Billed as a "variety show," it had a reputation locally as the toughest joint between Chicago and Leadville. A week seldom passed without a murder or barroom brawl.

93

In 1881, much to the surprise of the liquor interests, the state legislature enacted the Slocumb local option law, requiring a $1,000 license fee—it was $100 in Omaha at the time—and providing for compulsory closings on Sundays and election days. When Colonel Watson B. Smith, a federal court official in Omaha, advocated strict enforcement of the legislation, unknown assailants shot him to death in his office. Despite moves toward regulation, saloons remained a major feature of Omaha.

Violence was accepted as part of the everyday routine. Typical incidents of the 1870s epitomized conditions. One afternoon, a drunk caused a disturbance in the Variety Bazaar. Bouncers beat him and tossed him into the street. Passing policemen, called "stars," picked the unfortunate man up, placed him in custody, and carried him off to jail. This was an accepted procedure. Men found in gutters accounted for a high incidence of all arrests. Many disturbances never appeared on police blotters. In the rougher dives, pistol whippings and knifings happened all too frequently. The onslaughts aroused public ire only when local citizens got in trouble. After a popular Union Pacific railroad worker was stabbed in the stomach during a barroom brawl, his colleagues threatened those responsible, hanging one in effigy. Fights occurred every Saturday night. One time, a crowd of over a hundred spectators gathered at the main intersection to watch two men, both crazed by hard drink, flail away at each other. In a larger confrontation, soldiers and townsmen exchanged shots. A trooper caused another contretemps: a hair-pulling match over his affections, carried on by two prostitutes that erupted into a general row. In the most disturbing affair of all, toughs beat the Omaha police chief senseless at the Crystal Saloon with no resulting convictions. With some relish, a Kansas City newspaper reporter wrote: "It requires but little, if any, stretch of the imagination to regard Omaha as a very cesspool of iniquity, for it is given up to lawlessness and is overrun with a horde of fugitives from justice and dangerous men of all kinds who carry things with a high hand and a loose rein. . . . Mobs of monte men, pickpockets, brace faro dealers, criminal fugitives of every class find congenial companions in Omaha, and a comparative safe retreat from the officers of the law. . . . If you want to find a rogue's rookery, go to Omaha."

Prostitution flourished. "Many immoral women inhabited the tenderloin district in the vicinity of Ninth and Douglas streets," Alfred Sorenson, the Omaha journalist, reported. "Police raids on the disorderly houses were of rare occurrence, no arrests being made unless some serious disturbance required the presence of officers of the law." Once in a while, the police staged a raid to appease public opinion. In 1873 they temporarily incarcerated fifty-six members of the "frail sisterhood" for "social eviliance." When the police made arrests, there were frequently no convictions. One of the few actual closings of a disorderly house came when a police judge ordered the notorious Red Light shutdown and fined the owner twenty-five dollars. While some practitioners of the "oldest profession" free-lanced, the majority worked out of saloons or bawdy houses. A beautiful woman, Anna Wilson, the companion of a handsome gambler, became queen of the underworld. She lived lavishly, and once had $10,000 in diamonds stolen from her person after she drank too much champagne. Rumors claimed that she was a member of a respectable southern family. A shrewd business woman, on her death in 1911 she left an estate of $250,000 to charitable and public causes in Omaha.

Gambling was the mainspring of the corruption system. Faro banks, Keno games, and poker houses ran around the clock, seven days a week. "Evenings I sauntered leisurely around the city," Edward F. Morearty said, recounting what it was like in Omaha during the hot and dry summer of 1880, "and in so sauntering, curiosity prompted me to follow a crowd of men going up the steps of a two-story brick building located on the southwest corner of Twelfth and Douglas streets. . . . The crowd that was surging in there were gamblers, eager to get on the game run by Dan Allen; Gotley Brooker was dealing the cards." Many visitors found it surprising to see Keno and poker rooms going on in broad daylight; dozens of sweating men huddled around tables playing against the bank. Every saloon had gambling tables. Curses rang out as cards turned. At one place, an old "moocher" and self-styled frontier bully scared tenderfeet by pretending to draw a revolver and yelling, "You super-annuated son of a sea cook," or words to that effect. Many big rollers preferred different surroundings. One maintained a genteel room for high class players; another conducted a game that featured sumptuous lunches. The leading gamblers of Omaha customarily played every afternoon in a room over a Twelfth Street saloon. In 1887 the "Big Four" combination opened the Diamond in a two-story building on Douglas Street. The ground floor had an expensively furnished bar, a pool room, and a horse betting parlor; the second faro, hazard, roulette, poker, and other games. There were many more losers than winners in the wagering rooms of Omaha. Pawnbrokers did a good business, and tales of unsuccessful plungers abounded. In a much publicized incident, a deacon tried to explain his gambling away of church funds by claiming that he hoped to win money to buy books for a Sunday School library.

Losses from chicanery tarnished the name of Omaha gambling. Complaints by honest gamblers led to the closing of "Dollar Stores," which operated around the railroad stations. For one dollar a customer drew an envelope from a box, hoping to win a prize of from one dollar to fifty dollars. Of course, the "Dollar Stores" were pure bunco games, and patrons had no hope of winning. More sophisticated were the activities of a gang headed by Canada Bill, a former riverboat gambler capable of assuming several ruses. A favorite was that of a squeaky-voiced farmer in a slouched hat with one trouser leg stuffed into the top of a boot. His criminal band consisted of a clever crew of card artists, cappers, and confidence men. An able lieutenant, Sherman Thurston, ranked high as a capper. Another, Doc Boggs, had a national reputation as a bunco steerer. He dressed in expensive clothes and was an excellent conversationalist. Other members included two tough enforcers, John Bull and John Sullivan, plus several professional gamblers: Jim Shotwell, Rudolph of Milwaukee, and Grasshopper Sam. These men were among the best-known in Omaha. Their nefarious exploits received a great deal of attention. They followed their trade in the vicinity of the stations and in nearby saloons. Their favorite and most successful swindle was the three card monte trap. Bunco men and cappers befriended unsuspecting visitors, luring them into card games with Canada Bill and his fellow legerdemains. The enforcers lurked in the background, ready to help if needed. There was an actor for every part, ensuring a constant "run of suckers." Once in a while, members branched out into other areas: fixing horse races, rolling drunks, and plotting armed robberies. The Omaha police generally left them alone; most of their problems came from railroad detectives. The Canada Bill gang broke up in 1876. The members moved west to the gold fields but not before establishing precedents for illegal activities that continued in Omaha for many more years.

During the Gilded Age, there was no major call for political reform in Omaha. The closest the city came to having a crusader was Mayor William J. Broatch, and he had suspect motives. He arrested saloon owners who stayed open beyond the never previously enforced 1:00 A.M. closing time, double-crossing elements that had helped him get elected. Most politicos left well enough alone. They generally avoided the issues, although at times they had to take stands on questions that stirred the electorate: the condition of the streets, the need for a better water supply, the levels of protective services, and the awarding of traction franchises. When possible, they concentrated on state and national matters. Both Omaha Republicans and Democrats combined to help defeat proposed amendments to the Nebraska constitution that would have allowed women to vote and ushered in prohibition. Even Omaha Populists avoided calling for reform in local affairs; rather, they advocated national change.

Perfidy and vote buying were accepted as matters of course. Opponents denounced members of one council as "Corporation Cormorants and Venal Vampires." The 1887 Republican primary pitted privately-owned public utilities against the liquor interests. "Such a disgraceful primary was never held in any republic; men voted from three to five times and often ten times that day; wagons and all kinds of vehicles were used to carry men from one voting place to another, and there voted regardless of residence or political affiliations," a participant declared. "Every ward heeler was liberally supplied with money, whiskey and street car tickets; the voting places were amply guarded by the right kind of police officer, whose chief duty was to obey orders from the ward boss." Liquor was an accepted part of politics. In 1890, when William Jennings Bryan ran for Congress, he made an evening canvass of the saloons, sipping soda as an aide set each house up with a free round of beer. Those tactics helped Bryan, a prohibitionist, carry a predominantly Republican district by 10,000 votes.

Throughout the 1870s a small group of railroad executives controlled the dominant Republican party's organization in Omaha. Ward heelers who attempted to follow an independent course ran the risk of having their names listed in the black books, used for hiring and firing, kept by every corporation in town. In the 1880s there was a quiet revolt against what rank-and-file Republicans called King Caucus. After every national convention, local Republicans formed clubs to carry on the campaign. The dissidents, working through corporations interested in breaking railroad dominance, put forward successful slates of businessmen decided on in advance. Despite the breaking of the more oppressive aspects of the old system, the Union Pacific in particular remained an important force in the Omaha GOP. The Democrats did not have an organization until 1884, when they established the Samoset Club patterned after Tammany Hall in New York City. Members of the Samoset Club had stylish uniforms for use in frequently held political parades. The society, which succeeded in reviving interest in the Democratic party in Omaha, disbanded in 1890 following the formation of a broader based organization called the Jacksonian Club. The Populists worked through temporary organizations during their greatest days. In 1898, after the party had gone into decline, they formed the short-lived Peter Cooper Club. If nothing else, the Omaha politicians put on good shows in public complete with monster rallies, uniformed men on foot and horseback, marching bands, and torchlight parades.

Three of the most important Omaha political leaders of the period were all newspaper editors: Edward Rosewater, George L. Miller, and Gilbert M. Hitchcock. Of the group, Rosewater was the most colorful and controversial. A Bohemian Jew, he immigrated to the United States with his parents in 1854 when he was thirteen years old. During the Civil War he was a telegrapher in the United States Army Telegraph Corps. In 1863 he came to Omaha to work in the Pacific telegraph office. He soon became the local manager, holding the position for seven years. In the course of his duties, he acted as an agent for the Associated Press and as a correspondent for several eastern papers. He resigned from the telegraph company in 1870 to found the Omaha *Tribune*. His association with that venture lasted only a few months; he sold out after winning election to the state legislature as a Republican. He served only one term, receiving considerable publicity for successfully sponsoring a bill providing for an Omaha school board and for taking an active lead in helping to impeach the governor for misappropriation of state funds. To promote his political views, he started the Omaha *Bee*. Designed as a temporary sheet, it flourished, soon becoming one of the leading newspapers in Nebraska. Ultimately, it made Rosewater a wealthy man. At the time of his death in 1906, he was one of Omaha's most important citizens.

Rosewater's strong views, not always consistent, made him many enemies. Late in his career, vindictive state legislators denied him election to the United States Senate. Although a partisan Republican Rosewater opposed monopolies, frequently attacking the policies of the Union Pacific Railroad. Yet his opposition to power by the few did not extend to his own self-interest. Along with other Omaha publishers, he bitterly criticized printers when they struck for higher wages. Rosewater was a careful writer. He sometimes started an article more than fifty different ways before he was finally satisfied. Furthermore, he was a good debater. His appearances against national figures drew large crowds. In 1881 he out-pointed Susan B. Anthony on the question of whether women should be granted the vote. During the 1896 presidential campaign, neutral observers thought he outpointed Bryan in a debate on financial questions.

Over the course of a long career, Rosewater attacked thousands of persons in print. It was not unusual for him to break with associates. On occasion, this led to trouble. When he started to horse-whip the editor of the Omaha *Republican* following an exchange of insulting articles, his larger opponent slammed him to the ground and sat on him. Another editor accosted Rosewater on the street and hit him on the head with a billy club. A saloon keeper, Dick Curry, enraged when the *Bee* called his place of business, "A squalid place of resort; a wretched dwelling place; a haunt; as a den of business," received a four-year prison sentence for having a henchman beat Rosewater senseless. Rosewater prevented another physical attack by drawing a gun on James Creighton, who had taken exception to an editorial on a school board issue. The financier, a former overland freighter, then suggested a duel with shotguns—a challenge that Rosewater prudently declined. Rose-water was fortunate no one ever shot him; irate subscribers killed several frontier editors.

George L. Miller became a journalist after working as a physi-cian, politician, and army sutler. Born in upstate New York in 1831, he studied medicine and opened a practice in Syracuse. He migrated to Omaha in 1854, entered political life, and twice won election to the territorial council. During his second term he was president of the body. In 1860 he moved to St. Joseph, Missouri, where he submitted articles to local papers. By this time, he had decided to give up his medical pursuits. At the start of the Civil War, he received an appointment as post sutler at Fort Kearny. In 1864 he returned to Omaha and stood unsuccessfully as a Demo-cratic candidate for Congress. The next year he and another man, whom he bought out within three years, founded the Omaha *Herald*. He ardently championed the Democratic cause; he claimed friendships with two of the party's national politicians, Horatio Seymour and Samuel J. Tilden and rose into a position of leader-ship in Nebraska. For several years, Miller and J. Sterling Morton carried on a feud within the Democratic party. Miller increasingly combined his political fortunes with the promotion of Omaha and Nebraska. He was a member of the delegation that negotiated with Union Pacific leaders for a bridge at Omaha, and he invested

George L. Miller

heavily in real estate. He became a wealthy man, and had lost much of his crusading zeal when he relinquished his editor's chair in 1887. He hoped for a cabinet position that never came, so he devoted the remainder of his life to his Omaha business interests.

Gilbert M. Hitchcock, born in Omaha in 1856, was the son of an early Nebraska political leader. His father, Phineas Hitchcock, was first a territorial delegate and after that a United States Senator. Gilbert received his higher education outside of Nebraska. He attended school in Germany for two years and after that obtained a law degree from the University of Michigan. He burst upon the Omaha scene in 1882 when he debated a feminist, Phoebe Cousins, before a large crowd. Edward Morearty, a spectator, remembered: "I will confess it was the first time I had ever seen or heard of him; yet I am free to say that as the debate progressed he proved to be an agreeable surprise to the audience and to me. During the debate he became so enthused in his subject that he invoked the wrath of his opponent to such an extent that she arose from her seat to attract his attention, and pointing her long bony forefinger at him menacingly, exclaimed: 'Mr. Hitchcock, you are a disgrace to the mother who bore you.' He was applauded to the echo and won the debate on its merits." In 1885 Hitchcock helped found the Omaha *Evening World*. Four years later he purchased Miller's old *Herald* and merged the two papers into the Omaha *World-Herald*. Overnight, Hitchcock, the principal owner in the new morning and evening paper, became a major figure in Nebraska journalism. The *World-Herald* supported the Democratic party; Bryan was editor at the time of his 1896 presidential nomination. Hitchcock subsequently entered politics and served three terms in the House of Representatives and two in the Senate. Hitchcock was a transitional figure among the Omaha journalists with political ties and aspirations. While he took positions on local questions, he never ran for local office. He capped his activities by being the first Omaha newspaper publisher to make a mark in national political and international affairs.

Throughout the frontier period in Omaha, the bad condition of the streets caused many residents to experience lingering doubts about the idea of progress. Even though grading operations, called "surgical operations" by local residents, started at an early date, thoroughfares remained in terrible shape. For several decades the city council did little. It bowed to strenuous opposition from property owners who did not want to pay for improvements. During rainy periods wagons sank up to hubcaps on main roads,

Gilbert Hitchcock

and residents wore knee-high boots to wade through the ruts and potholes. One spring someone put an open barrel in the middle of a flooded stretch of an intersection with a sign warning persons not to fall in, because they would go straight to China. At times the streets became rivers. "Streets are in bad condition, and are daily getting worse," a reporter warned in 1876. "The water is ploughing them out right smart, leaving deep furrows here and there." Trying to use the wooden sidewalks was a frustrating undertaking; during the winter people used the planks for firewood. In 1880 only a quarter mile of Omaha's estimated 118 miles of streets had any paving. The city, which spent approximately $11,500 annually on road work under an inefficient contract system, owned neither a stone crusher nor a roller. Improvements came slowly. Downtown Farnam Street was one continual mud hole until the laying down of what was known as a Sioux Falls granite surface in 1883. All over town makeshift repairs and general inefficiency continued to frustrate Omahans until well after the end of the frontier.

Poor municipal cleansing contributed to inconveniences experienced by pedestrians. The streets were a dumping ground for waste paper, ashes, garbage, and other items. Beasts lay where they expired. "The dead mule, which was lying a short distance northeast from the Union Depot, for several days, and from which a thousand double stinks was emanated every second, has been removed much to the relief of the offended First Ward nostrils, but greatly to the regret of the dogs, cats and rats who were taking their regular square meals off the deceased animal in delightful harmony," Rosewater wrote in 1872. For many years, only a good strong wind improved matters. Authorities gave up; until the 1880s they never attempted to clean the streets. They justified inaction by pointing out that few other western cities bothered with the problem. This failed to impress outsiders, and Omaha gained a reputation as a dirty and unkept town.

Information provided by the city to the 1880 census — the last taken by the federal government prior to the frontier's close — indicated that Omaha had many sanitary problems. There was no system of sewerage. Human excreta accumulated in privy vaults, hardly any of which were watertight. Chamber, laundry, and kitchen slops normally went into dry wells or cesspools, mostly porous and without overflows. There were no regulations governing the disposal of manufacturing by-products. Householders had the sole responsibility of removing garbage and ashes. No uniform way existed of disposing of ashes; garbage piled up on the banks of the Missouri River. Some observers justified the crude method by claiming that the dryness of the climate lessened the danger to health. Another source argued that Omaha was simply experiencing growing pains. "All these things will be speedily changed," an Omaha judge contended. "Thus far the city has grown too fast for public improvements to keep up." Unfortunately, such sophistry did not bring about solutions to serious quandaries.

Many Omahans believed a waterworks the solution. As late as the 1870s water for domestic use came from wells. Firefighters and scavengers depended on water pumped from the river into cisterns, located at intervals throughout town. For many years the city council declined to take any action, citing high costs. Bids submitted by outside interests were allegedly far too high; the project became bogged down in politics. By the late 1870s, public sentiment, as expressed in mass meetings, seemed to favor a reservoir and gravity system proposed by the Holly Company that had built similar waterworks for many other towns. A controversy evolved over ownership, Rosewater and other leaders charged that the "solid eight" on the council had received bribes to grant a franchise to the Holly Company. After sensational charges, judicial actions, disputed ordinances, and a hotly contested election, a group of local businessmen won a twenty-five year franchise. In September of 1881 the City Waterworks Company went into operation, solving a vexing difficulty. Whether or not it led to a cleaner city remained open to question.

Serious problems plagued the new works, even as local boosters praised the combination direct pressure and gravity system, which featured a powerful pumping engine that brought up water from the Missouri River to a ten-million-gallon-capacity reservoir on Walnut Hill. The water distributed through the mains contained too many dead fish and two much raw sewage to satisfy customers. To compound matters, there were no meters, resulting in an enormous wastage of water. During 1886 the original owners, unable to capitalize on their monopoly, sold out to a Boston syndicate. A year later, a Chicago group acquired the works, and carried forward an ambitious project. This was the construction at a cost of $1.5 million of a new pumping house and reservoir at Florence, on high ground north of Omaha. The new facilities did not lead to better management; people remained bitter about service. In 1891 New Jersey interests bought the firm and renamed it the American Waterworks Corporation. Unsuccessful attempts by this company to gain a franchise extension in 1896 touched off a bitter political battle over public ownership. It eventually went beyond the boundaries of Omaha, involving the Nebraska state government and the United States federal courts. The conflict extended into the twentieth century and did not end until the city purchased the works for $6.5 million in 1912.

During the 1880s and 1890s Omaha had increasingly required more efficient and comprehensive urban services. It was no longer enough to have a few jerry-built sewers, wooden pipes, or hastily dug ditches that carried everything from street runoff to human excrement. Nor could Omaha function effectively with impassible streets during much of the year. As the town expanded in physical size and the first of many suburban components appeared, there was a need for different kinds of transportation. Changing conceptions of technological progress caused complications. Growth and change came too fast for long-range planning and careful deliberations. Indeed, it was no longer possible or fashionable to blame inaction on rapid growth. A condition and not a theory confronted those responsible for setting policy. While franchises became political footballs and many citizens grumbled over the level of services, Omaha — just as the other new cities of the West — overcame the worst of its problems, succeeding for the most part in providing citizens with services comparable to those in the older portions of the land.

Andrew Rosewater, the brother of *Bee* editor Edward Rosewater, was the most influential of Omaha's late nineteenth century city engineers. He played a major role in determining the quality of life in the community, representing the city in the building of the first waterworks, and starting in 1881, supervising construction of a system of sewage. With modifications, Rosewater followed plans for "separate systems." George Waring, Jr., the leading American sanitary expert of the day, advocated this approach. He had rebuilt the sewers of Memphis following a devastating yellow fever outbreak. In Omaha, Rosewater supervised the construction of a $1 million dollar system of sixty-nine miles of storm and sanitary sewers. When rapid growth overwhelmed the sanitary parts of the sewerage, Rosewater changed the basic design, adopting a plan of building large trunk sewers with lateral branches. This abandonment of "separate systems" worked reasonably well, solving Omaha's sewage problems until well into the twentieth century.

Unlike many contemporaries, Rosewater saw a direct connection between sewers and streets. Following 1883 he directed a comprehensive program of street improvements. Within a few years, Omaha had forty-four miles of pavement, mainly asphaltum, Colorado sandstone, Sioux Falls granite, and wooden blocks. Even though a local leader exaggerated in claiming that by 1889 Omaha had a reputation as having some of the better thoroughfares in the United States, there had been a considerable improvement over the previous sorry state of affairs. Rosewater was in the vanguard of a nationwide movement that saw sanitary engineers take the lead in the professionalization of city management. He followed policies and practices advocated by early national organizations in the field. This led to a somewhat uniform approach: a faith that technology would solve problems associated with rapid urban growth. The efforts of Rosewater and his colleagues generally went unrecognized; politicians took credit for improvements and blamed bureaucrats for mistakes. Probably the biggest notice Rosewater gained came when he died in 1906. His obituary said he expired in an apartment in a local hotel an hour after following his wife's advice to drink a milk shake for chest pains. Few Omahans thought of Rosewater when they flushed toilets or drove down paved streets, unaware of his considerable contribution.

Omaha's street railway system developed without a master plan. In 1868 the territorial legislature granted a twenty-five year franchise to the Omaha Horse Railway Co., incorporated by a large number of local businessmen. The firm, prohibited from using steam power, soon had two miles of track in operation, all along a main street. From the first, the line barely made operating expenses. The cars, which ran every twenty-eight minutes when on schedule, were very slow owing to the poor condition of the roadway. Potential patrons found it easier to walk. The bulk of riders were stockholders and politicians, all of whom rode free. A drop in the fare from ten to five cents failed to attract new customers. To compound matters, the horse car drivers, described as deaf and nearsighted by the press, passed by many potential users. The concern underwent several ownership changes, and finally in 1878 was sold to the highest bidder for $25,000 at a sheriff's auction. The new owner extended the line, regularly cleaned the notoriously dirty cars, and laid wooden planking between the tracks to improve the speed of service. In 1880 the line boasted impressive dimensions: 5 miles of tracks, 10 cars, 70 horses, 20 employees, and 495,000 passengers annually. These statistics tended to hide the company's poor reputation, which would shortly result in drastic changes in transit services.

An increase in the size of Omaha from twelve to twenty-four square miles in 1887, as a result of the first annexation since 1869, created opportunities for the expansion of transit lines. The Omaha Horse Railway Co. added routes and switched from horses to mules, but such measures as painting cars canary yellow and improving schedules had little effect on its indifferent-to-bad image. More importantly, the owners lacked the necessary political connections to prevent competition. Between 1884 and 1888, five new lines received franchises. Within a few years, the Cable Tramway Co., the only cable car line ever built in Omaha, had four miles of tracks in operation. It had a bad image, because frequent cable breaks disrupted schedules. More serious difficulties befell a line built by real estate agents to serve a development called Benson Place. The street railroad started with a "dummy" steam engine, which had to be withdrawn from service when it frightened horses. After using horse power for a short time, the concern converted to electricity, changing its name to the Benson & Halcyon Heights Railroad. The owners rushed construction of another electric line, the Omaha Railway Co., because of opposition by residents to overhead wires. A short line, the Omaha & Southwestern Street Railway Co., served the growing west side of town. In 1888 the Council Bluffs & Omaha Electric Line started service over a Missouri River bridge owned by Council Bluffs interests. More lines, including the Metropolitan Street Railway Co. and the Interstate & Street Railway Co., followed in the 1890s; and to further complicate matters, several that were never built received charters.

Omaha had a chaotic transit situation. There seemed almost a mania for organizing and operating street railroads. Many short lines had very limited purposes. One ran to and from a park; another supported a baseball team that played in a field at the end of its tracks. The whole business greatly confused and frustrated passengers. Many doubtless hoped that someone would take advantage of an 1889 measure passed by the Nebraska legislature providing for consolidation. Nothing happened until Gurdon W. Wattles purchased the Omaha Railway Co. shortly before McKinley's election. By 1901 Wattles had combined all the traction firms into the Omaha & Council Bluffs Street Railway Company, with 150 miles of track and over fifteen hundred employees. He later wrote that he pushed for consolidation after making a bad business decision. He said he bought a street railway on the assumption that he would make a fortune in real estate by laying tracks into developing parts of town where he already owned property. He soon realized that there would not be a quick recovery and that he should have put his money into depressed downtown real estate. However, once committed, and faced with the drain of running a street railway upon which he had never expected to make money, he reluctantly promoted the creation of a single system. He hoped to salvage something out of his investment. There was no politics involved; the legislative groundwork had been laid over a decade earlier. Indeed, Wattles, whatever his actual motives, found himself hailed as a community benefactor. Few persons in Omaha paid much attention to the ramifications of the gigantic local traction merger; all they wanted was better service, which was what they received. The Omaha & Council Bluffs Street Railway Company gave greater Omaha a comprehensive transportation system, supplemented by commuter trains and interurbans. At the time of its inception, it seemed a model of free enterprise and a public-spirited solution to a serious problem — a view that would change markedly in later years.

Obtaining adequate lighting was another hard-to-solve matter complicated by rapid technological change. The Omaha Gas Manufacturing Company, granted a fifty-year franchise by the city council, started operations in November of 1869, soon gaining a reputation for terrible service. It used such cheap coal that one year the gas gave out at dusk on an average of three times a week. This enraged Omahans, and at one time the works had less than two hundred commercial and residential customers. Only the supplying of gas to a hundred street lamps (a status symbol among growing cities of the time) prevented bankruptcy. Conditions gradually improved; so that by 1880 the plant produced 30,000 cubic feet daily, charging consumers $3.50 per 1,000 cubic feet, which was in line with national averages for cities in Omaha's class. The firm's retorts produced 900,000 cubic feet every day in the 1890s, and more than double that amount by World War I; but by then, the gas works sold hardly any illuminating gas.

During the 1880s Omaha acquired a number of electric plants. The Union Pacific electrified its station; a hotel had its own generating plant. The gas company built a power station, converting the street lights from gas to electricity. In 1903, after the perfection of dynamos and distributing systems, the Thomson-Houston Co., an early Omaha electricity producer, gained control of all the small competing electric companies in Omaha. Monopoly had become an accepted practice in the industry; and Omahans took that and electric lights for granted, as indications of continual progress.

The telephone added a new dimension to Omaha's role as a communication center. The first phone call in Nebraska came in 1877 when two telephone pioneers, L. H. Korty and J. J. Dickey, spoke to each other over a line between Omaha and Council Bluffs. The two men strung a number of private lines in Omaha, before the establishment of an exchange. In 1880 the Omaha Electric Co. had 179 miles of wire and an estimated annual net income of $4,000. Many problems needed solving. The original method of signaling required thumping the transmitter diaphragm with a pencil; later, cranks and shrill bells became the rule. Early switchboards were large and cumbersome. Transmission lines frequently broke, and wires made strange sounds. As with most innovations, initial costs to consumers were quite high. The first subscribers were professional persons, commercial establishments, and a few wealthy individuals. Frequently, physicians had direct lines to drug stores. During the 1890s, when the initial patents expired, the telephone business temporarily became more competitive. Some people in Omaha believed that telephones would never have more than specialized purposes. After a successful Omaha storekeeper sold his establishment to work for a phone company, friends said he had made a serious error, arguing that the bulk of commercial pursuits would always be carried on by mail or word of mouth. Thirty years later he headed the Northwestern Bell Telephone Co. which served 640,000 patrons in five states and had 11,000 employees.

With the introduction of long-distance lines, Omaha had emerged as a major national transmitting center. When President William McKinley stayed in Omaha for several days in 1898, he used a special station at the Omaha Club to talk regularly with officials in Washington. By the turn of the century the telephone, a novelty only a short time earlier, was taken for granted by Omahans and their contemporaries in other cities throughout the country.

The evolution of protective services represented another important element in the rise of Omaha. The fire department moved rapidly from a volunteer to professional status following a disaster. On September 4, 1878, the five-story Grand Central Hotel, built five years earlier by leading businessmen and a symbol of community aspirations, caught fire in the early evening hours. A workman apparently kicked over a candle on an upper floor during a renovation project. After the ringing of the fire bell, tragic errors followed. An eyewitness reported:

Durant Engine and Hose Co., May 1875

The engines came promptly to the scratch, and sparks and cinders were by this time raining down from the roof. At this moment the scenes in and about the burning building baffled description. Firemen, hose, and streams of water were indescribably mingled; the first floor was crowded with a vast throng of men, many of them bareheaded and in their shirt sleeves, all talking, shouting and offering advice, above which the hoarse calls of firemen could be heard, creating a pandemonium of discord, no pen can describe. At that hour the entire roof had fallen in, and masses of tin roofing, burning debris of every conceivable nature, etc., fell to the pavement, making the work of saving the surrounding property dangerous in the extreme.

110

Five firemen died when they went onto upper floors obviously in danger of collapse. Only the arrival of firefighters from Council Bluffs prevented the burning of Omaha's downtown. In the wake of the catastrophe, viewed by thousands of persons, the fire chief lost his job. By 1880 Omaha had phased out all except one of its volunteer units. The backbone of the reorganized force consisted of an authorized unit of sixteen professional firemen, who manned four engines, including a hook-and-ladder. From the 1880s onward, despite an occasional terrible fire, such as the burning of the Omaha Hardware Co. in 1892 and the Boston Store two years later, the Omaha Fire Department enjoyed a good reputation.

The police department had trouble overcoming the taint of corruption. By the 1880s, Omaha's force consisted of eighteen patrolmen and a chief, called a city marshal. "All policemen, including the marshal," an observer claimed, "were appointed by the mayor, subject to confirmation by the city council, and it being no unusual thing to have an entire new police force following the election of a new mayor and council, as the police force was the reward of the faithful ward heelers, regardless of physical, intellectual or moral fitness for the position; in fact, it was but a political football." In 1887 the state, in a controversial move that ran counter to prevailing national trends toward "Home Rule," took control of the Omaha police, establishing a police board appointed by the governor. This resulted for a short time in better police, but frequent changes in the state appointed board led to demoralization inside the department. Most appointees were political discards or businessmen interested only in the title of commissioner. Favoritism and political regularity rather than competence became the criteria for hirings, promotions, demotions, and dismissals. The "moral squad" decided what was corrupt and what was not. The only consolation was a general belief that circumstances were probably about the same in other emerging cities.

The motto of the Omaha Board of Health, "In time of peace prepare for war," had little relationship to reality. A formally constituted board, created by the council in 1871, had minimal authority. In 1878 a reorganization made the board more efficient on paper. It included the mayor, the president of the council, and the city marshal. Annual expenditures totaled $240, hardly enough to carry on a comprehensive program. There was no full-time investigator. The only board member with police powers was the mayor. There was no special program concerning the inspection and correction of nuisances. The city did not own an isolation hospital. Except for

111

Grand Central Hotel, early 1870s

minor outbreaks of smallpox, cholera, diphtheria, and malaria, Omaha remained relatively free of epidemic disease in the nineteenth century. This was more good luck than anything else. In the 1880s, even after authorities devoted more attention to cleaning streets, heaps of decaying vegetation and large ponds of stagnant water accumulated in the river bottoms during summer months. About the best that could be said was that most other communities in the country were equally negligent in spending money on public health. The typical pattern was a poorly-financed board capable of acting with energy and dispatch only in an emergency.

Omaha did not have a coordinated welfare system. The city ran a poor farm, and from time-to-time, the council appropriated small amounts of money for relief. Church and voluntary organizations aided their needy members. Several hospitals maintained charity wards. Some factory owners, during periods of layoffs, felt an obligation to provide food baskets for loyal employees. Various private agencies augmented the welfare picture. Three national societies that operated in Omaha, the Young Men's Christian Association, the Young Women's Christian Association, and the Salvation Army, carried on a wide variety of activities. Several local groups had specialized functions. The Omaha City Mission and the Nebraska Society for the Prevention of Cruelty to Children and Animals concentrated on helping abused and underprivileged children. The Omaha Charity Association had a day care center. Unwed mothers received aid from the Child Saving Institute and the Home of the Good Shepherd. The Rescue Home Association attempted to reform prostitutes. The City Mission and the Associated Charities of Omaha ran rescue halls and soup kitchens. While in some instances wealthy citizens accepted welfare obligations—the Omaha Women's Club played an important role in founding the Visiting Nurse Association of Omaha—there was no general outpouring of support for welfare causes. Most unfortunates were left to fend for themselves. During the depression years of the 1890s, countless thousands took the clearest course open to them. They moved away from Omaha.

Omaha schools received considerably more attention. The rapid growth of the city necessitated an almost yearly expansion of the public school system, and voters responded by passing the necessary bond issues to finance new school construction. A harbinger of progress was a $250,000 high school completed in 1872 on Capitol Hill, the former site of the old state house. The four-story building contained seventeen classrooms, four large recitation halls, small offices, commodious library facilities, four apparatus rooms, and quarters for a janitor. Each of the classrooms had a capacity of fifty-five students. The spire was 390 feet above the Missouri River, making the school easily the most visible landmark in Omaha. In 1883 five full-time instructors had the responsibility of teaching 140 students, the vast majority males. There were recurrent discipline problems, and a graduate recalled that the principal's office was "frequently ornamented with boys and girls waiting to be called on the carpet or to offer excuses." Few students were diligent about pursuing a curriculum that had little relevance to life on the Middle Border; it included physiology, astronomy, Latin, and moral philosophy. Sometimes there was retribution, as a girl who neglected her lessons discovered. "Yes, I did have a jolly time skating and playing and thinking my wits would carry me through," she wrote. "They didn't, and I paid for my fun by making up my lessons so I could go on to graduate with my class." Part of the problem with a lax attitude toward school work lay at the primary level. Overworked and undertrained teachers in the elementary schools frequently had to instruct several grades in the same room. Small Roman Catholic and Episcopalian primary schools augmented the public system.

Only one of several plans to establish a university succeeded. In 1878 a $50,000 bequeath from the will of Mary Creighton, widow of the telegraph builder, led to the establishment of Creighton College. Under the leadership of Father Michael Dowling the Jesuit institution, originally a preparatory school, admitted its first college class in 1887. Philanthropist John Creighton placed the school on a firm financial foundation by giving $2 million in cash, donating land, and building a medical school. The state of education, after a sorry start in the early years, was a further indication of Omaha's modernization.

Religious institutions in Omaha continued to show great diversity, reflecting trends in the nation as a whole. In 1890, the first year that the Federal government took what its experts considered a successful religious census, there were 95 different organizations in Omaha. These denominations reported 81 edifices and a total value of church property of almost $2 million. Communicants numbered 18,658, as reported by religious leaders. Roman Catholics numbered 7,675, far and away the highest total which was consistent with figures elsewhere, particularly in growing places that required unskilled laborers. The largest Protestant denominations in Omaha were the Methodists (1,859), the Presbyterians (1,708), the Luth-

Omaha High School

erans (1,277), the Episcopalians (1,228), and the Baptists (1,107). There were 1,035 Jews, an impressive total. It reflected the efforts of both early orthodox and reform leaders to establish strong Hebrew assemblies, despite a relatively small number of Omaha Jews. Ethnic groups of the same denominations often formed separate congregations. Of two Roman Catholic churches, St. Joseph's parishoners were predominately German, while St. Patrick's mostly Irish. While religious institutions were well established in Omaha, there appeared room for considerable improvement, at least in the eyes of religious leaders of all denominations. The listed percentage of communicants, thirteen percent, was the lowest for any American city of over 10,000 population west of the Mississippi River. By way of contrast, the total for San Francisco was thirty-one percent, for Kansas City twenty-four percent, and for Denver thirty-one percent. As in many other growing metrop-

115

olises, the floating nature of Omaha's population obviously was part of the reason. Still, there seemed little doubt to religious leaders that Omaha posed both a challenge and a fertile ground for evangelistic crusades.

A proliferation of voluntary associations served as further indication of a search for community identity. Several of the groups had clear commercial aims: the Board of Trade, the Real Estate Owners' Association, the Manufacturers' and Consumers' Association, the Commercial Club, and the Live Stock Exchange. The Woman's Christian Temperance Union and the Independent Order of Good Templars promoted prohibition in Nebraska. The latter's only lodge in Omaha, Life Boat Lodge No. 150, disbanded after working unsuccessfully for a statewide prohibition amendment to the Nebraska constitution in 1890, but the WCTU survived as a force to be reckoned with later. Fraternal orders included the Masons, the Odd Fellows, the Knights of Pythias, the Moose, and the Elks. Among the leading ethnic organizations were the Hibernians, the Sokols, the Danish Brotherhood, and the German Turnverein. Another society, the Woodmen of the World, was founded in Omaha in 1890. The Grand Army of the Republic had several posts in Omaha; the Daughters of the American Revolution had the Isaac Sadler Chapter. Two organizations, the Social Art Club of 1881 and the Western Art Association of 1888, represented short-lived attempts to advance artistic pursuits. The oldest social club was the Omaha Club, organized with an initial membership of 245 in 1884. It served as the prototype for a number of country clubs formed in later years.

Of all the societies, the one that had the most lasting impact was that of the Knights of Ak-Sar-Ben. Founded in 1895, it had from the start both economic and social purposes. "The organization was the result of an admitted need of stimulus and was designed to promote patriotism among the citizens, advertise the city and create a friendly feeling among neighbors," an Ak-Sar-Ben secretary wrote. "At the annual ball, the crowning social event of the year, one of the members of the board of governors is crowned 'King' and a young society woman 'Queen'. . . . During carnival week. . . . one hundred thousand people or more come to Omaha to witness the gorgeous parades and partake in the festivities." The heart of the Ak-Sar-Ben was "The Den," the large building where the Populists had launched their crusade in 1892. Ak-Sar-Ben epitomized the booster spirit that infected the Midwest in the years following the

Creighton College

end of the frontier. It also was as an indication of growing stability and maturity.

Parks served as another sign of progress. Omaha was fortunate that in 1872 two civic leaders, Andrew J. Hanscom and James G. Megeath, donated seventy-three acres for a park. Some observers suspected their motives; the unimproved tract, which the deed of gift required the city to develop, lay at the end of their horse car line. Still, they left Omaha with a legacy and tradition of park development that in the long-term outweighed personal considerations. Hanscom Park became a show piece. "The circular drives, the shady nooks, the tables and seats, and the dancing platform, large enough to accommodate about twelve sets, combine to make it the largest picnic ground anywhere to be found in this vicinity," a reporter for the Omaha *Bee* claimed in 1874. Numerous improvements made over the following decade and a half, some supervised by City Engineer Rosewater, enhanced the park's beauty and usefulness. There were two lakes, a waterfall, extensive flower beds, macadamized roadways, fountains, and magnificent stands of trees, plus a pavilion, bandstand, and greenhouse. In 1891 a $400,000 bond issue enabled the city to purchase more park land. Much of it, along with other parks acquired through the years remained unimproved; although one, Riverside Park, had a small zoo.

While Omaha did not have a comprehensive beautification plan, the board of park commissioners managed to acquire jurisdiction over a couple of boulevard streets. In their 1898 report, the commissioners claimed that they needed more money to create systems on a par with those in other cities in the vanguard of the "City Beautiful" movement. However, the commissioners believed that recent enthusiastic support for parks by property owners and improvement clubs harked well for the future. "We believe our work is generally approved," they concluded. "Those who criticize it will be found to be those who would have no parks at all, who never visit parks, and who really have the most need for the revivifying influence of a day in the parks." Certainly, there were firm foundations upon which to build.

Architecturally, Omaha experienced a boom that lasted from the late 1870s until the Panic of 1893. At the start of the upsurge, the *Bee* interviewed local architects about construction trends. One saw things from a narrow perspective predicting that in order to remain competitive, store owners would have to pay more attention to the interiors of their establishments. Another, A. R. Dufrene, made

Riverview Park

thoughtful and broader observations. "There has been too much sameness," he said. "People would insist on having a house just like some other one. Now, although there is a decided tendency towards better styles, such as the Queen Anne and the Gothic, there is more room for good effects in these styles. On a whole a better class of dwelling is called for than formerly. And this demand is not alone for dwellings, but also for stores. Patterned and colored bricks are now used in fronts with good effect." His statement applied to the homes of the affluent. His firm of Dufrene and Mendelsohn designed the three-story Fred Drexel residence, built in 1884 at a commanding point above the Missouri River. The $27,000 mansion was of English Gothic design. The exterior featured ornamental stone carvings and a porch running around the sides. The interior plan made elaborate use of wood finishings. There was an oak reception hall, a chestnut drawing room, a cherry main hall, and an ash kitchen. In 1889 F. M. Ellis of Omaha designed the $40,000 twenty-five room Henry W. Yates home, a three-story dwelling with a stone exterior and a slate roof. All the interior woodwork was solid with no veneer. It had four bathrooms and nine fireplaces. Few persons in Omaha could afford or wanted such opulent domiciles. Most of the thousands of homes built in the 1880s were the work of tract developers. The dwellings had the monotonous sameness that Dufrene hoped was past. They were wooden one- and two-story square or rectangular boxes of five to six rooms. Usually, carpenters planned them on the spot. It was small solace to professional architects that they resembled houses throughout the Midwest.

The large downtown buildings built during the time of expansion shaped Omaha's urban design for many decades to come. Public buildings, banking houses, business blocks, hotels, theaters, and offices showed architectural forms characteristic of Midwest cities. The conspicuous new Douglas County Courthouse—built after Omaha officially became the county seat in 1882, although most county offices had been in the city since territorial days—was 140 feet from base to dome. Fireproof, it had dark marble-bordered corridors and elaborately finished iron stairways. The rectangular seven-story First National Bank of Omaha had a solid look that featured relatively clean lines, with some conspicuous terra cotta, particularly on the upper footings and over the doorways. An exterior of Ohio cut stone was the dominating feature of the J. J. Brown Block, a four-story 33-by-102-foot downtown building. Goo's Hotel was four stories high, of rectangular design. It had an elevator, running water, steam heat, and alarm bells. Boyd's Opera House sat seventeen hundred persons. Constructed in Modern Renaissance, it had a large stage capable of holding up to twenty sets of scenery. The regional headquarters of a prestigious eastern insurance company, the New York Life Building, was among the most imposing edifices in Omaha. A striking feature of the ten-story building, which had nearly four hundred rooms, was the entrance and rotunda. Two polished Norfolk pink granite pillars guarded the vestibule, which had floors of Lake Champlain marble, walls of Tennessee and French marble, and ceilings of gold and silver. None of the hundreds of buildings in the central business district won any architectural prizes; but taken together, and lining the streets wall-to-wall, they gave Omaha a metropolitan appearance.

An important aspect of the construction activities involved the

Farnam Street, 1889

erection of jobbing houses in a five-block area on the east side of the downtown. The numerous warehouses in the area were undistinguished; they were great brooding beasts of buildings dedicated to commerce. A wide variety of items passed through them on the way to stores and dealers throughout a wide expanse of the country. The warehouses stood as monuments to the success of objectives stated in the 1881 report of the Omaha Board of Trade. "We are endeavoring to make Omaha the great distributing point of the extreme west, and as far as possible the depot of purchases of the northwest and southwest sections," the report stated. By the nineties, this vision had become reality. Hundreds of "Knights of the grip" sold the products that served as the warehouse district's reason for being. In many ways, the grey buildings helped to explain why Omaha experienced such rapid growth in a short span of time.

One characteristic of Omaha in the last half of the nineteenth

121

century was that it had a large floating and rapidly changing population. In 1860 it had an enumeration of 1,883, including 985 white males, 876 white females, 20 free colored, and 2 Indians. The number of persons in 1870 stood at 16,083. Of these, 9,763 were natives and 6,320 foreign-born. Blacks totaled 446. Census figures for 1880 showed 30,518 inhabitants of Omaha. Females made up 44 percent, foreign-born 33 percent, and blacks 3 percent. These percentages were in line with those for other communities in the urban West at the end of the frontier.

Omaha's listed population in 1890 was 140,452. Critics later claimed this represented a gigantic over-enumeration of close to 40,000 people. They based their case on other indices such as school returns and tax rolls. The official returns cut two ways. In 1890 it suited the purposes of Omaha leaders to inflate returns; in 1900 following drastic losses — the census listed a populace of 102,555 — it was in the interests of promoters to minimize losses by claiming mistakes had been made a decade earlier. In any case, the 1890 statistics, representing a spectacular enlargement of 360.23 percent over the previous canvass, remain suspect. Officially, Omaha had 80,108 males and 60,344 females. Foreign-born numbered 35,039, blacks 4,566, Chinese 89, and Indians 3. The most foreigners came from Germany (8,279), Denmark (4,242), Ireland (4,067), and Bohemia (2,675). Omaha's main suburban component, South Omaha, had 8,062 citizens, of whom 2,554 were foreign-born.

Many factors, besides the possibility of improperly conducted enumerations, complicated conclusions in Omaha about the population. By law, census takers counted individuals in places where they were domiciled on the day of the enumeration. This automatically meant the missing of thousands of railroad workers and drummers. On the other hand, no one systematically tallied inmates of saloons and houses of ill fame, along with the hundreds of rooming houses near the railroad tracks. At any given time, there were thousands of transients in the city. The best that could be said was that the "official" population was mobile and volatile.

The attitude of ethnic and religious groups toward each other changed markedly as Omaha moved through the frontier period. In the beginning, there was considerably cooperation and an acceptance of the "melting pot." Josie McCulloch, who grew up in Omaha in the 1870s and 1880s, had vivid memories of the early days. "In that neighborhood Swedish, Bohemian, Italian, Irish, and Negro children all contributed to the process of Americanization," she recalled. "Often we children were sent running to the emigrant wagons to hand the children a Sunday school paper or to invite them to church."

By the 1890s things were different. The American Protective Association, a national organization that opposed certain forms of immigration, appeared in Omaha. Edward F. Morearty, a member of the city council, felt that the local APA was primarily a device to get individuals of Irish descent out of politics.

While some Irish politicians were hounded from office, their plight hardly compared with that of a black man falsely accused in 1891 of assaulting a white child. Despite pleas by the governor of Nebraska and other officials, a howling mob took the innocent man from the jail and lynched him from a telephone pole. Moreover, Morearty failed to mention a political reality that had helped to fan nativist sentiment. Almost all local political candidates were either Irish or native-born Americans, a circumstance that continued for many more years.

Omaha had changed markedly within a few decades. Police, fire, and health services had reached professional norms. Day and night, huge presses spewed forth thousands of newspapers all destined for local and regional distribution. The sound of the printing machines competed with that of the streetcars that rumbled down the paved streets. Large buildings dominated the downtown landscape; throughout town church spires rose toward the heavens. Warehouses held goods and produce scheduled for distribution throughout the vast expanse of the American West. Within Omaha, thousands of houses stood on property that was a few years earlier open country. Urban services had advanced along acceptable if not dramatic lines. Water and sewer lines had replaced wells and ditches. Telephones were rapidly becoming an accepted and necessary means of communication. Parks and boulevards attested to a growing interest in esthetic values. Of course, as the frontier ended, old problems remained unresolved and new ones appeared. Gambling and prostitution continued to flourish; Omaha was still a "Wide Open" town by any definition. Indeed, this seemed an enduring legacy. And, there were the vexing issues raised by the activities of the APA and the vicious lynching of a black man. Was Omaha, even as it reached an established state, on the verge of social disintegration? Some experts believed that rapid immigration created "Social Dynamite." Would the Omaha area, with the massive influex of foreigners, be a testing place for the theory? As a new century dawned, that was a problem for Omahans of all stations.

Part Three

1900-1930

5

A Future Rich with Promise

Omaha entered the twentieth century as an important part of the American urban mosaic. It was one of the key gates of entry into the West; its packing plants served a national market. The wealth of western mines filled the coffers of leading businessmen. Behind lay the milestones and episodes that shaped the city: the capital fight, the quest to obtain the Union Pacific terminal, the machinations involved in gaining the Missouri River bridge, the manipulations that brought in the Chicago packers, and the glories of the Trans-Mississippi Exposition. The city had survived depressions, dry weather, population losses, and insect infestations. Every setback had been followed by a sudden advance, and the city emerged as a regional metropolis. Council Bluffs was part of Omaha's suburban ring which included the factory center of South Omaha, the residential community of Benson, the old Mormon camp of Florence, and the fashionable development of Dundee. Former challengers—Bellevue, Plattsmouth, and Nebraska City— had lost in significance, relegated to the status of moderately successful farm marketing towns. The rapid growth of Lincoln from an insignificant village in the 1870s to a prosperous capital city of over 40,000 by 1900 afforded Omaha an impressive satellite. Other Nebraska cities added luster to Omaha's urban crown: Grand Island, North Platte, and Columbus. Omaha continued to enjoy a special relationship with Denver and to exploit connections in Sioux City, Sioux Falls, and Rapid City. The opening of the Northwest held promise of new ties. "Omaha is awake, alert and reaching out eagerly for new business," a report by a local commercial organization declared. "The businessmen of the city are heartily co-operating in efforts to extend Omaha's trade and to make this city the most important commercial and industrial center of the west."

Between 1900 and 1910 a "Golden Age" of agriculture in Nebraska boded well for Omaha. The years of trial that accompanied early settlement appeared over. "The slack farmer moved on," Nebraska novelist and social historian Willa Cather claimed. "Superfluous banks failed, and money-lenders who drove hard bargains with desperate men came to grief. The strongest stock survived, and within ten years those who had weathered the storm came into their reward." Some indicators did not reflect the optimistic aspect of the changed conditions. Nebraska's population only advanced from 1.1 million to 1.2 million, almost all as a result of urban growth. The most significant agricultural increase came in the northwestern Sand Hills, after federal legislation enlarged homestead land grants. Throughout the state, mortgage debts and farm tenancy rose sharply. Even so, changing production patterns, coupled with growing knowledge about the capability of Nebraska farming, led to an era of progress and prosperity. The initial phase of agricultural experimentation had ended on the northern plains.

Steady agrarian progress characterized the first decade of the new century in the Cornhusker State. The listed value of farm property jumped from $748 million to $2.1 billion. Farm buildings and land per acre rose in value from $19.31 to $49.95. Livestock valuations enlarged from $145 million to $222 million. Increased mechanization, labor saving techniques, and the introduction of new crops helped improve productivity and profits. Gang plows replaced walking plows; manure spreaders and horse forks reduced labor hours. Development of a serum for hog cholera helped to almost double swine production. The Agricultural Experiment Station at the University of Nebraska successfully promoted the growing of alfalfa as a major forage crop. Of even greater significance were the changes wrought by the introduction of Turkey Red winter wheat brought to the plains by the Mennonites. The various strains failed to gain acceptance until an adroit advertising campaign by the experimental station, the railroads, and the newspapers. These and other advances came during a lucky ten years.

128

Adequate rainfalls—except for 1907 the annual mean was 22.84 inches—led to a succession of good crop yields, coming when the market was in a generally upward spiral. Wheat prices went up 67 percent, oats 78 percent, corn 140 percent, and hogs 133 percent. In keeping with the high returns, cattle on the Nebraska plains peaked at over three million.

Omaha interests sought new gains through the organization of the Omaha Grain Exchange. Chicago railroad magnates encouraged the exchange as a counter to those in Kansas City and Minneapolis. In 1909 F. P. Manchester, secretary of the Omaha exchange, predicted a great future. He based his conclusion on the possibility of more equitable freight rates coupled with the continued rapid development of adjacent agricultural territories.

The resurgence of the Union Pacific Railroad was a primary cause of optimism. The railroad fell into desperate straits following exposures of corruption and the administration of Jay Gould. Reform president Charles Francis Adams told congressional investigators that speculators intended to loot the road and leave behind "two rusty streaks of iron on an old roadbed." After a period of receivership, a brilliant capitalist picked up the road and made it not only an integral but a successful part of the American economic system. The person responsible for the change was a man few except insiders noticed before he acquired the Union Pacific. He was E. H. Harriman, a small and unobtrusive individual with a moustache. There was a temptation to write him off as just another office clerk, which was what he had been at the start of his career in Hempstead, New York. Such a view would have ignored his ability to evaluate and acquire railroad properties. Without fanfare, he made a fortune dealing in railroad stocks and gained the backing of powerful New York banking interests. In 1900, after two years of purchasing common issues in the Union Pacific at relatively low prices, he acquired control of the railroad. Given the road's history, there was a tendency to equate Harriman with the previous management—either as a "crooked renegade" or a "do good reformer"; yet he was much more. He wanted to consolidate western roads into vast monopolistic combinations, and he thought of improving service. His policies, which challenged those of the federal government, directly aided the Omaha business community.

Harriman's first step in his campaign to create a western railroad empire was to revive the moribund Union Pacific. Through his financial connections, he had the necessary money to make extensive physical improvements. Furthermore, he determined to plow

129

any initial profits back into the railroad, a policy that in the long term served stockholder interests. His engineers replaced light rails, widened embankments, rebuilt roadbeds, reduced grades, eliminated curves, and improved trestles. To upgrade passenger service Harriman built dozens of new stations, including one in Omaha, added modern rolling stock, and ran trains on time. Double tracks and the institution of block signals improved safety standards. The changes allowed for the introduction of heavier and more powerful locomotives, greatly improving hauling capacities per unit. As these policies went ahead Harriman set about reacquiring auxiliary lines, many of which were still in receivership. When he took control of the Union Pacific, the former eight thousand mile system had been reduced to the main line from Omaha to Ogden, the division from Kansas City to Cheyenne, and three hundred miles of branches. In a short time Harriman regained the suddenly profitable agricultural feeders, leaving old Colorado mining roads, called "suckers," to fend for themselves.

With the Union Pacific secure, Harriman quickly broadened his horizons buying the six thousand mile Southern Pacific Railroad. In a single stroke he became one of America's men of power. Through complicated manipulations, Harriman also moved into the Northwest taking over the Oregon Short Line and the Oregon Railroad and Navigation Company. He operated these short roads, plus the Southern Pacific, and the Union Pacific, as a single unified line: the closest thing yet to a western railroad monopoly. Although Harriman was temporarily checked by the famous antitrust case, *Northern Securities Co. v. United States,* he remained the nation's greatest railroad baron. Undismayed by the setbacks, he went right on acquiring railroad stock. He gained a dominant voice in the management of the Illinois Central Railroad and he told the Interstate Commerce Commission that he would go after the Santa Fe and other railroads if allowed. "In comparison with him, the Vanderbilts, the Goulds, and the Garretts, and the Huntingtons represent the parochial period in our railroad history," an economic expert wrote. "They consolidated small railroads into kingdoms, Harriman is federating their kingdoms into empires." His rise had great implications for Omaha. The Union Pacific had apparently achieved its promise, emerging as a major force in American economic life.

Harriman's critics argued that he used unscrupulous tactics in the daily operations of the Union Pacific Railroad. Just as other railroad owners did, he gave free passes to politicians, rebates to favored shippers, and freight differentials to large producers. He continued the policy of long and short hauls, under which big interests received lower rates for thousand-mile hauls than individual farmers did for ones of a hundred miles. When pressed he retorted with a standard line followed by his colleagues; he did not like discriminatory practices but had to resort to them in order to compete. People who had no choice except to ship on his tracks found it very difficult to accept such a rationalization.

Dislike of the Union Pacific throughout Nebraska continued well after the death of the Populist movement. About the only place in the state where the road had any support was in Omaha. Even though competition continued between the Union Pacific and the Southern Pacific in regional parts of the system, more through business went via Omaha than ever before. Certain railroads in which Harriman had holdings, notably the Illinois Central, stopped soliciting transcontinental business from other routes. This helped Omaha, as did increased activities in the shops and the headquarters. Then, too, Omaha business leaders ultimately made money from the road's increased profitability. When Harriman died suddenly in 1909, he was in the eyes of many Americans a malefactor of great wealth. He was a transitional figure in railroading and a bridge between rugged individuals like Jay Gould and such corporate bankers as J. P. Morgan.

Omaha's business leadership also underwent a transition. Two towering figures, William A. Paxton and John A. Creighton, passed away in 1907. Paxton was a prime example of the unbridled self-determination that helped to build the city in its first half century. The mule skinner turned capitalist had been involved in everything from wholesale groceries to real estate. A mover in the establishment of the stockyards and of South Omaha, he was essentially his own man despite a talent for organizing syndicates. He was not averse to taking unfair advantage of business opponents, and he knew how to drive hard bargains. A rough-talking man, he was willing to use whatever tactics necessary to achieve his ends.

Creighton, honored as a papal count, was a former overland freighter turned financier. For over twenty-five years he managed extensive family properties and made a great deal of money through his own business affairs. His Montana mining holdings brought large returns, as did his Omaha real estate investments and speculations. His principal position was that of president of the First National Bank of Omaha. Like Paxton, he helped make Omaha a livestock and packing center. Unlike his colleague, he was a devout Roman Catholic with a social conscience. He gave liberal portions of his fortune to Omaha institutions. Of particular note were donations of hundreds of thousands of dollars to St. Joseph's Hospital and to Creighton University. Privately, he assisted numerous worthy charities and individuals. He received many honors from Catholic organizations, including a Laetare medal awarded by Notre Dame University. When the white-bearded Creighton died at age seventy-five in 1907, he was among the most revered men in town. He and Paxton represented contrasting styles of business leadership. One, a hard driver of the William Rockefeller mold, saw no reason to share his money with anyone. The other, like Andrew Carnegie, believed that he had an obligation to use wealth to advance society. Whether the two Omaha business pioneers were "Industrial Statesmen" or "Robber Barons" remained a moot question, although no one disputed their contribution to the raising up of the city.

Gurdon W. Wattles picked up their fallen standards. The former Iowa banker, who did such a successful job of running the Trans-Mississippi Exposition, was a leader for the twentieth century. He had all the right credentials to direct Omaha's fortunes in the post-frontier era; humble beginnings, outstanding ability, a fine intellect, impeccable manners, driving ambition, and a ruthless streak. He looked the part of a business leader. Official photographs showed him with the stern features and dark clothing expected of a successful banker. Wattles had the skill of being able to define complex problems, to reach solutions, to organize the means to carry things out, and to bring affairs through to a satisfactory conclusion. He enjoyed reading books and had a more scholarly bent than many of his contemporaries. His second wife was a professor of home economics at the University of Nebraska, and he considered it a great honor that Iowa State College awarded him an honorary degree. Wattles belonged to just about every social organization in Omaha; he saw the value of such connections in building a career. In 1905, in an elaborate ritual viewed by thousands of fellow townspeople, he was crowned king of the Knights of Ak-Sar-Ben. Prior recipients of the annual award received their titles in recognition of civic contributions and social connections. In Wattles' case, it seemed an official coronation.

Wattles was head of the state commission that had responsibility over the Nebraska exhibition at the 1904 World's Fair in St. Louis; a moving picture he commissioned extolling the state's economic development received wide acclaim. A few years later, in 1908 and

Gurdon W. Wattles

1909, Wattles was president of the National Corn Exposition, a regional show designed to publicize the role of Omaha as a grain center. Although he was a delegate to the 1904 Republican National Convention, he was not an extreme partisan. During World War I he served a Democratic president, Woodrow Wilson, as food administrator of Nebraska. Promotional and political activities advanced Wattles' business fortunes. His growing banking interests allowed him to branch out in other directions. He represented eastern financial institutions in Omaha and was a director of the Chicago Great Western Railroad. In 1913 he built the Fontenelle Hotel, which quickly became an Omaha landmark. His skill at consolidating businesses had served him well when he organized the Omaha & Council Bluffs Street Railway Company. This made him a traction king; he was the local version of Charles Yerkes, the controversial owner of Chicago street car lines. Included in the responsibility of running a transportation monopoly was the task of dealing with labor. Here, Wattles refused to compromise. Indeed, he took such a hard line in favor of the rights of management that it hurt his standing in Omaha.

In 1903 Wattles organized the Omaha Business Men's Association. The exact membership was a well-kept secret, although Wattles claimed it was at least 260. The purpose was to keep labor unions out of Omaha, and to maintain the open shop. Wattles described the aims as "purely defensive and made necessary . . . by the apparent determination upon the part of labor organizations in the city to either control or ruin every business enterprise." More specifically, Wattles was probably concerned about stopping efforts to unionize his traction workers. Shortly before the formation of the management alliance, he had barely headed off organizing attempts by the national Amalgamated Association of Street and Electric Railway Employees.

Labor troubles had steadily increased as the city became more industrialized. In the 1880s and 1890s the governor had sent militia into Omaha during smelting, railroad, and packing house labor disputes. Sometimes the workers won limited victories. Employees of the Omaha & Grant Smelting and Refining Works gained an eight-hour day and higher wages as a result of the 1891 walkout. More often the strikers lost. In 1893 the packing companies, helped by six companies of militia and by strikebreakers, swiftly broke a strike by beef butchers. By the early twentieth century packing workers had unionized, greatly furthering their bargaining position. They won pay increases during an 1898 stoppage and achieved another

Hotel Fontenelle

round of raises five years later through strike threats. Under the circumstances, it was no wonder that Wattles's call for a united group of businessmen to stand against labor found an enthusiastic response.

A test between management and labor came in September 1909 when the Amalgamated Association of Street and Electric Railway Employees made another attempt to organize the traction workers. Wattles secured a unanimous resolution from the Business Men's Association executive committee approving any "attitude" he decided to take, and he made a contingency arrangement with Waddel and Mahan, a New York firm that engaged in strikebreaking. After that, Wattles refused a demand by the streetcar men for recognition and a contract, adamantly rejecting arbitration. He said, "There are some things in this world that you cannot arbitrate." Following a discussion of several hours with labor representatives, he issued a statement clearly expressing what he intended to do if his workers walked out. "Now," he declared, "I am not a timid man either . . . I say to the Union men, if they quit the employ of this company, there will never be another union man employed by this company. . . . I have prepared this company for a strike, and I have men employed waiting to take the place of every man who quits . . . this company will go right along and operate its cars; *if necessary under the protection of the government itself."* Wattles proved a man of his word.

When the streetcar men struck, Wattles acted swiftly and with characteristic resolution. On September 19, 1909, the first strikebreakers arrived. Over five hundred armed men established headquarters in the car barns which had been equipped with barricades, cots, and commissaries. The hardened veterans of numerous labor disturbances disdainfully ignored police deployed to protect them. Few who saw the men believed company claims that they were motormen and conductors recruited from the ranks of the Brooklyn Rapid Transit Company. Wattles called them a "jolly lot of disreputables. . . . always ready for a fight." The public stayed off the cars and sided with the strikers. When the cars rolled at intervals, many were demolished by angry mobs. Wattles, undismayed by the violence, brushed aside attempts at negotiation.

The strikers refused Wattles's offer to return to work without penalty if they would agree not to belong to a union; so he went ahead with the process of breaking the strike. In the middle of October he won the inevitable victory. He took back only the men he wanted, providing they signed "yellow dog" contracts. The strikebreakers moved on to other centers of labor unrest. "No compromise was made, and the strikers were defeated," Wattles proclaimed. "The union was destroyed." He proposed a national "standing army" to break traction strikes and violently attacked unions in a privately printed publication, *A Crime Against Labor: A Brief History of the Omaha and Council Bluffs Street Railway Strike, 1909.*

The traction strike showed the strength of the Omaha Business Men's Association. It stood united against labor, at one time fighting fourteen unions in separate actions. There were violent strikes in the meat packing industry; forty-five hundred men left their jobs in 1917 and six thousand in 1921. Strikebreaking became an accepted way of life in Omaha; management broke several strikes, including a short 1918 traction work stoppage and a 1919 walkout by teamsters. During a lengthy labor dispute in the building trades, the governor of Nebraska actually appointed a member of the business association to investigate the situation. This kind of favoritism was a symptom of a carefully nurtured anti-union attitude in Nebraska that produced a 1921 anti-picketing law, a prohibition that was retained easily in a referendum held the following year. The provision had the desired effect. It completed what Wattles started: the shattering of the union movement in Omaha for many years to come.

Wattles dealt with other aspects of economic life. He took advantage of the agricultural boom to strengthen hinterland ties in Nebraska, and he extended his city's influence in other directions. These activities also countered efforts by increasingly aggressive Kansas City businessmen. The Missouri city, which had enjoyed a development strikingly similar to Omaha's, wanted to broaden its markets from Kansas to other parts of the plains. So, Wattles needed a defensive strategy to keep the Kansas City Board of Trade, which had operated a grain futures market since 1877, out of Nebraska. This was no mean task given the power of the organization. Wattles had little chance of making inroads into North and South Dakota. The powerful Minneapolis Chamber of Commerce, a combination of great flour mills, controlled sources of supply, working in league with railroads and grain elevator companies. Chances for Omaha seemed better in Iowa. Wattles believed that excellent opportunities existed to compete successfully with Cedar Rapids, Des Moines, Ottumwa, and Sioux City for livestock and grain. The National Corn Exposition, in addition to promoting the growing of corn, demonstrated Omaha's interest in Iowa markets.

Wattles had no illusions about breaking the hold of Chicago capitalists over Iowa's economy. However, he did see commercial opportunities, if orchestrated correctly.

The extension into Nebraska of a regional Chicago railroad helped to improve Omaha's fortunes as a grain market. In 1903 A. B. Stickney, president of the Chicago Great Western Railroad, succeeded with the help of Omaha businessmen in financing and constructing a branch line across western Iowa to Omaha. This gave the Great Western a direct route between the city and Chicago. More importantly, it touched off a violent rate war. Prior to the coming of the Great Western, the railroads serving Omaha had their price structures so arranged that the city had no profitable way of handling grain destined for outside Nebraska. Rates from interior points to distant markets were far less than those from the same points to Omaha. It cost less to ship from Broken Bow in central Nebraska to Chicago than it did to ship from Broken Bow to Omaha. In addition, prices increased if grain stopped in Omaha prior to reshipment.

Stickney changed this long haul arrangement. He worked out a plan under which the through rates were made equal to the sum of the local rate in and the proportional rate out. In short, he charged what the traffic would bear. The other roads had no choice except to compete if they wanted traffic. At one time corn carried from Omaha to the Mississippi River dropped to three cents per hundred pounds, an incredibly low rate destructive to the shippers. Stickney received very strong support from Wattles and Omaha business interests that did not have direct ties either with the Union Pacific or the Burlington. The railroads, which had compromised earlier over Kansas City rates when faced with competition from Stickney, did so again. A general agreement overhauled the rates in and out of Omaha, making it feasible for Omaha to function competitively with older grain centers.

In November 1903 Wattles had taken the lead in organizing the Omaha Grain Exchange. Receipts in the first year amounted to sixteen million bushels, an unimpressive total by national standards. Poor area elevator facilities hampered the new exchange. The one-million-bushel Union Elevator burned to the ground, leaving storage space for only 2.3 million bushels. New construction improved matters, but it was several years before local elevators came close to meeting demands on their services. They had a capacity of six million bushels in 1906 and almost seven million in 1909, and in the same span receipts advanced from thirty-five million to

Omaha Grain Exchange

fifty million bushels. By the end of the decade, Omaha ranked overall as the nation's fourth largest grain market. Totals for corn were especially impressive; over twenty million bushels annually made Omaha the world's second largest handler of the commodity. Wattles, then president of the exchange boasted in 1909:

> These results have been obtained because of the enterprise and business acumen displayed by the grain men who comprise the Omaha Grain Exchange. The market has been, from the start, an active and open market. There has been a buying interest here from the beginning that has taken every bushel of grain offered, no matter how small the quantity, and has paid for it such prices as naturally attracted further business. . . . It is pleasant to reflect that this growth and development has been based upon Nebraska and Iowa grain only, and that a large field outside of the territory we have reached in these two states still remains to be invaded by the Omaha dealers if only the transportation charges can be adjusted to a proper basis.

Wattles failed in his primary goal of making Omaha the nation's second greatest grain market. The Omaha Grain Exchange never traded in futures. Instead, it bought and sold grain shipped to the city. Still, Wattles had created an economic institution that added a new and profitable dimension to Omaha's economy.

Wattles made a mark on Omaha. His civic activities enhanced the city's image. He fought hard to establish its economic independence. On one hand, he successfully challenged unions. He looked upon outside organizers as interlopers eager at a small price to gain power in a community that they had nothing to do with building. On the other, he maneuvered to free Omaha from domination by the railroad companies. He placed the men who used their monopolistic position to fix rates in the same category as labor agitators. Unlike the packing house owners, who brought money and jobs, they took without giving much in return. Thus he opposed what he believed unfair designs by both outside capital and labor. Of course, he saw nothing wrong with pushing an aggressive strategy of creating a larger and more secure productive and distributive region for Omaha. Wattles was neither a philanthropist like Creighton nor a rough-and-tough capitalist like Paxton. He had no real social conscience and no sympathy for the rights of laborers. He could not understand those who criticized him for bringing in strikebreakers or forcing the signing of "yellow dog" agreements. He confided to a friend in 1918, "I don't enjoy being the target for attack by all socialistic and anarchistic elements, but when attacked there is only one road to follow, and that is the road that leads to justice and honest dealings." In the early 1920s he moved to a large mansion in Hollywood, California, where he continued to tend his extensive interests until his death in 1932. No one raised any statues or named parks in his memory. Still, he had convinced some Omahans of their city's greatness.

Edward F. Morearty, explaining why he wrote *Omaha Memories: Recollections of Events, Men and Affairs in Omaha,* articulated the sense of purpose that Wattles gave the city.

> Because it is in the geographical center of the United States through which passes the channels of commerce from the rock-bound coast of Maine to the Golden Gate of California, and from the snow-capped mountains of Canada to the pleasant glades of Florida; because it has the most even and healthful climate of any spot in the United States; because it is the second primary livestock market of the world; because it is the fourth primary grain market of the world; because its jobbing trade in 1916 was $188,000,000; because its factory out-

put for 1916 was $219,000,000; because it is the greatest cream-
ery producing city in the world. Because in 1999 it will have a
population of 1,000,000 people; because it is the greatest lead
ore reducing city in the world; because it is the second primary
corn market in the world; because it is the greatest sheep feeding market in the world; because it has the broadest streets and
best kept of any city of her size in the United States; because it
has more palatial residences and the greatest number of home
owners in proportion to population than any other city in the
world; because it has the most extensive, best equipped, best
service street car system in the world; because it has the most
schools and most efficient teachers in this nation.

This kind of extravagant exaggeration was more than boosterism.
It represented an attempt to articulate aspirations in a context that
would gain widespread community support and spur city building
for the furthering of common goals.

An important element in promoting Omaha's future were the
thousands of salesmen based in the city. They had to hold old territory and pioneer new, all before growing competition. The best
drummers met the challenge, adjusting their methods to conform
with the changed circumstances. Selling a tractor in Ankeny, Iowa;
negotiating an agreement to supply shirts in Hastings, Nebraska;
and writing an order for tacks in Mitchell, South Dakota: these
meant the difference between success and failure. The salesmen
acted as spearheads of commerce that brought gigantic amounts of
money into the city. They covered areas well beyond the 150-mile
radius considered by business experts as standard territory for convenient sales operations, making it possible for the hundreds of
wholesale and jobbing houses in Omaha such as M. E. Smith &
Company in wholesale dry goods, the Omaha Baum Iron Store,
Inc. in hardware, and the Carpenter Paper Company in paper to do
immense amounts of business. During the 1910s and 1920s aggregate annual sales rose from $100 million with the way led by auto-
mobiles and accessories, groceries, building materials, and agricultural implements. In 1929 an Omaha promotional pamphlet, published by a business organization, claimed that a tradition of service
and aggressive marketing had combined to make the city "the logi-
cal jobbing capital of the central United States." A generation of
salesmen working the plains gave a semblance of reality to that conclusion. They were the unsung heroes of the Omaha story.

The livestock market remained one of Omaha's greatest
strengths. In 1915 South Omaha became part of Omaha, adding
over 25,000 persons to the city. Most laborers in South Omaha

worked in the livestock yards or the packing houses. The "Big Four" packers, modified from earlier days by name changes and mergers, were Armour, Cudahy, Swift, and Morris. There were a number of smaller plants: the Higgins Packing Company, Hoffman Brothers, Mayerowich & Vail, Roth & Sons, and the South Omaha Dressed Beef Company. Cumulatively, the big and small companies employed over 13,000 men, with an annual payroll of $13 million. The slaughterhouses needed large facilities. Armour's buildings sprawled over several acres. A new structure erected in 1915 was one of the largest in the region. The building contained a sheep killing and cooling department, an engine room, a machine shop, and a car shop, all prerequisites for improved operations. The yards were equally impressive. They covered 200 acres of which 175 had a paved surface. There were 4,298 pens all equipped with concrete watering troughs, supplied by the stockyards' own water department. Annual receipts for livestock traded rose in 1900 from 830,000 cattle, 2.2 million hogs, and 1.3 million sheep to 1.2 million cattle, 1.9 million hogs, and 3 millon sheep in 1910. There was a gradual upturn; in 1925 receipts amounted to 1.6 million cattle, 3.4 million hogs, and 2.4 million sheep. By that time, freight charges on Omaha livestock and packing products totaled over $17 million yearly.

The Omaha Livestock Exchange, which had about 250 members, handled almost all the necessary transactions. The Union Stock Yards Company of Omaha, Limited, continued to have major responsibilities. Its general manager from 1907 until 1923 was Everett Buckingham who previously had been a high official of the Union Pacific Railroad. His presence suggested continuing railroad involvement in Omaha business undertakings. Another indication of outside influence was that a large minority of shares in the stock yards company were in the hands of the Armour family of Chicago. Economic relationships were such that no one in Omaha, Wattles included, could obtain complete fiscal independence.

Other manufacturing pursuits moved forward in Omaha, as indicated by figures for 1915, a representative year. The Union Pacific shops employed over fifteen hundred operatives. The sixty-acre complex, besides building and repairing rolling stock, chemically treated over 500,000 ties to improve durability. Another large concern, the American Smelting and Refining Company, operated a thirty-one acre smelter, which refined metals and by-products with an estimated annual value of $39 million. Aside from a few major foundries — the Paxton & Vierling Iron Works and the Omaha

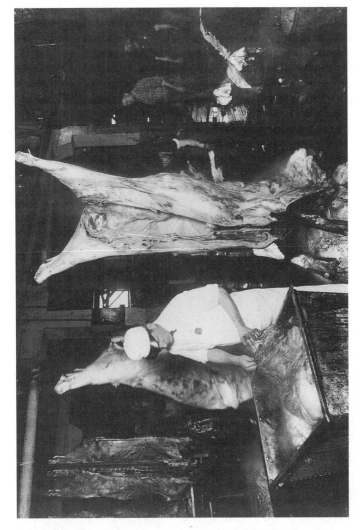

Beef Killing at the Cudahy Packing Co.

General Iron Works – plus the Bemis Omaha Bag Company that produced burlap and cotton bags for the grain industry, most industrial activities were extractive in nature. Five breweries had an output valued at $3 million, almost all for the local market. The largest were the Fred Krug Brewing Company, Metz Brothers, and the Storz Brewing Company. All were owned by Omaha interests unlike another firm in the liquor business, the Willow Springs Distilling Company, which was part of a national distilling group. There were five large creameries; they had a product in excess of $7 million, most of which was "process butter." Two establishments, the M. C. Peters Mill Company and the Krogh Alfalfa Mills, mixed alfalfa and molasses to make stock food, sold throughout the plains. Other important business lines were flour and mill products ($3.2 million), bakery ($2.4 million), grocery specialty items ($2.3 million), and clothing goods ($1.3 million). School children in Omaha learned a litany: "Omaha macaroni is sold in Italy! . . . Omaha pig lead is sold all over the world!" Pleasing to factory owners, the words failed to hide that Omaha had not developed much in the way of manufacturing outside of the agricultural sphere.

American Smelting and Refining Co.

World War One was an interlude that had little immediate impact on Omaha. The preparedness movement was of no consequence. Given the nature of the local industrial system; there were no munitions plants. Hostilities lasted too short a time, from April of 1917 to November of 1918, to cause significant changes. The establishment of an army balloon school near Omaha elicited much comment, resulting from the novelty of manned balloons drifting over the city, but generated little money for the economy. While close to 20,000 Omahans served in the armed forces, creating local labor shortages, the most serious hardships experienced on the home front were "wheatless" and "meatless" days. A sharp increase in railroad passenger traffic brought some new business; many soldiers and civilians had to lay over for several hours between trains. The livestock and packing industries were already operating at around full capacity when war came to America. Receipts remained at high levels, with livestock that could not be handled diverted to other markets.

During and immediately after hostilities there was a massive expansion of agriculture throughout the Great Plains. Cultivated land in Nebraska rose by three million acres, with most going into wheat and corn. The vast enlargement, which related to good crop yields, high prices, and patriotism, greatly increased the grain trade in Omaha. At the same time it stimulated commercial and jobbing pursuits. Few persons seemed concerned that much of the new farm land was in areas that defeated farmers had left late in the previous century. Wartime demands and prosperity took precedence. Omaha businessmen held their own, maintaining their city's prewar position against rivals. No place in the region gained any appreciable advantage over another because of the war. The plains were prosperous at the conflict's end, and so was Omaha. Its leaders looked ahead to further prosperity in the 1920s.

A recently developed industry, electric power, led Omaha into what many believed the climax of the machine age. Just as in the not too distant past, with the transcontinental telegraph and railroad, Omaha seemed in the vanguard of a modernization that would change conditions in North America. By the postwar period, electricity was taken for granted as a source of light. More importantly, generators no longer had to be constructed close to users. Technological advances enabled the transmission of electricity through power grids over long distances. Indeed, it was possible to transfer electricity from one grid to another, and a whole new national industry arose. Those in on the ground floor, such as capi-

145

Union and Burlington Depots, ca. 1920s

talist Samuel Insull of Chicago, who developed large holdings throughout the Midwest in the twenties, wanted neither government handouts nor interference. Their needs were totally different from those of the original owners of the Union Pacific Railroad. Insull and his colleagues were perfectly content to have a new agency, the Federal Power Commission, limit its activities to the licensing of dam sites for private power purposes. The power interests argued that federal involvement would lead to higher rates. Critics claimed that it was the other way around; increased governmental regulation would lead to lower rates, because power monopolists gouged consumers. One of the shrillest critics was a Nebraska progressive Republican, Senator George W. Norris of McCook, a small community in the western part of the state. He championed public power for reclamation projects and argued in favor of the "yardstick" principle under which pilot federal projects would be used to measure power costs. Norris was particularly incensed by the practices of the new darling of Omaha's business constellation, the Nebraska Power Company.

Reformers found it easy to dislike the Nebraska Power Company. They did not even approve of its slogan, "Electric Service is Cheap." To them, the firm embodied objectionable business practices. In 1917 a powerful national holding company, the Electric Bond and Share Company, had acquired an Omaha power producer and changed the name to the Nebraska Power Company. As a result of this transaction, Electric Power upped the fixed capital in Nebraska Power from $6.4 million to $13.5 million. Some $5 million of a resulting common stock issue went directly to another Electric Bond subsidiary, the American Power and Light Company. This stock transition, worthy of any undertaken by Jay Gould in Union Pacific issues, paid handsome dividends. According to an investigation by the Federal Trade Commission, the rate of return on ledger value was 96.8 percent over the ensuing ten years. Dividends for one year amounted to 160 percent. Following a rate cut and in a year of depression, 1930, dividends reached $1.2 million.

Nebraska Power added local businessmen to its executive group. At one point, nine out of fifteen members of the board of directors were Omahans. Nebraska Power produced roughly sixty percent of the electricity in the state. Its Omaha power stations had major responsibilities in the operation of the national transmission network. Such considerations guaranteed criticism under the best of circumstances. Nebraska Power reacted by mounting a massive ad-

148

vertising campaign designed to counter the view that it was an insensitive monopoly run by outside forces only concerned with taking profits out of Nebraska. The person responsible for improving Nebraska Power's image was James E. Davidson. A pioneer in the industry, he was the firm's vice president and general manager. Born in 1879, he grew up in Port Huron, Michigan, where his father owned a small electric business. Davidson quit high school prior to graduation to take a job at the Port Huron Light and Power Company. He became superintendent at the age of twenty-one, starting an executive career. He moved up rapidly and soon headed an American Power and Light Company subsidiary in Portland, Oregon. He assumed his Omaha responsibilities in 1917 and quickly became a prominent figure in the community. In addition to gaining respect as an able manager, he was a likeable man with a genial personality. He gave a great deal of time to civic activities and belonged to the major social clubs and service organizations. Twice he directed community chest drives. His adopted city gratefully appreciated such altruism and, accordingly, honored him. He was king of Ak-Sar-Ben in 1923 and named the outstanding Omaha citizen of the year in 1929.

Although he held several local directorships, Davidson devoted most of his business activities to Nebraska Power. Unlike Wattles at an earlier date, Davidson had little interest in using civic connections as a means to gain footholds in a wide variety of Omaha businesses, with the purpose of achieving community power. Rather he did it for enjoyment and self-fulfillment, at the same time helping Nebraska Power. It served the controversial monopoly well to have a highly visible public spirited leader. After all, during the dark winter months, Nebraska Power occasionally turned off the power for the non-payment of bills at the homes of widows and orphans. And almost every storm brought breaks in lines, frequently throwing whole towns into darkness. Davidson was aware of the general reaction to such circumstances; every session of the state legislature saw the introduction of bills, defeated or swiftly tabled through intensive lobbying, calling for municipal ownership.

Davidson's specialty was public relations. He was instrumental in establishing the Nebraska Committee of Public Utility Information. This organization did such a successful job of improving the image of private power in Nebraska—it produced a textbook glorifying the community contributions of private electric companies and equating foes with the "Red Menace"—that Davidson received national recognition. In 1925 his colleagues in the industry elected him president of the National Electric Light Association and awarded Nebraska Power a prize for the "Most Constructive Public Relations Campaign carried on by a Light and Power Company in Local Territory." Davidson remained in the electric business in Omaha for many more years; he gained a reputation as the "Number One" power salesman in the country. He was cognizant of the means of promoting consumer products in a hostile environment.

During the 1920s Omaha businessmen used advertising to further the fortunes of the city. On one level, there was a need to uphold the community image as a growing regional metropolis. This involved boosterism, emphasizing statistical virtues: thirty-sixth in area, thirty-fourth in population, fourth largest railroad center, first in home ownership, second livestock market, intersection of sixteen motor highways, home office of thirty-one insurance companies, and $2.3 billion in bank clearings. Of more immediate economic consequence were efforts to call attention to Omaha's standing as a place to shop. The quick adoption of the automobile on the Middle Border changed conditions. It became practical for farmers in eastern Nebraska and western Iowa to reach Omaha and return home the same day. To encourage them to come, adroit publicity proclaimed the wonders of the downtown district: "Omaha's main retail market covers an area of a little more than two square miles. Here are the department stores and exclusive shops, to be counted by the hundreds, where all the latest merchandise gathered from the marts of the world is offered to the thousands of daily buyers. The last word in styles and merchandise from Paris, Vienna, London and other world markets in as great variety, and at prices commensurate with those to be found in any other of America's great metropolitan retail markets, are stocked by these Omaha stores to meet the demands of a prosperous and discriminating customer clientele."

For many persons who grew up in the Omaha region in the first quarter of the twentieth century, their first lasting memory of the city was going with their parents to the Brandeis Stores. It was the successor to the Boston Store, started in the late nineteenth century by pioneer merchant Jonas Brandeis. His three sons, Arthur, Hugo, and Emil, all of whom played major roles in Omaha commercial real estate development, erected the huge emporium in the heart of downtown, making it the apex of their extensive holdings. The Brandeis Stores was the finest department store on the northern plains. The seven-story establishment covered an entire block. From the commodious bargain basement to rooftop

Brandeis Stores

151

restaurant, there was a dazzling array of merchandise; carpets, corsets, furs, blouses, laces, embroideries, drugs, books, men's clothing, umbrellas, linens, hardware, toys, china, and notions. The three restaurants suited the needs of tired shoppers and were relaxing places to spend the noon hour. A generation of children remembered the lavish Christmas displays. The main floor, with its high ceilings, white fluted Corinthian columns, broad aisles, large potted ferns, and unobstructed sight-lines, created a pleasing atmosphere for the displays of high class merchandise. The escalator system, the only one in the area, attracted considerable attention. For the convenience of customers, the store offered a free area telephone service, a post office branch, a check room for packages, and a cashier's desk. The Brandeis Stores acted as a magnet that brought buyers to the city in droves. It was a community institution that helped the whole downtown, contributing in many ways to furthering Omaha's annual retail trade of several hundred million dollars. The department store was a local version of Marshall Field's in Chicago and Macy's in New York City.

By 1929 Omaha seemed to many on the verge of another of the rapid advances that had characterized the past. The first portion of the twentieth century had been basically a period of the consolidation of earlier gains, the keeping of regional metropolitan status, and the laying of foundations for future progress. Wattles consolidated important activities, battled to make the Omaha business establishment independent from outside forces, and helped define and articulate community aspirations. Davidson directed a business that appeared the means for furthering regional designs and the acquisition of untold new wealth. The Ak-Sar-Ben had become a means of unifying a wide variety of groups to carry through social and political projects. The grain and livestock exchanges traded in the products of a gigantic region. Jobbing and retail businesses appeared to have unlimited potential. The stockyards and packing houses served as tangible evidence of Omaha's rise as an agricultural center. Passage of a bond issue to construct a municipal airport north of downtown in the Missouri River bottoms seemed to assure Omaha a role in the rise of regional and even national air transportation. The resurgence of the Union Pacific and the "Golden Age" of Nebraska farming added to a general picture of economic optimism. The wave of national prosperity that swept across the country in the 1920s worked to the benefit of urban areas, while rural regions fought losing battles to maintain their economic footing.

Omaha experienced a building boom in west side districts annexed earlier in anticipation of future development. A master plan produced in 1919 by the Omaha City Planning Commission called for widening heavily traveled streets to carry increased automobile traffic. The following year Omaha's first zoning ordinance contained stipulations designed to prevent commercial and industrial encroachments on land designated for residential purposes. A zone of apartments and duplexes separated downtown from the west side housing tracts. Several thoroughfares, among them Dodge, Harney, and Leavenworth, provided arterial connections with the central core. Two of the west side subdivisions catered to the wealthy. Builders, emphasizing the advantages of the automobile and the prospects of a cycle of rising land prices, lured rich Omahans away from the older north side enclaves of Kountze Place and Miller Park to western Fairacres and Buena Vista on the Gold Coast. Developers sought to construct self-contained garden suburbs patterned after those in Chicago and elsewhere. Happy Hollow, near the site of a former country club, contained rolling hills, lush shrubbery, manicured lawns, numerous trees, Tudor-style homes, and winding streets. In one year alone, 1922, over fifteen hundred new homes appeared in west side neighborhoods. West Dodge Acres, Bensonville Place, Beverly Hills, and Elmwood Gardens attracted buyers. So did the older suburban towns of Dundee and Benson. American intellectuals found little to praise about the housing trends; Sinclair Lewis attacked suburban values in *Babbitt*. However, Happy Hollow and other sections exemplified how many Americans wanted to live in the 1920s, a decade of urban prosperity.

The problems that increasingly afflicted plains agriculture in the 1920s, related to overproduction, adverse climatic conditions, shrinking overseas markets, increased costs, and downward prices, caused little concern in Omaha. Those involved in making economic decisions rode the trend of general prosperity risking that periodic adjustments, realignments, and reallocations would straighten things out. Enormous purchases of material items by hinterland residents—everything from automobiles to radios—more than compensated for lower quotations for livestock and commodities on the exchanges. Studies of previous achievements convinced Omahans that the past was prologue. Seventy-five years after the formation of Nebraska and the founding of Omaha, at the time of the diamond jubilee for state and city, the slogan adopted by the Chamber of Commerce, "Onward Omaha," summed up the objectives of the business community. A promotional publication emphasized:

> Omaha faces a future rich with promise of continued domination in field, garden, and stock-yard. Omaha faces a future in which the great economic battles will be fought and won by cities with transportation facilities and quick contacts. Omaha is the country's center. Already it is the fourth railroad center; already it commands the highways; but now commerce is to travel by water and air. A navigable channel, down the Missouri and Mississippi to the Gulf of Mexico, will be the gift of the next few years, and when it comes, it will open a new avenue to the markets of the world. Omaha, according to aviation experts, is ideally situated to become the capital of the skyways. In the geographical center of the United States, Omaha is built on level, rockless and comparatively treeless land which lends itself naturally to flying fields. No mists, little smoke, and rare fogs hinder the free movement of airplanes in the Midwest. Omaha leaders have been quick to grasp their opportunity, and the city is riding the rising tide of aviation. Omaha faces the future backed by all of her old allies, and fortified with the strength of two new ones — water and air!

Then, the New York stock market collapsed, starting a tidal wave of adversity that swept over the United States. Omahans in all walks of life had more to worry about than the advance of air and water transportation. A network of bankrupt railroads, idle factories, and empty stores stood as testimony of what befell the plains. As in the 1890s abandoned farms were the rule rather than the exception. The ruin of agriculture seemed to spell an end to glory for Omaha. The city, in lieu of prosperity, faced instead the onslaught of depression. The fabric woven over many years faced severe testing. Under the circumstances the people of Omaha and their social institutions undertook new significance, transcending that of the standards advocated by the business community.

6

Laws that People Don't
Believe in Can't
Be Enforced

Omaha underwent numerous changes in the first thirty years of
the twentieth century. Many decades later, experts, after studying
technological trends, would describe the process as "modernization." At the time, people equated developments with normal community progress or else took them for granted. As it was, the altering of forms in Omaha as throughout the United States related to
several considerations; the transformations wrought by the
machine age, the positive attitude of the voters toward improvements, the growing professionalism among those responsible for
urban services, and the gradual evolution of social and cultural institutions.

The success of a number of bond issues at the polls, always in the
face of opposition charges that the increased costs would ruin the
city, facilitated the implementation of vast improvements that
Omaha needed, as it increased in physical size. By 1929 the community covered 25,000 acres. It had seven hundred miles of streets and

six hundred miles of sewers. The Omaha Fire Department met the challenge of community enlargement with mechanized equipment, outlying stations, and better training methods. The police also became more efficient, adding motor traffic control to their responsibilities. The public schools added many teachers, and Omahans established a municipal university. Religious bodies enjoyed membership increases, and a number of new churches and synagogues graced the skyline. There was interest in providing adequate public funding for a library and for furthering the arts in general. Several cultural institutions elicited favorable comment. "The cultural future of Omaha," an Omaha *Bee* staff writer wrote on the eve of the Great Depression, "seems as certain of greatness as the commercial future.... The symphony orchestra, the Art institute, the Community Playhouse and other organizations are on firm foundations and Omaha is destined to be not only a bigger, but a better city, both financially and culturally."

Underlying the quest for a state of refinement were four concerns that threatened and ran counter to the quest for stability. Sometimes, they shaped policies in fundamental ways, at other times they were more subtle. Some had deep roots in the past. A few were of relatively recent origin. The first prolonged query involved the character of the population. The mixing of ethnic groups, in addition to giving the city a diversified cultural heritage, caused numerous tensions. A second serious matter, which evolved from the first, was interracial violence that twice in ten years shook the town to its foundations. Third was Omaha's enduring and well-deserved reputation as a wide open town, a stigma that increasingly disturbed citizens in other parts of Nebraska and culminated in political action. The fourth question centered around the nature of the political system. Omaha acquired a boss whose political machine controlled local politics for close to three decades. Supporters argued that the machine ameliorated pressures toward community disintegration by creating a consensus and giving people in the lower strata of society a voice. Critics viewed it as a disgrace that prevented solutions to ethnic, racial, and vice problems. In any event, the boss system touched upon many aspects of the body politic in Omaha, either directly or indirectly. Whether this was for good or bad remained in dispute.

Omaha's ethnic mix seemed to many observers a key to understanding the nature of the city. Evaluations were not always positive. When Rudyard Kipling passed through the town in 1889, he concluded that it "seemed to be populated entirely by Germans,

Poles, Slavs, Hungarians, Croats, Magyars, and all the scum of the Eastern European States." In 1900 when the recorded population for Omaha was 102,555, there were 23,552 immigrants, accounting for twenty-three percent of all Omahans. Most were Scandinavians (6,710), Germans (5,522), Danes (2,430), Bohemians (2,170), and Irish (2,164). A total of 56,430 persons had at least one foreign-born parent. South Omaha counted 5,607 foreign-born, for twenty-two percent out of an enumeration of 26,001.

By 1910 Omaha had 124,096 persons. Of these, 27,179, or twenty-two percent, were from overseas. The larger numbers came from Germany (4,861), Sweden (3,805), Austria-Hungary (3,414), Denmark (2,652), Russia (2,592), and Italy (2,361). The most dramatic change was the rising number of Italians. Many people from central Europe were Bohemians, listed by the census as Austrians or Germans. South Omaha, in the last count prior to its 1915 annexation by Omaha, had 26,259 people. The "Magic City" had grown by only 258 inhabitants in the first decade of the century. After construction of the packing plants and the establishment of levels of production, there was little need for additional workers. Even so, the numbers and percentages of foreigners moved upward markedly. There were 8,021, accounting for thirty-one percent of the total, with 3,551 individuals hailing from Russia constituting the largest single bloc.

After 1910 Omaha's demographic characteristics started to stabilize. In 1920 there were 191,601 inhabitants; and only 35,385, or nineteen percent, were foreign-born. However, changes in countries of origin showed up in the census despite little new immigration. Many persons previously listed as coming from Germany or Austria-Hungary now claimed new nations created out of World War One, particularly Czechoslovakia and Poland, as places of birth. Three other countries contributed in excess of ten percent of Omaha's population. There were 4,270 persons from Germany, 3,825 from Russia, and 3,708 from Sweden.

Both numbers and percentages fell in the 1920s, when the United States government enacted measures that drastically curtailed immigration. The 1930 population of Omaha was 214,066; and the foreign-born percentage had declined to fourteen percent, the lowest figure in the century. By nationality the largest aggregates were Czechoslovakians (3,946), Germans (3,700), Italians (3,221), Swedes (2,977), Danes (2,561), Poles (2,546), and Russians (2,084). The statistics presented a general picture of Omaha's primary population trends. There were things that they failed to show. Estimates placed the number of persons of Danish extraction at 10,000 and of Bohemian at 7,000. Many of the Russians were Jews who had fled the country to escape religious persecution. The Italians were primarily from southern Italy and Sicily. A majority of immigrants of all nationalities were males. Throughout the period 1900-1930 Omaha's foreign-born percentage was larger than that of the nation as a whole and much larger than in other cities in the Missouri River Valley and watershed. Although hardly comparable to Chicago, Milwaukee, and Detroit, there was no doubt that Omaha qualified as an "immigrant city."

In the 1920s, when roughly fifty percent of the population were immigrants and their children, Omaha reached the zenith of its ethnic diversity. There were numerous ethnic neighborhoods, all in older sections near downtown and in South Omaha. While the vast majority of Germans, Swedes, Danes, and Irish had dispersed throughout town, there was still a Little Germany. Other nationalities were either voluntarily or involuntarily segregated. In turn, Irish, Germans, and Italians lived in an uninviting area of several blocks on the flood plain, just to the southeast of downtown near the factory and warehouse districts. Some Italians had already left Little Sicily, southeast of the business district. Rigid segregation patterns restricted blacks to two ghettos, a small one next to the stockyards and a larger one on the Near North Side close to the Union Pacific shops. The original Bohemian district was along South Thirteenth Street, a north-south thoroughfare. Newer Czech districts were on South Omaha's east side. Sheeley Town, on Omaha's southwest outskirts, was the first Polish district. Poles soon spilled over into South Omaha, creating a Little Poland on Golden Hill. Greek immigrants had dwelled near the packing plants in a district later inhabited by blacks and Hispanics. Another neighborhood on South Omaha's south side, directly in the path of prevailing winds from the stockyards and packing plants, was a "zebra striped" dumping ground for poor immigrants from eastern Europe. Serbs, Croatians, Lithuanians, and others all endured the squalid rooming houses of the polyglot precinct before moving away as quickly as possible. Even so, other immigrant sections, from their ethnic churches to distinctive architectural forms, acted as forces of stability in Omaha.

Some of the Omaha foreign-born groups moved without much trouble into the mainstream, the Germans serving as a case in point. They started coming early in Omaha's history, and their transition to American life was eased by the presence of thousands of residents of German extraction. German immigrants settled in the older parts of Omaha and in the suburbs of South Omaha, Benson, and Florence. Many acquired their own homes and businesses, rising quickly to important positions in the community. They generally tried to keep Germanic customs, teaching their children the German language, worshiping in German churches, reading German papers, and keeping traditional German mores. On Sunday afternoons they liked to go in family groups to beer gardens to socialize and listen to brass bands. Among their organizations were the Platt-Deutschen Verein, Omaha Musik Verein, and German Turnverein.

Efforts to keep Teutonic cultural forms alive in Omaha, while at the same time embracing American economic and political values, gradually broke down. World War One was a contributing factor. Unknown parties defaced a statue of Johann von Schiller. Federal legislation required Germans who were not American citizens to register as "Alien Enemies." State-encouraged patriotic organizations placed them under observation. To prove loyalty to their adopted land, many Germans abandoned the old ways, going out of their way to oppose the Kaiser. The Omaha *Tribune,* a German language journal, ardently championed the Allied war effort. Prohibition brought a further blow, forcing the closing of beer gardens. Immigration fell off sharply, and older people passed away. By the end of the 1920s there was little outward evidence of German culture in Omaha.

Bohemians, too, arrived in Omaha when it was a young community. In Civil War days, a small party came to the city from Cedar Rapids, Iowa. Throughout the 1870s controversial newspaper editor Edward Rosewater, who put forward an unverified claim as Omaha's first Czech immigrant, helped advertise the virtues of Nebraska among Bohemians. Two other men furthered his efforts: U. L. Vondicka, a railroad land agent, and John Rosicky, editor of the Omaha *Pokrok Zapadu.* During the last twenty years of the nineteenth century, many Bohemians moved into South Omaha. Some came directly from abroad; others had given up trying to farm in Nebraska. While a majority never advanced beyond the packing houses, fully three-fourths owned homes and a few rose in professional and business fields. They were one of the best organized nationalities in Omaha. Of special importance were Sokols, societies that promoted gymnastic and cultural activities. An annual summer festival featured folk dances performed by young people and in the 1920s Czechoslovakian independence day became a major holiday. Even so, social activities became increasingly American. Many second and third generation Bohemians continued to take pride in their roots, but so did the members of other immigrant groups. Among Czechs, the assimilation process was virtually over by the Great Depression.

Swedes and Danes, the chief Scandinavian elements in Omaha, quickly Americanized. The first Swedes arrived in the late 1860s, at the start of large-scale immigration from Sweden into the United States. Many who came to Omaha found employment in the Union Pacific shops. When they migrated, they had little education and few skills. They worked hard, but having little money to start with they had trouble getting ahead, and the vast majority remained unskilled workers. Although the Swedes had ethnic lodges, notably the Independent Order of the Vikings and the Order of Vara, they showed little interest in preserving former customs. The same was true of the Danes. Their clubs were almost entirely social. The major one was the Danish Brotherhood, a national organization. Economically, they did about as well as the Swedes, advancing slowly. The Danes had come to the United States in immediate post-Civil War times to escape the German military occupation of their native provinces. Many men left out of fear of being impressed into the German army. Almost all of the Danes and Swedes who lived in Omaha were former peasants. They hated their feudal monarchs and landlords and had no sense of nationalism. In the United States, they rejected their past life to the extent that few made an effort to teach their children the rudiments of Swedish or Danish. This resulted in almost complete acculturation by the second and third generations.

The Irish constituted another major component of Omaha's foreign-born community. The largest single body came originally to help build the Union Pacific. Those who stayed in Omaha went to work in the railroad shops or secured jobs as common laborers. Very few, almost all of whom were men, had come directly to Omaha from the "Old Sod." By the 1890s, when the American Protective Association singled them out as targets in an unsuccessful attempt to drive immigrants and their children out of Omaha, the Irish lived throughout town. They had intermarried and adopted American ways to the extent that they had virtually lost identity as a separate ethnic group. Even though they observed St. Patrick's Day, they showed no positive interest in the bitter fight over home rule for Ireland. In Omaha they moved into all levels of society, being particularly influential in politics and city government. They greatly strengthened the Roman Catholic Church. Many early church benefactors were Irish immigrants or their sons and daughters.

Omaha had a significant Polish community before many other American cities. Early in the 1870s the first Poles came to Sheeley Town to work in a small packing house. More Poles came in the 1880s and 1890s. Few spoke English or had skilled occupations. They toiled in the packing plants, stockyards, and worked on the railroads. The vast majority were hard-working people with strong family ties. They owned small homes and raised many children. Polish social life revolved around the Roman Catholic church and fraternal organizations. There were Polish schools and recreation centers, sponsored by a number of societies: the Polish Roman Catholic Union, the Polish Union of the United States, the National Alliance, the Pulaski Club, the Polish Welfare Club, and the Polish Citizens' Club. The Poles, as other central Europeans, enjoyed music and dancing. A major event was the wedding dance, a festive affair open to the public. Older Poles were clannish and showed little inclination to learn more than the rudiments of English or to make drastic changes in their life styles. The younger Poles reacted in an opposite manner. They eagerly adopted American values, showing a great interest in sports. During the 1920s Sheeley Town produced powerful amateur baseball teams. Strong clubs featuring Frank Konicki, Ben Stahurski, "Long Hip" Dargaczewski, Joe Slizewski, and others afforded ample evidence of the acceptance by Poles of America's national pastime.

In the early 1880s there was an influx of Russian Jews into Omaha as part of a general immigration that followed the Kiev Massacre. In Omaha many started anew as peddlers and small shop owners. Some went on to become outstanding merchants, known throughout the community. Initially, most Russian Jews settled in a few neighborhoods in the older sections, although they never lived in ghettos. They had a strong tradition of education and had a reputation as being keenly intellectual. Their cultural life centered around the Jewish Community Center which had a library, gymnasium, auditorium, and Talmud Torah. The Hebrew religion remained a strong force among them, but they showed no interest in preserving Russian customs. After all, pogroms—the organized massacre of helpless people promoted by the authorities—had prompted the Jews to leave Russia.

The Italians, who did not start arriving in large numbers until after 1900, were very individualistic. Fears of restrictions on immigration helped to spur the immigration of thousands of uneducated and unskilled Italians into the United States; a number who moved to Omaha were from feudal-like southern estates and villages. Many were young men who lived together in crowded rooming houses. Most had temporarily left their families behind in Italy. They gained employment almost exclusively as day laborers and showed little interest in American customs. Their ways brought recriminations from older residents who called them "dagos," "guineas," and "wops." A leadership group, mainly from the ranks of the few Italians who had lived in Omaha prior to rapid immigration, gradually emerged. Their influence, along with that of the Roman Catholic Church and the arrival of Italian women and children, brought a measure of stability. By the 1920s almost all the Italians in Omaha belonged to one or more of twenty-four societies. These organizations, united under the auspices of the Italian consul, sponsored a wide variety of undertakings. Predominantly Italian Roman Catholic churches held large festivals, including the annual summer feast of St. Lucia. Most of the stresses and strains related to a desire of Italian immigrants to keep old ties while at the same time becoming loyal Americans. "Though America must be first does not mean that we cannot cherish a love for our mother country," Giulio Agazzoni, a patriarch of the community, said. "A man does not need to hate his mother because he loves his wife." These were brave words, echoing what German immigrant spokesmen had said earlier. Agazzoni's statement had little effect upon the assimilation process, which moved ahead at a rapid pace in the ensuing ten years.

There were numerous other immigrant groups in Omaha. Several hundred English and Canadian immigrants lived throughout town. So did Norwegians, Welsh, French, and Belgians. Other nationalities were in small colonies in South Omaha. Lithuanians, Serbs, and Croatians resided within the shadow of the packing plants, where almost all of them worked as common laborers. The same part of town contained Romanians, Hungarians, and Austrians. They were too few in number to have much in the way of an impact on the city. Several hundred Syrians, the first of whom arrived in 1890, occupied a tightly-packed South Omaha neighborhood. Few Syrians worked in the livestock district. The men started as street merchants, hawking shawls, carpets, and clothing, after a time acquiring small shops. The Syrians clung tenaciously to their old customs, with their community concerns centering around two fraternal orders, the Knights of Furzol and the Syrian-American Club.

Shortly after World War One, the packing houses brought in Mexican strikebreakers during a labor dispute. After helping to break the strike, a couple of hundred stayed on in Omaha. Some continued to work in the packing industry. Others sought employment on the railroads and during summer months in Nebraska beet fields. The Mexicans had a strong sense of unity, and they soon had their own Roman Catholic Church, the Neustra Señora de Guadalupe. Immigrants of all nationalities worked together on the job and then went their own ways after quitting time. Usually they got along well, but there were barroom brawls or shouting matches. The possibility of a major clash was always present, such as the one that led to the eradication of the Greek community.

Large numbers of Greeks moved into the Omaha area during the first decade of the twentieth century. The packing houses hired some to break a strike; the railroad brought in others as contract laborers. While contract labor was illegal in the United States, there was no serious attempt to enforce the law. By 1909, Greeks constituted a significant ethnic group. Several hundred lived in a small area in Omaha. These were permanent residents. They owned shops and had regular jobs and congregated at a combination tavern and pool room. The majority of the Greeks, however, resided in crowded rooming houses in South Omaha, in a district originally called "Indian Hill" which quickly acquired the new designation of "Greek Town." The section's population doubled to approximately two thousand persons in the winter months when the railroads laid off section hands.

Almost all the temporary residents of "Greek Town" were men, ages fifteen to thirty-five. They intended to return to their native land at a future date, so they made no pretense of adopting American ways. Having nothing to do, they spent their days in coffee houses, drinking thick Turkish coffee, arguing Greek politics, and playing cards. Other working men in South Omaha resented their apparent indolence, not stopping to consider the long and hard hours that the Greeks toiled in the summer on remote stretches of railroad track. Adding to resentment of Greeks was the fear that they corrupted South Omaha women. The Greeks did not help matters by making lewd remarks to passing females. Moreover, at least forty Greeks lived openly with American women. The Greeks, hardly any of whom spoke English, rapidly gained the status of unwelcome intruders. These proudly nationalistic people who traced their heritage back to classical times never realized that trouble brewed until it was too late to reverse the tide.

In February 1909 two Omaha newspapers launched bitter attacks against the Greeks of South Omaha. An article in the Omaha *Bee* declared, "The thing that sticks in the craw of the anti-Greek element is that they work cheap; live even more cheaply, in groups, are careless of many of the little details that Americans set much store by; once in a while are imprudent, ignore the restrictions of American law that lay heavily on the true patriot — in short, do not mix, are not 'good fellows' like the citizens we get from northern Europe, for instance." Joseph Pulcar, the editor of the Omaha *Daily News*, was even more explicit in discussing the habits of the Greeks. "Their quarters," he said, "have been unsanitary; they have insulted women; in many ways they have made themselves offensive in the eyes of the great majority of the people of South Omaha, too." After that denunciation, Pulcar called the Greeks threats to the workers of Omaha. "Herded together in lodging houses and living cheaply," he stressed, "Greeks are a menace to the American laboring man — just as the Japs, Italians, and other similar laborers are." All that was needed was an incident, and that soon came.

A popular South Omaha police officer met a violent death in the course of apprehending a Greek. Patrolman Edward Lowery was forty-two when he died in the line of duty. He left a wife and two children, one a University of Nebraska student. Lowery and his wife were both Irish immigrants. He was a foreman in the Cudahy Packing Company's lard department for several years, until he walked off the job in sympathy with strikers in 1904. Summarily fired, he experienced a lengthy period of unemployment before securing an appointment in the South Omaha Police Department. He soon gained a reputation as a respected and understanding officer, frequently helping drunks home instead of arresting them. He was a rising and respected member of the Irish community when he acted on a complaint to arrest John Masourides for vagrancy on the early evening of February 19, 1909. Masourides was already under police surveillance because of an arrest for gambling. His new troubles stemmed from information that he possibly had an illicit relationship with a seventeen-year-old minor, Lillian Breese. She was a Grand Island, Nebraska girl who claimed to make a living teaching English to immigrants. Lowery surprised the couple in a rented room and apprehended Masourides. The circumstances enraged Masourides, and there was an altercation. Before witnesses attracted by the disturbance Masourides pulled a gun; he later claimed he intended to throw it away to avoid charges of having a concealed weapon. Lowery drew his service revolver and both men fired. Lowery fell, fatally hurt; Masourides, slightly wounded,was easily subdued by bystanders. Word of the incident spread quickly. The South Omaha police had to transfer Masourides to an Omaha jail to prevent a lynching. The ambulance carrying him ran a gauntlet of five hundred enraged persons. Shots rang out as horses, running hard, pulled the vehicle out of town. It was a portent of things to come.

On Saturday, the Omaha *World-Herald* carried a banner headline: "ED LOWERY, SOUTH OMAHA POLICEMAN, IS SHOT AND KILLED BY GREEK." The story of the incident contained the text of a petition hastily drafted by Joseph Murphy, an Irish leader in South Omaha:

> Whereas, Many instances of their flagrant disregard and insolence of our laws and ordinances of this city have occurred during the past years, and Whereas, The so-called quarters of the Greeks are infested by a vile bunch of filthy Greeks who have attacked our women, insulted pedestrians upon the street, openly maintained gambling dens and many other forms of viciousness . . . Therefore, be it resolved, That we, the undersigned citizens and taxpayers of the city hereby believe that a mass meeting should be held on Sunday afternoon, February 21, 1909, at the city hall to take such steps and to adopt such measures as will eventually rid the city of the Greeks, and thereby remove the menacing conditions that threaten the very life and welfare of South Omaha.

As if this were not provocative enough, the Sunday morning edition of the *World-Herald* carried a "Proclamation of Mourning" issued by Mayor Frank Koutsky of South Omaha. "Grief unspeakable watches the bier of the martyred hero today," it began. "A Greek, one who in his own native land was never accorded the privilege of lifting his head and looking outward and upward, murdered Officer Lowery." Going on to discuss Masourides's past, the proclamation continued, "His life was filled with the brightness of freedom and his pockets filled with easy gold. He grew fat in arrogance and pushed aside the native sons or used them as mere rungs of his ladder of success. . . . And then when a gentle hand sought to restrain him for a moment from wrong doing his thought was only to kill, and to kill craftily. And he killed." Murphy and Koutsky may not have agreed on most issues, but in this instance they held a common belief: Greeks must go.

The thousand men who assembled on Sunday afternoon on a vacant lot near "Greek Town" turned into a mob. They passed resolutions directed against the "outlawry and viciousness of Greeks," and the "scurvy Greek assassin." In addition, they heard speeches eulogizing the fallen officer and condemning Greeks. An Irish politician said, "It is about time for the citizens to take steps to rid the city of this menace." Thus prompted, the crowd stormed "Greek Town." As if under orders, the howling horde systematically looted and burned buildings, beating senseless any Greeks in their way. During the worst of the rioting, the South Omaha police mobilized but stayed at their headquarters. Mayor Koutsky informed the governor of Nebraska, but requested no troops. Authorities in Omaha declined to intervene. In the wake of the rampage, the South Omaha Greeks left town as quickly as they could. Many went over the bridge into Iowa, carrying belongings on their backs. After a meeting, the bulk of the Greeks in the untouched Omaha community packed and left. By the end of winter there were hardly any Greeks in the Omaha area.

There was a national reaction to the disturbance. Newspapers around the country tended to view the Omaha Greeks as victims. An editorial writer in the Chicago *Record-Herald* claimed that orators of "recent origin" had incited the mob by discriminating between Greeks and Americans. A writer in the Fort Worth *Record* cautioned against the "evil consequences" of a combination of racial and popular feeling. Closer to home, the Omaha *World-Herald* said that the rioters were the "dregs" of South Omaha. Masourides, after two trials, received a fourteen-year sentence for second degree murder. He served five and a half years before being furloughed and deported. The United States Justice Department carried on an investigation of the events in South Omaha. No indictments resulted, although the government paid over $80,000 in indemnities to Turkey, Greece, and Austria-Hungary. A committee of the Nebraska legislature gave "certificates of excellence" to two members who spoke at the pre-riot rally, exonerating them of responsibility.

A black lawyer, H. J. Pinkett, analyzed the causes of the affair in a letter to an Omaha newspaper. He wrote, "It is too bad that we have to admit that our civilization is so veneered and that men cannot see that the real crime is committed by the men higher up who foster and encourage those agencies which bear crime and shame and misery and death. These are the real offenders against the state; the ones to be punished for the wrongs committed by the creatures of their system." Whether he realized it or not, members of his race were the next victims of a massive explosion in Omaha.

The blacks of Omaha had deeper roots than those of many of the immigrant groups. Early in the history of Omaha, blacks found employment as service workers on the railroads and in the hotels. Dining car personnel, chair car attendants, mail car workers, and Pullman conductors made their homes in Omaha. They had steady jobs and a generally good family life. The railroad employees were in many cases respected members of the greater Omaha society, despite having little to say in affairs and very little material wealth. They played a major role in servicing the passengers who traveled over the great rail network that radiated out of the city. The census listed the black population of Omaha at 3,443 in 1900 and 4,425 in 1910. These figures were probably a little low. People were counted in place at the time of the enumeration; so some Omaha blacks, on trains all across the West and Midwest, showed up in the returns as residents of towns, usually division points, far away from Omaha.

On the surface, the black community appeared quite stable. Its center was a several-block district north of the downtown. There were over a hundred black-owned businesses, and there were a number of black physicians, dentists, and attorneys. Over twenty fraternal organizations and clubs flourished, and the National Association for the Advancement of Colored People had a strong chapter. Church life was diverse. Of more than forty denominations, Methodists and Baptists predominated. On past occasions, whole congregations had come north in mass, the way blazed by their pastors who had gone on ahead. Of course, outward appearances of solidity failed to hide a number of depressing realities: white resentment, nominally segregated facilities, low levels of education, marginal housing, abject living standards, poor salaries, and few opportunities. Prejudice over color negated any initial advantage that blacks had over other elements in the Omaha melting pot.

The Omaha black community experienced dramatic changes in the World War One decade. Of great significance was the loss of political influence. During previous years, black leaders had made certain small but significant advances. An Omaha black served as a justice of the peace in the 1880s; and in the 1890s another, Dr. M. O. Ricketts, was a two-term member of the state legislature. Ricketts was an adroit politician, and he succeeded in gaining a number of patronage positions for blacks. In the 1900s he moved to Missouri and Jack Bromfield emerged as the leading black political leader in Omaha. Critics charged that he displayed more interest in promoting and protecting gambling enterprises than in furthering the status of his race. He acquiesced to the replacement of blacks on public bodies, and before long they had almost entirely disappeared from places of influence; there were, for example, no black teachers or educational policy makers. Concurrently, there was a large influx of blacks into Omaha. They came as part of a World War One migration of rural southern blacks to northern cities. In Omaha many of the newcomers obtained employment in the packing houses. They performed a variety of tasks including those of skilled butchers and trimmers. The 1920 census reported that Omaha had 10,315 blacks; 5,598 males and 4,717 females. The number of blacks in the city had doubled in ten years.

The pressures created by the influx gradually moved toward a disastrous confrontation. Whites returning from service sometimes found their jobs taken by blacks. This automatically caused tensions. Complicating matters was the breakdown of local black political influence. Recent migrants had little respect for the older leadership. At the same time, a new reform government in Omaha had few lines of communication beyond the business community. The administration's enemies, especially those associated with the vice elements, sought incidents to discredit it. Conditions started to deteriorate in the summer of 1919 — a Red Summer in American race relations. Blacks died in violent disturbances from the crowded tenements of the South Side of Chicago to the shantytowns of East St. Louis. In Omaha daily newspapers launched a crusade against black lawbreakers. As the campaign intensified, the targets became alleged black rapists. Even though cases collapsed under investigation — one man arrested was over a hundred miles away when an attack on a white woman occurred — the newspapers continued to make sensational charges. The Reverend John Williams, the editor of the weekly *Monitor,* Omaha's only black owned paper, tried to calm fears. He contended that what happened elsewhere could not possibly happen in Omaha. Events proved him wrong.

Early on Friday, September 26, 1919, nineteen-year-old Agnes Lobeck reported a serious incident. Her story was as follows: while out walking with a "crippled" acquaintance, Millard Hoffman, a black man suddenly leaped out of the bushes. After slugging Hoffman senseless, he assaulted her and ran off into the night. What followed was a disturbing event in the history of Omaha. Decades later it still remained a source of controversy. On the day after the alleged crime the police arrested a suspect, William Brown, an itinerant packing house laborer from Cairo, Illinois. Detectives took him to Miss Lobeck's house, where from a sick bed she identified him as her assailant. A crowd gathered, and the officers had trouble getting Brown away to a jail cell on the upper floors of the Douglas County Court House, located in the heart of the business district. Pinkett talked to Brown and observed his physical condition: Brown had severe rheumatism and moved with great effort. It seemed hard to believe that he had either the dexterity or energy to stage a mugging and rape. If anything, he seemed an innocent victim. The major Omaha papers did not bother with such particulars. Extra editions reported that still another assault had occurred, and that the culprit was under lock and key in the courthouse. By Saturday night the city seethed with self-righteous indignation; and Brown was the talk of the town. Afterwards, an official report noted, "It is known that at least one party on Saturday night went about to the various pool halls in the south part of the city and announced that a crowd would gather at Bancroft School and from there would march to the courthouse for the purpose of lynching the colored man." Those responsible for these activities were never identified.

On Sunday afternoon several hundred teen-age whites assembled on a South Omaha school grounds. Goaded on by Millard Hoffman, Miss Lobeck's companion at the time of the alleged attack, the crowd marched on the courthouse. Their purpose, according to a participant, was "to get the Nigger." They were led by two students beating on drums. A squad of police who tried to stop the march were cursed and brushed aside. When the marchers reached the courthouse, they found it protected by thirty police officers. For an hour nothing much happened, except officials ordered a black detective inside after he infuriated the throng by drawing his revolver in response to a racial slur. After that there were friendly exchanges between police and demonstrators. It looked as if there would be no serious trouble. The four-story courthouse, built at a cost of $2 million in 1912, was one of the sturdiest buildings in town. Supposedly the imposing structure was both "mob proof" and "fire proof." Brown, housed with 120 other prisoners on the top floor, appeared in no danger. The police chief was not even present; nor had he seen fit to take any extra precautions, such as securing gun shops in the downtown district. He assumed that the crowd would disperse and go home at the supper hour. It did not.

Things started to get out of hand shortly after 5:00 P.M. News of the trouble at the courthouse quickly spread throughout Omaha. Swarms of people, estimated well in excess of five thousand, converged on the building. Leaders began to emerge. Older and more determined men, identified as from the "vicious elements," took the place of the boys. They seemed to know exactly what to do. Some looted sporting goods stores and pawnshops for guns and ammunition. Others ordered people to get gasoline to burn the building. A young man on horseback appeared, brandishing a heavy rope. Two girls distributed stones out of tin buckets. The police, showered by pellets, withdrew inside the building. When an assault party stormed the south entrance, the police beat it back by using two powerful streams of water from fire hoses. Bricks crashed through the courthouse windows and random gunfire echoed in the streets, as the crowd continued to grow by the minute. The chief of police and two commissioners had trouble getting into the building, even though escorted by twenty officers. When the chief tried to make an appeal from an upstairs window he reeled back, hit on the head and slightly injured by a stone. The reform mayor of Omaha, Edward Smith, arrived, making an unobtrusive entrance. Not long after that, fire bombs started to crash through the windows, setting afire county offices on the first floor. When firemen came, the mob overpowered them and took their ladders, preparing to use them to storm to upper floors. As smoke poured into the jail, guards took the prisoners to the roof, where they lay flat to avoid gunfire. A more desperate situation could hardly be imagined for the city government of Omaha. Over a thousand active rioters surrounded the courthouse, screaming, "Give us the Nigger." Some 5,000 spectators blocked all the streets in the business district, making immediate police reinforcements impossible. The mayor and key safety officials were trapped in the burning building. Discipline disintegrated around them. Officers became passive; and some, reconciled to disaster, made farewell telephone calls to their families.

Mayor Smith was running out of options. His "law and order" government was in a shambles. His personal popularity had fallen since earlier in the year, when he had apparently condoned the use of strikebreakers. He was a short, stocky man, with a strong tie to the business community. He was also a man of courage. He walked out of the courthouse to face the mob, but never had a chance to speak. A man cried, "He can give us the nigger if he will and save the courthouse." A youth yelled something about a gun. Several thugs assaulted Smith, knocking him to the ground. When some horrified spectators tried to help him, a husky youth yelled: "Don't let them get Mayor Smith away. Let's string him up. Shoot him. He's a negro-lover. They elected him. He's not better than they are!" The mayor, covered with blood, shouted: "No, I won't give

up this man. I'm going to enforce the law, even with my own life."
That further enraged mob members. They set fire to a car sent to
help him escape and pushed and shoved him through the main
streets of his city. At an electric pole, men dropped a noose around
his neck and threw the end of the rope over a beam. An unidentified man cut the rope as it was being drawn tight, and ran back into
the crowd. Another person pleaded: "He's a white man. For God's
sake, use a little judgment. Don't do something you'll be sorry for.
Don't be a bolsheviki." The vigilantes listened for a moment and
then resumed the work of lynching the mayor. Thousands of spectators looked on. At that point, police appeared with drawn pistols.
They formed a ring around the mayor and without further incident
took him away to a hospital, where he was to undergo a lengthy
recovery. The mayor's rescue happened so quickly that he was gone
into the night before his attackers had time to react. After realizing
what had happened, they retaliated by burning a police car and
launching a violent attack on the courthouse.

The frenzied mob went from room to room in the unburned
parts of the large structure, smashing furniture and starting small
fires. The chief and the commissioners stood aside and watched
helplessly. The sheriff defended a stairway, which the mob by-
passed and cordoned off. A group of prisoners took Brown, clad in
blue prison overalls, and pushed him down a flight of stairs into the
arms of the mob. Reports said he went willingly, realizing that
there was no hope. Men passed Brown head over head to the outside of the building as police watched, their attempts to save him
defeated. By the time Brown reached the ground, he had been
beaten unconscious, castrated, and stripped. Someone threw a rope
around his neck, and men attached the other end to an auto
bumper. As the vehicle dragged Brown through the crowd, persons
fired bullets into him. At a major intersection, Eighteenth and
Harney Streets, Brown's battered and bleeding remains were
lynched from an electric light pole. Crazed white men fired hundreds of bullets into the body before it was cut down. Then it was
pulled behind an auto to another crossing. While a news camera
flashed and thousands watched, boys poured oil out of street lanterns stolen from a construction project onto the remains which
were then ignited as those present roared approval. Incredibly, the
horrifying events had not yet ended. Men tossed a rope around the
heap of charred flesh and bones and dragged what was left through
the streets for close to two hours, as crazed spectators hooted and
cheered. Before the riot ran its course, a white boy died, killed by a

stray bullet; and many other persons received injuries. By dawn, Omaha was peaceful; its night of shame over.

The aftermath of the "Court House Riot" was predictable. Too late to do any good authorities dispatched sixteen hundred heavily armed federal troops, supported by machine guns, into the city. General Leonard Wood, commander of the soldiers, initially blamed the disturbance on the newspapers. "One of the first steps toward the preservation of law and order should be the suppression of a rotten press where there is one," he announced. "I am strong for the freedom of the press where it is honest and fearless; gives facts, not lies." A few days later, he reached another conclusion. After praising local unions for their support of the legal process, he turned to the lynching, stating that "just one agency was to blame for this — that was the I. W. W. and its red flag, the Soviet organization of this country." Eventually, the troops left and conditions returned to normal. The county spent $500,000 repairing the courthouse, and soon no outward trace of the riot remained. Miss Lobeck recovered in time to marry Millard Hoffman. Rumors circulated that the mob action was planned in advance; that the assault was a hoax and that Brown was the victim of a sinister conspiracy either plotted by the mayor to make himself appear a hero or by his political enemies to discredit him and all his works. Formal investigations collected data that failed to prove any conspiracy existed. A number of suspects arrested for participating in the riot eventually went free. Nothing was done to protect Brown's rights; a wire service report indicated without verification that someone answering his description had abandoned a wife five years earlier.

Newspaper editorials tried to explain what happened and to analyze its significance. Under the heading, "Omaha Bows in Shame," the black editor of the *Monitor* wrote: "It all seems as though it were a hideous nightmare, a disturbing dream that must vanish when one awakens. And would be to God that this were true! But, unfortunately, it is no dream, but an awful reality that has horrified and stunned the community." He concluded that Brown's lynching was an isolated incident and not a race riot. An editorial in the *World-Herald* attacked "jungle rule" and the "mob spirit" of the "wolf pack." It intoned: "It is over now, thank God! Omaha henceforth will be safe for its citizens, and as safe for the citizens within its gates, as any city in the land. Its respectable and law-abiding people, comprising 99 per cent of the population, will

Rioters at Courthouse, 28 September 1919

173

see to that. . . . There will be no more faltering, no more freckless-
ness, no more procrastination, no longer the lack of a firm hand."
After denouncing "red handed criminals," the editorialist warned
Omaha blacks to obey the law. The *World-Herald,* which had
attacked black lawbreakers prior to the riot, received a Pulitzer
Prize for the editorial. The paper's publisher, Gilbert Hitchcock,
was Minority Leader of the United States Senate. On the day of the
Omaha disorder, he was deeply involved in Washington trying to
persuade the Senate to ratify the Versailles Treaty, which would
have brought American entry into the League of Nations. The
editor and publisher of the *Monitor,* John Williams, was a vicar
relatively unknown outside of Omaha. And so, following a major
award, the incident ended, with the mutual consent of most concerned. Few remembered the name of the victim in the racial
tragedy.

The riot finished the ruin of Mayor Smith's hapless administration, and he declined to seek reelection. He had been elected in 1918
under a unique commission plan adopted six years earlier. In a non-
partisan general canvas, the voters elected seven commissioners.
Once installed, the commissioners selected a mayor and department
heads from their own ranks. Candidates normally ran on slates and
announced beforehand what functions they wanted to fill if
elected, be it mayor or fire commissioner. Smith had headed a
divided Allied Slate. One wing, consisting of the Committee of Five
Thousand, favored prohibition and a crusade for moral purity.
Another had a strong business orientation. The members considered themselves "moderate progressives." They stood for
changes in the structure of government and for efficiency and
economy. A "Good Government" group, sponsored by the Omaha
Church Federation and the Douglas County Dry League, supported the Allied Slate, with the exception of one Jewish candidate.
A "Good Government" official explained, "The state must stand
for Christianity." Smith was the only Democrat on the Allied Slate;
the rest were Republicans. Smith, a strong supporter of Woodrow
Wilson, had a local reputation as a progressive reformer. He had
much support among the "better elements." Smith and four other
members of his slate, including the man not endorsed by the Good
Government group, swept to victory on election day. The Allied
Slate ran best among "old stock" whites and worst among blacks
and newer immigrants. The victory was very popular with commercial interests. The Omaha *Trade Exhibit* explained the reform victory by stating that "the business men of this city, the big men who

Burning of William Brown's Body

are responsible for the city's rapid growth and wonderful progress determined to have a four-square city, a well regulated and well balanced city, and one whose political machinery and city government would be a true representation of the place in business and social affairs in this great trade territory that Omaha now holds."

The new city government experienced serious problems almost from the beginning. The commissioners had differing social and economic philosophies, and they soon fell out over a wide variety of issues. They failed to agree about the location of a settlement house, schemes to catch bootleggers, and whether or not to keep a women's detention hospital. A commissioner opposed the settlement house as an unwarranted interference with immigrants' control over their children; another claimed that strict enforcement of prohibition would give Omaha a bad name. Police Commissioner J. Dean Ringer, a member of the Committee of 5,000, opposed the hospital. "I don't want Omaha advertised as a place where diseased prostitutes can be cured," he objected. "I want the burglar, the bootlegger, the pickpocket and the prostitute to understand that we will not tolerate their presence in Omaha if we can help it." Ringer hoped to use the police department as a vehicle for a moral crusade. As for Mayor Smith, it turned out that he had a rather limited view of his duties. He told an assembly of ministers, "I have no desire or ambition to have my administration known as a 'reform' administration. . . . My role is to sit on the lid of expenditures."

Controversies ended with the September 1919 disaster. After that the commissioners, reconciled to the impossibility of consensus and demoralized by Mayor Smith's refusal or inability to exercise further leadership, concentrated on staking out positions for the 1921 election. When it came, the reformers choice for mayor was prohibitionist Abraham L. Sutton, who had been defeated for governor on the Republican ticket in 1916. The campaign of the "Progressive Seven" concentrated on saving Omaha from sin. Ringer, a candidate for reelection and leader of the slate, said the "morals of the youth of the city are at stake," and contended, "In my mind the moral issue in the city is the greatest of them all." Other appeals, such as one entitled, "To the Mothers of Omaha," failed to have an impact. The voters threw out the reformers in favor of the United Seven, headed by former mayor James C. Dahlman. Reform government ended, foundering over ideological differences and an inability to develop a workable program.

Dahlman, except for Smith's tenure, was mayor of Omaha from

his initial election in 1906 until his death in 1930, winning seven out of eight mayoral campaigns. He sought to obtain Home Rule and to control the excesses of private utility interests. The first campaign platform he ran on called for the reduction of gas prices. He was later a key figure in the city's acquisition of the waterworks. A slender and brown-eyed man, he brought an unusual style to the mayor's office. He lived without ostentation with his wife and daughter and refused an official car, preferring to use public transportation. When he needed an automobile for official functions, particularly the entertaining of visiting dignitaries, he rented one out of his own pocket. He ate sparingly; his favorite meal was a sandwich, milk, and a piece of pie. Almost always he wore cowboy boots, putting the right one on first out of superstition. Routine administration bored him, and he turned most paperwork over to his secretary. During office hours he talked to anyone who came by, holding what one observer called a sort of open house. On a regular basis he saw anywhere from ten to a hundred constituents a day and talked to many more over the telephone. He took "cranks" in stride, calling them "enthusiasts."

Dahlman, a patient man who listened attentively to long and involved stories, strongly favored family life. He frequently pardoned husbands in jail for drinking or minor offenses, if their wives explained what happened. "If it was the man alone who paid the penalty for the offense I would let him stay in jail," Dahlman often commented. "I cannot see a mother and children suffer because the husband and father drank a little too much." People contacted him about all sorts of matters, all of which he handled himself. He saw nothing wrong with attending to complaints about potholes, chickens running wild, and uncut weeds. Critics argued that there was little substance to his administration and that he had little control over the machinery of government. He ignored such remarks and continued to enjoy direct contacts with constituents. He went about his tasks, earning the title of "the perpetual mayor of Omaha" and keeping an earlier sobriquet, that of "Cowboy Jim." Few mayors of major cities served longer or were closer to the people.

Dahlman had an extraordinary career. Born on a Texas ranch in 1856, he had little formal education. At age seventeen, he won a statewide riding tournament in Texas. He became a cowhand, earning a reputation as an expert with the lariat. When he was twenty-two, he fled to Nebraska after killing his brother-in-law during an argument. Dahlman, who used an assumed name until he

Mayor James C. Dahlman

learned a judge ruled the killing self-defense, went to work punching cows on the large "N-Bar" ranch. Dahlman was a cowboy for several years, working his way up to range boss. He was proud of his occupation and critical of the popular view of cowboys, which depicted them as swaggering, hard-riding men who spent their free time drinking, gambling, wenching, and fighting. "The cowboy is of entirely different makeup," he claimed. "While he is usually a strong, hardy fellow and can ride any sort of horses, he is not looking for spectacular performances on horseback. His business is the expert handling of cattle – this is what is expected and demanded by his employer."

In the 1880s Dahlman married a refined eastern woman who had come west to teach and settled down in the remote western community of Chadron, Nebraska. He worked as a brand inspector for the Wyoming Stockmen's Association and entered Democratic politics. For several years he was on the Chadron City Council. After that he was first sheriff and then mayor. During the 1890s he embraced Populist doctrines, but although a delegate to the 1892 Populist convention, he remained a Democrat. He supported William Jennings Bryan, and ran the Democratic statewide campaign of 1896 in Nebraska. Following the election Dahlman left Chadron, living for a short while in Lincoln, where he was secretary of the state transportation board. In 1898 he moved to Omaha and worked in the livestock commission business prior to running for mayor. He had statewide aspirations and in 1910 ran unsuccessfully for governor. A contributing factor to his defeat was his stand against prohibition. Bryan, by then an avowed dry, opposed him. Even so, Dahlman and Bryan remained the best of friends and continued to cooperate on other matters. Dahlman seemed to get along with just about everyone. His acquaintances included such diverse personalities as Theodore Roosevelt, William "Buffalo Bill" Cody, and Sioux chieftan Red Cloud. Several times Dahlman was a delegate to national conventions of the Democratic party, the last time in 1928, when he supported Alfred E. Smith.

No one ever questioned Mayor Dahlman's integrity, though there were charges that he was a front man for sinister elements. His critics said that he performed routine and ceremonial functions, and in exchange for support at the polls allowed a crooked machine to dominate local politics. In 1911 the editor of the Omaha *News* charged that Dahlman's backers were "crooks, bums, outcast negroes, gamblers, frequenters of dives and pool halls, parasites on fallen women, and other men of that stripe." Such charges implied a continuance under Dahlman of a traditional relationship that had existed in the nineteenth century between politicians and vice elements. Dahlman felt comfortable with a wide open Omaha; he frequently even went down to the jail in the middle of the night to bail out cowboy visitors who had celebrated too much and run afoul of the law. There was no doubt that Dahlman accepted machine help. The question, never answered, was to what extent it influenced his performance as mayor. It could be argued that he simply took support where he found it, and that he looked upon the dives of Omaha as business operations that contributed to the city's economy in much the same way as Gurdon W. Wattle's transit line and James E. Davidson's power company. Yet it was probably more complex. He appeared to have a mutually advantageous relationship with a man he never associated with in public, Thomas Dennison, Omaha's political boss.

Dennison, called "the Old Grey Wolf" or "the Boss," was a shadowy figure in the life of the city. Physically, he was a large and powerful man with a weather-beaten face and a cauliflower ear. At the height of his power he dressed immaculately and wore large diamond rings. He had steely eyes and a narrow smile. Born in Iowa, he grew up on farms in that state and in Nebraska. As a teenager, he toiled for several years as a farm laborer, winning a cornhusking contest. He went west at age twenty and worked as a blacksmith, a railroad section hand, and a prospector. After a time, he gravitated to Leadville, Colorado, one of the roughest towns in the country. In 1880 the city of 14,000, perched high in the Rocky Mountain mining district, had over a hundred dance halls. Dennison started as a bouncer in the large and notorious Texas Saloon "gambling hell," advancing within a short time to a quarter owner.

He became a professional gambler and ran dance houses in several mining towns before moving to Omaha in 1892. He arrived with a great deal of money and may have represented a gambling syndicate. After running a profitable policy game, he invested in several "dens," including the Budweiser Saloon, which he used as a headquarters. When some leading gamblers left town near the turn of the century after police harassment, which Dennison may have instigated, he emerged as leader of the Third Ward. It was in that part of town, the old First Ward, where vice activities centered. Quickly solidifying power he served as middle man between gamblers and saloon keepers, established a satisfactory arrangement with the police force, developed ties with Omaha *Bee* owner

Edward Rosewater, and dealt through intermediaries with important businessmen. Dennison also founded a "charitable organization," financed with money he collected in the Third Ward from fellow gamblers and others, through which he regularly distributed clothing, food, and other goods to the needy. In return, he "expected value received" at the polls, and he usually got it. Grateful recipients voted for his ticket; and that, plus ballot stuffing and intimidation, enabled him to influence city elections. He never held office, but police officers chauffered him about town, and few doubted that he was "the Boss."

Dennison preferred to stay in the background, particularly after he won acquittal on two charges in the 1900s. He was accused of stealing jewelry and of trying to dynamite an enemy. A teetotaler, he lived quietly with a wife and daughter. As a hobby, he raised champion wire-haired terriers. "I like dogs," he said. "They're honest and don't try to double-cross you." He believed that legislation had no effect on human conduct. He explained: "Some people are good and some are bad. Laws can't change them. Laws that people don't believe in can't be enforced if whole armies tried it. There are so many laws that lawyers are either lawbreakers or hypocrites. For my part, I hate a damn hypocrite." As for gambling, he compared it to accepted business practices and minor law violations, stating: "People are always getting excited about little things, like minor lawbreaking and misdemeanors. Take gambling, for example. A dinky crap game or penny-ante poker causes a hell of a racket. But the stock market gambling was all right." Dennison took a practical approach toward politics. Talking about the possibility of a reform government, he supposedly ruminated: "I think we better let the bastards have it their way for awhile. Let's just lie low for the next election . . . they'll be glad to see us back."

For many years an Omaha printing company president, Frank B. Johnson, supposedly acted as Dennison's conduit to the business community. Some persons thought Johnson the boss, speculating that he gave Dennison "daily marching orders." Probably, it was the other way around. Dennison, in any event, remained in the limelight, receiving considerable publicity from time-to-time, particularly in 1930 when, following the death of his wife, he married seventeen-year-old Nevajo Truman. In the early 1930s Dennison's health declined, and he underwent the strain of a federal prosecution for conspiracy to violate the prohibition laws, which ended in a mistrial. In May of 1933, his ticket went down to defeat in a local election. Campaign workers for his opponents had

181

Thomas Dennison and his Bride Nevajo Truman, October 1930

sung, "The Old Gray Wolf, he ain't what he used to be, he ain't what he used to be." Less than a year later, he died in California of a cerebral hemorrhage. Over a thousand persons attended his interment in Omaha's Forest Lawn Cemetery. It was hard to sum up his contribution. An editorial in the Omaha *World-Herald,* which consistently opposed his machine, concluded on February 16, 1934: "There were quite the makings of another sort of man in Tom Dennison. . . . He had . . . the qualities of natural leadership, of the fighter, and he was industrious and persevering. . . . Suppose he had been directed into a better path for a better end. . . . Our guess is that he would have gone far and won for himself a deservedly honored name."

The Omaha of the Dennison-Dahlman era was wide open by any stretch of the imagination. Gambling, though outlawed, continued to flourish throughout the Third Ward. Police raids occurred only when an establishment's owners had run afoul of the organization. An illicit drug traffic existed, although its scope remained a carefully kept secret. Professional criminals frequented the vice district, using it as a haven and base of operations. Saloons increased markedly in number during the ten years before World War One. Opponents considered them the cornerstone of vice in Omaha. A critic stated: "The saloon is a preparatory department in the school of social evil. . . . It is a wonderful system which is able to make the same money serve two purposes, that of *degrading and educating,* in other words, which can successfully serve both God and the devil at the same time." An 8:00 P.M. closing law enacted by the state had little effect. Juries refused to convict alleged violators. A state constitutional amendment authorizing prohibition that passed by a wide margin in 1916 contained no provision for implementation. National prohibition flopped in Omaha, owing to Dennison's satisfactory relationship with the police department and total disinterest on the part of the business community in pushing for energetic enforcement. A survey made in 1929 claimed that at least fifteen hundred places, including many drug stores, sold liquor. A state attorney general, C. A. Sorensen, prepared a report on vice in Omaha and told city officials, "Clean up Omaha or I'll come and do it for you." His campaign resulted in some well-publicized raids and forced many liquor interests under cover. Vice activities dispersed throughout town, ending the heyday of the Third Ward. The saloon vanished, replaced at the end of prohibition by cocktail lounges and taverns. Still, despite cosmetic changes, Omaha remained a boisterous town.

Prostitution continued a reality of Omaha life. However, things were not as open as early in the century when a huge resort, the Arcade, a four-block area of brick houses and paper shacks, operated in the Third Ward. Three hundred women paid $2.00 a day for "cribs" in surroundings protected by security men, bright lights, and iron fences. Mae Hogan, a successful madam, started as a lady barber, using that occupation as a means of meeting clients. She made enough money to open a "house of assignation," where men brought their girl friends, and later established a large house in "Scandal Flats" across from a hotel frequented by cattlemen. By 1910 Omaha had twenty-six hundred professional "ladies of the night," plus many more irregular free-lancers in the "army of vice." Most of the latter had no connections with houses and worked out of dance halls. "Few of these girls are bad, they are simply inexperienced," a reformed prostitute explained. "These unsophisticated girls do not realize the danger they encounter. . . . The dance hall, or Sunday dance, where a promiscuous collection of people meet, where drink is dispensed and dope used as a refreshment and stimulant to the dancers cannot but bring about new recruits to the district." Some of these amateurs graduated to professional status, acquiring pimps or ending up in one of the hundred or so major houses. Estimates claimed that collectively these places had average annual incomes from 1905 to 1911 of $17.5 million, a portion of it generated by liquor business.

In 1911 legislators in the "Holy City" of Lincoln passed the Albert Law closing the houses. The only effect was to disperse the harlots throughout Omaha to rooming houses and hotels. One streetwalker told a reporter, "It's a poor girl on the street who can't make at least five dollars a night in Omaha." A Dennison lieutenant, Billy Nesselhous, a former jockey, coal hauler, and street gambler, usually accompanied in public by a beautiful call girl or actress, left an estate of $2 million upon his death in 1937. The lavish pleasure palaces were gone, but as long as the machine operated, men seeking prostitutes had no trouble finding them.

By the end of the 1920s, Omaha was a cosmopolitan city with a violent and bawdy reputation. The spectre of machine rule hung over the community. Outstate politicians railed against vice and crime in Omaha, contending that the existing conditions gave Nebraska a bad name. Some concluded that a tornado that had smashed through Omaha in 1913, killing 170 persons and causing $7 million in damage, was an indication of God's displeasure. The town's ethnic heritage came under attack. There were charges that the foreign-born were clannish and that they were not true Americans. Racial purists believed that immigration had made Omaha a cauldron of discontent, contributing to a host of problems. Some observers saw what they believed a direct connection between corrupt politics and immigrant groups, arguing the foreigners provided the votes that kept the machine in power. Omaha leaders objected, claiming that the existence of vice was much overemphasized and that the vast majority of residents were law-abiding persons living and working together with a minimum degree of friction. They said that the city was no different from other metropolises and better than most. After all, Omaha had no Al Capone; and many more people died in other racial disturbances than in the "Court House Riot," the line of reasoning went. Civic image builders dwelt on the stability of family life and talked about the contribution of religion, the richness of numerous ethnic celebrations, and the enlightened influence of education.

184

Sporting District, 1908

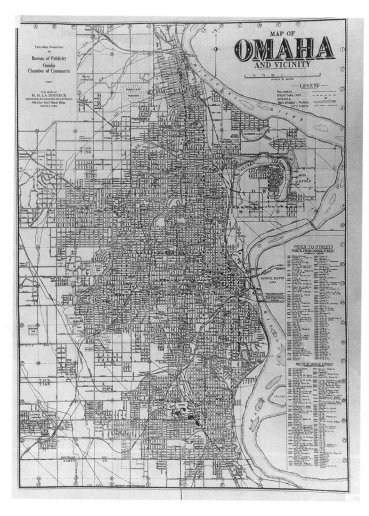

Map of Omaha, 1926

186

The Joslyn Memorial, a magnificent art gallery, served as a positive symbol of community. The $3.5 million structure opened in 1931 after almost a decade of planning and construction. It was a gift of Mrs. Sarah Joslyn, intended as a memorial to her late husband, George Joslyn, who had made a large fortune in a variety of businesses. He was president of the Western Newspaper Union, which furnished ready-prints and ready-to-print plates to over five thousand weekly newspapers. His holdings had included thirty-two printing plants, seventeen wholesale paper houses, and several paper mills. The huge gallery had proportions and features befitting a paper king. Its Georgia marble exterior had a modified classic design, unrelieved by wall openings. Bas-relief panels at the four corners of the building depicted such themes as "The Pioneer Press" and "The Indian Prayer for Life." The entrance pavilion was a colonnaded loggia, flanked by Ionic columns, with polygonal shafts and caps done in Indian Thunderbird motif. Decorations on the entrance door portrayed the virtues of Charity, Courage, Faith, Hope, Industry, and Vision. The entrance lobby contained two great columns of Porto Oro black and gold marble imported from Italy. The focal point of interest in the interior was a floral court, where fountains splashed into an octagonal pool of blue-green faience tiles. A concert hall on the main floor, decorated in soft shades of rose and gray, had a seating capacity of twelve hundred persons. Other rooms — reception halls, library units, and galleries — had the Thunderbird as the dominant decorative theme. The Joslyn contained many permanent collections, including those of the Art Institute of Omaha and the Helen Wells Seymour collection of oriental textiles.

Numerous lectures, concerts, demonstrations, and traveling art shows made the Joslyn, from its opening day, a cultural center. The memorial was what Omahans wanted visitors and others to remember; it provided a much more desirable cultural image than gambling casinos, speakeasies, and whorehouses. And so, almost four decades after the official closing of the frontier, Omaha leaders felt compelled to reemphasize that their city was not a roaring camp but a place of high culture. Their efforts harked back to early attempts to establish a genteel identity, particularly those of the Omaha Library Association of the 1850s. In the 1920s a successful community playhouse and a poorly financed symphony that died at the end of the decade received publicity out of proportion to their actual contributions. The whole process related to a development unclear at the time; Omaha had become a mature community.

Joslyn Memorial

Somewhat embarrassed by a stormy past, its boosters reacted defensively to criticism. There was a groping for a set of values that could bring together second and third generation Omahans, establishing social forms that would help a continued rise. The city remained on the move; hardly anyone thought of a decline. The way things transpired, it would have been a good idea to have considered that possibility.

Part Four

1930-1960

7

The Heart, Mind, and Body of Our Country

One reason for the success of Omaha was the positive attitude of the business community toward newcomers. The first promoters, the Creightons and Kountzes, had worked together to gain the Union Pacific terminal. A generation later, William A. Paxton and his associates had gone to considerable lengths to bring in the packing plants. In the 1890s Gurdon W. Wattles had quickly gained entrance into Omaha's economic life, soon rising to the top. James E. Davidson had a similar experience in the late teens and early twenties. If either Wattles or Davidson had gone to one of the many smaller thriving towns of the region, they might have encountered serious problems trying to break into the dominant groups. Established interests tended to discourage outsiders from coming in, even if they had ability and money. Critics in the 1920s believed that the approach stifled small town social development, but many small town capitalists felt comfortable with existing patterns. As long as they remained "big fish in a small pond," they were perfectly content to live in a "one horse town." The Omaha entrepreneurs never felt threatened, nor had they been content to accept a settled state of affairs. Of course, in part this was because Omaha was not a front office town; executives from the outside were always coming and going. So Omahans welcomed new blood and money, considering the risks much less than the gains to themselves and to the city.

William Randolph Hearst's purchase of a major Omaha newspaper was a continuation of the process. No one in power in the city expressed concern about a non-resident controlling a major organ of public opinion. What they wanted was his money and support. In 1928 Hearst bought the *Bee-News* which had combined the old *News* and *Bee*. In 1920 the Rosewater interests had sold the *Bee* to Nelson B. Updike, a local grain dealer. He acquired the *News* in 1927, only to sell his holdings the next year to Hearst's empire. Peter Hamilton of the *Bee-News* told the public that the change of ownership demonstrated Hearst's faith in Omaha. According to Hamilton, his boss believed the past history of Omaha demonstrated that there were firm foundations for further advance. Hamilton declared, "Mr. Hearst shares with the people who preceded him to Omaha optimism for the future and commends to persons elsewhere seeking a place to live happily and prosper in, this city in the heart of the United States which so typically personifies the heart, mind and body of our country." This was certainly what the Omaha business leaders wanted to hear. A fanatical booster could hardly have said it better.

The problem was that Hearst soon decided that he had made a bad investment. In 1937 he sold the *Bee-News* for $750,000 to the *World-Herald*. The new owners promptly folded the *Bee-News,* bringing to an end an era in Omaha journalism. Edward Rosewater's old *Bee,* Nebraska's first regional paper, had played an important part in building the city. The journal's rise had coincided with that of the town. Demise of the newspaper had grim implications, or so it seemed. Hearst, cutting his losses, had become one of the first well-known American capitalists to invest heavily in Omaha and then pull out. To make matters more disconcerting, he destroyed a regional institution. After professing faith in Omaha, he left town.

Hearst's decision came after the euphoria of the 1920s had given way to the despair of the 1930s. The Great Depression shattered confidence. Tub-thumping statements of a few years before about a grand future based on land and sea transportation suddenly appeared classic examples of pro-business Babbittry, rather than attempts to articulate community aspirations in modern advertising jargon. None of this harked well. Had Omaha reached the limits of its success? Was it experiencing an inevitable decline? How far could a place created by speculators progress? Could a promotion that owed much of its success to "artificial lines" of commerce survive in the long run? Would industries leave in droves? The answers to these and other questions—all reflections of past queries— rested, as before, on the ability of the hinterland to sustain Omaha's transportation network, commercial pursuits, and industrial operations.

During the first years of depression, the agricultural economy of Nebraska collapsed. There was a temptation to blame the disaster on the materialism of the 1920s and to conclude that automobiles, radios, and telephones had corrupted a generation of young Nebraskans. The building in 1923 of a 35,000-seat football stadium on the University of Nebraska campus in Lincoln epitomized a changing value structure. Instead of working in the fields on Saturday fall days, many farm families concentrated on following the fortunes of the Nebraska football team. It somehow did not seem right to numerous oldsters who had sacrificed to build a state. Willa Cather, author of the pioneer epic *My Antonia,* now wrote: "Too much prosperity, too many moving picture shows, too much gaudy fiction have colored the taste and manners of so many of these Nebraskans of the future. There, as elsewhere, one finds the frenzy to be showy; farmers boys who wish to be spenders before they are earners, girls who try to look like the heroines of the cinema screen; a coming generation which tries to cheat its aesthetic sense by buying things instead of making anything. There is even the danger that that fine institution, the University of Nebraska, may become a gigantic trade school." There was no denying that the vast majority of Nebraska farmers enjoyed a higher standard of living than their forefathers, but the economic adversity that befell the state had deeper causes than a desire to see football games or to go to town in automobiles on Saturday night. Financial distress would have afflicted Nebraska in the 1930s regardless of farmers' living styles or social values.

Overproduction and rising costs were two fundamental causes of Nebraska's agricultural failures. The "Golden Age" had come to an abrupt end. Just before the start of the 1920s, wheat prices fell from $2.02 per bushel on December 1, 1919, to $1.31 per bushel a year later. The problem was that grain was a renewable resource. Production gradually returned to normal in areas of the world affected by hostilities, and trade patterns resumed their former characteristics. Foreign demands underwent a gradual decline, falling off sharply after the middle of the decade. Wartime price levels made it difficult to assess what was going on; in terms of the pre-war market, Nebraska farmers appeared to be doing well. The average state farm price index from 1922 to 1929 was almost thirty-

195

five percent higher than before the war. The figures were deceptive; they did not take in larger operating expenses, the loss of federal wartime price guarantees, or higher taxes. Despite a rise in gross farm income near the end of the decade, net income per farm had declined to an annual average of $1,795, compared with $3,087 during the period from 1914 to 1919. Throughout the 1920s land values fell; in one Sand Hills' county prices dropped from $29.00 to $10.00 an acre. Farmers with mortgages had trouble making payments and refinancing proved difficult. The temporary or permanent closing of more than six hundred state banks in Nebraska from 1924 to 1929 demonstrated the seriousness of the developing situation. Only a Bank Guaranty Fund, created by the state legislature back in 1911, had staved off an immediate calamity. These considerations, part of a larger problem, caused national concern. The McNary-Haugen bill, designed to subsidize grain farmers, passed Congress on three different occasions, falling victim each time to a presidential veto. A farm marketing measure enacted under Herbert Hoover was too far reaching to provide immediate aid. Although some had believed that the prosperity of the "Roaring Twenties" was permanent, the Crash of 1929 showed otherwise.

Early in the Great Depression, already deflated farm prices plummeted to the lowest levels in Nebraska history. Previous record lows of the mid-1890s seemed almost high in comparison. Between December of 1929 and the same month in 1932, corn dropped from 67¢ to 13¢ per bushel, wheat from $1.00 to 27¢, oats from 38¢ to 10¢, and barley from 49¢ to 13¢. By the hundred weight, beef cattle went from $10.50 to $4.10, and hogs from $8.20 to $2.30. Using 1914 to 1919 as base years, with a parity of 100, the purchasing power of Nebraska agriculture products averaged 87.22 throughout the 1920s and then dropped all the way to 54 in 1932. On top of this collapse came several drought years. Especially poor were 1934 and 1936, when rainfall fell below fifteen inches. The lack of rain affected the whole Great Plains, and great dust storms swept over the Nebraska prairies. Even in a year of normal rainfall, 1935, growing conditions were not good, and yields were much smaller than usual.

Some farmers left, but there was no general exodus on the scale of the 1870s and 1890s. New Deal programs saved the day. From 1933 through 1940, the Franklin Roosevelt Administration pumped more than $200 million into Nebraska agriculture. The Farm Credit Administration alone advanced $185 million to the state's farmers. Another agency, the Farm Security Administration, gave slightly over 15,000 farm families rehabilitation loans amounting to $12.7 million. Over eighty percent of all the farms in Nebraska profited from the first and second Agricultural Adjustment acts. In 1939 over 129,000 farms received $20 million. Even so, the agricultural aspects of the Great Depression had a devastating impact. The authors of *Nebraska: A Guide to the Cornhusker State* stressed this point, stating: "The condition of the farmers affected Nebraska merchants, lumber dealers, realtors, school teachers, laborers, and artisans. Housewives stocked their pantry shelves with the simplest essentials; construction lagged; school administrators curtailed their programs as tax receipts went down; day laborers, formerly sure enough of a place on Nebraska farms and in Nebraska industries, began the long trek of the unemployed."

Omaha's business community first assumed that the depression would not have a serious impact on the city. At the time of the 1929 Crash, the Omaha newspapers had not headlined the debacle, placing detailed stories on the business pages. There was unjustified faith that agriculture would hold up, enabling Omaha to ride out the storm. When the crisis became prolonged, Omaha began to suffer severely. Bank clearances fell from $2.9 billion in 1929 to $997 million in 1933. In the same period, deposits dropped from $115 million to $83 million. While no Omaha area banks failed in the 1920s, four state banks that combined held six percent of all deposits in the city, went under in August 1931. However, the three largest Omaha banks–First National, Omaha National, and U.S. National–remained open. Total grain receipts for 1930 were 78 million bushels, the highest ever. Then they plunged to 57 million bushels in 1931 and cascaded downward to 26 million in 1932, before starting back upward to 45 million in 1936. At the bottom, in 1932, it was unprofitable for farmers to market their crops. Wheat receipts only amounted to 17.5 million bushels, as opposed to 44.6 million bushels three years earlier. For corn, the figures were 6 million bushels against 24 million bushels, and for barley 133,000 bushels against 1.3 millon bushels. Livestock receipts also dropped, and so did production. From 1929 to 1933, cattle moved downward from 1.4 million to 1.3 million, hogs from 3.7 million to 3.1 million, and sheep from 3 million to 2.4 million.

What the market meant in human terms was brought home in dramatic fashion in 1933 when farmers tried to stop the flow of milk into Omaha. The milk strike failed, but low prices persisted until the impact of federal price support programs. Much to their sorrow, the leaders of Omaha business discovered that regional agriculture proved unable to withstand the onslaught of a national economic debacle. Under the circumstances, Omaha's great transportation network became a liability rather than a strength. It served a collapsing hinterland.

There was the expected search for scapegoats and a longing for older, more prosperous times. Some critics claimed that the sons and grandsons of the original Omaha leaders had gone soft, and that they had neither the brains nor the desire to drive the city forward to new triumphs. Other observers blamed the disaster on outside factors. An elderly capitalist, discussing the days when the railroad companies made many major decisions in Omaha, much to the profit of certain interest groups, recalled: "We were like an army; we obeyed orders and got in on the gravy. I used to wear a uniform and I wish to God I was wearing a uniform now." He could only watch in dismay as railroads throughout the middle of the United States fell into receivership. When this happened before, back in the 1880s and 1890s, it had been a combination of unscrupulous or inept managerial practices and a building of tracks into unsettled areas. Now, it was different; railroads running through what only a few years before had been prosperous farming territory lost business and fell into bankruptcy.

In Nebraska the depression seemed like a renewal of sinister manipulations by Wall Street plutocrats of the same kind that William Jennings Bryan had warned against decades earlier. With more pride than accuracy, a Nebraska economist claimed: "The major part of the capital which has been used to develop Nebraska towns has not been brought in from outside the State. . . . In the final analysis the railroads, factories, residences, business blocks, and other improvements of Nebraska have been built quite largely with Nebraska capital. In all probability the capital taken out of the State exceeds in amount the capital brought into the State." The New Deal soon came under attack by Omaha business interests. New Deal programs were financed in part through loans from the great eastern banking institutions. The bottom line of recovery as determined in Omaha board rooms was a further shift of the economy to the East at the expense of the Midwest.

Unemployment in Omaha mounted steadily in the early years of the Great Depression. Industrial and commercial establishments laid off large numbers of workers. There was a corresponding loss of public jobs. New entrants into the work force found few available positions. Employed men and women faced dismissals, severe pay cuts, and deteriorating conditions. Under the weight of prolonged mass unemployment, private, local, and state relief broke down. A $500,000 expansion project at the municipal airport, authorized by a 1930 bond election, made only a small dent in overall employment.

In the first three years of the depression, little help came from the federal level. President Herbert Hoover adamantly opposed direct relief by the United States government, but the New Deal quickly abandoned the old discredited policy. The Federal Emergency Relief Act and the measure establishing the Civil Works Administration provided temporary help for millions of Americans. During the first months of Roosevelt's presidency, over 11,000 unemployed Omahans registered for federal relief. This was a high total for a community that had 94,000 gainfully employed persons in 1930. As the New Deal progressed many federal relief functions in Omaha fell under two more permanent agencies, the Public Works Administration and the Works Progress Administration. Both the PWA and the WPA provided employment for thousands of Omahans, having an important effect on the economy prior to the upturn caused by World War Two.

The New Deal programs prevented a repeat of the disaster that befell Omaha in the aftermath of the Panic of 1893. Census statistics indicated that Omaha gained over nine thousand residents in the 1930s. The increase came despite a steady drop in manufacturing jobs from 16,000 in 1929 to 11,000 in 1939. Other areas — transportation, wholesale, retail, and personal service occupations — held up, with significant losses in industry compensated for by federal employment during the Great Depression. The government directly expended several million dollars in Omaha. The funds went for a variety of projects, most of which contributed to cultural, beautification, and urban services concerns. Matching PWA monies helped construct a 360-room building for the Municipal University of Omaha. Other large undertakings included erecting a bridge over the Missouri River at South Omaha and changing the river's channel. In addition, appropriations went to landscape parks, lay sewers, and improve streets. In the late 1930s the United States Housing Authority sponsored construction of two projects, the Logan-Fontenelle Homes in North Omaha and the South Side Terrace Homes in South Omaha. By 1940 roughly 16,000 people over fourteen years of age in Omaha either received unemployment benefits or engaged in emergency work.

The Omaha business interests tried to salvage what they could. Like other American businessmen, they first became displeased

Transient House, ca. 1930s

with Roosevelt's vehicle for a business revival, the National Recovery Administration, in the spring of 1934. Conditions started to improve, and they saw no further need for government controls. The *World-Herald*, long a Democratic journal, denounced FDR. The NRA's "Blue Eagle" emblem, displayed to show compliance, became a target of scorn. Inconsistencies and piles of regulations involved in attempts to regiment business under "codes of fair competition" led to widespread opposition to the agency long before a 1935 Supreme Court decision declared it unconstitutional. In Omaha, employer condemnation of Roosevelt and all his works failed to hide the obvious. They had lost control over a measure of their own affairs. Much of the careful work of many decades had apparently gone for naught.

It made little difference that Omaha businessmen could get whatever state legislation they wanted, whether related to manufacturing or agriculture. Few outside capitalists showed interest in 1936 when the Industrial Bureau of the Omaha Chamber of Commerce tried to attract factories by announcing: "The State Manufacturer's Association maintains headquarters at Lincoln, Nebraska. One of its primary objects is to be especially vigilant during the legislative sessions to see that no legislation harmful to industry is enacted." There was a marked shift in power toward Washington, where Omaha business had little influence.

In Omaha new villains appeared in the form of government officials, "brain truster" Rexford Tugwell and WPA head Harry Hopkins. They personified all the vexations of Omaha's dominant group. High ranking bureaucrats were hard to oppose. They were difficult to see and issued countless regulations, many contradictory or hard to understand. It was all very frustrating. However, a common resolve existed to keep alive the boast of the Omaha Business Men's Association, "Omaha is the best open-shop city of its size in the United States."

The battlefield was an old one, the Omaha traction lines. Here Gurdon W. Wattles had smashed unionization activities in 1909. Now buttressed by Section 7A of the National Industrial Recovery Act, which recognized the right of workers to organize, the Amalgamated Association of Street and Electric Railway Employees decided to force the Omaha Traction Company to grant recognition and other demands. These included a pay increase for operators from fifty-two cents to sixty-eight cents an hour. A short strike in April of 1934 ended after only a few days. Both sides agreed to federal arbitration. The arbitrator, Richard L. Blume of the National Labor Board's Kansas City office, wrote a report granting a five cent retroactive pay increase. Nothing was said about union recognition. In July the workers rejected the settlement by a vote of 359 to 1 and walked out for the second time. Their spokesman attributed the cause to "continued discrimination against members of the union by officials of the company." Blume hurried to Omaha and after a few days effected an uneasy peace. The men went back on the job in exchange for minor wage concessions, promises of a board to settle grievances, and assurances that further arbitration would solve other outstanding issues. Implicit in the settlement was the possibility of an election on collective bargaining. It appeared that organized labor was on the verge of sweeping away the open shop in Omaha. Unfortunately for those favoring unions, the old ways of management did not die easily.

The Omaha Traction Company had no intention of giving in; it merely wanted to buy time to prepare for the next strike and to solidify support from Omaha businessmen and politicians. Through its new co-counsel, Richard L. Blume — the NLB arbitrator in the previous two strikes — the company contended that no election was necessary, arguing it had negotiated with the union during the previous two strikes. In the spring of 1935 the National Labor Board agreed, saying that there was no need for an election. Buttressed by the ruling, and with its advanced planning completed, the Omaha Traction Company took a hard line. It broke off all negotiations with the Amalgamated Association of Street and Electric Railway Employees, refusing further arbitration of demands for union recognition, seniority rights, a six-day week, and new wage increases. On April 20, 1935, the streetcar and bus drivers went on strike, assuring a major confrontation with their employers. There would be no industrial peace in Omaha.

A long and bloody strike ensued. The Omaha Traction Company fired all the men who walked out, adopting what it called "Our New Plan." Advertisements announced the retention of an Omaha private detective bureau, the Midwest Adjustment Company, to "protect the company's property." Midwest Adjustment, backed by an arsenal of submachine guns and sawed-off shotguns, provided a force of one hundred men. The agency's director, Benjamin Danbaum, a former state law enforcement official, had a close working relationship with the Omaha police; during the strike he helped them obtain a consignment of tear gas from an Ohio chemical concern. It was a situation reminiscent of 1909, except that this time the traction line employed local instead of outside strikebreakers. As before, many persons in Omaha sympathized with the strikers.

When the Omaha Traction Company asked Mayor Roy Towl, a civil engineer elected on a "reform" ticket, to guarantee adequate protection to cars put back into operation, he replied that the decision to resume service rested solely with the company. This was a course that the company was ready to follow. The first streetcars, complete with windows screened by heavy wire, rolled on the morning of April 24. Heavily armed police and company guards were on board. Heavily armed automobiles preceded and followed each car. The trams, which attracted few passengers, negotiated their routes without opposition. Following this elaborate show of force, the company rejected a city council resolution calling for arbitration. It gradually resumed spasmodic day and night service over most lines employing 250 strikebreakers, all protected by Midwest Adjustment Company personnel. Violent events soon occurred. A striker fired on a car; others attacked two trains and beat up a strikebreaker. Dynamite bombs damaged the home of an Omaha Traction Company official and blasted two streetcars. These incidents were almost innocent precursors to what lay ahead.

In the middle of June heavy rioting swept across the south side of Omaha. For three straight nights, mobs roamed the streets burning streetcars, causing an estimated $400,000 in damage, and looting a grocery store owned by a man suspected of riding on a trolley. There were two deaths and a hundred injuries. The city council voted a $50,000 emergency fund for added law enforcement; but before anything further could be done, the police lost control of the situation. On the morning of June 15, as gutted streetcars smoldered in the streets, Mayor Towl and the sheriff reluctantly sent a joint wire to the governor's office to request troops. Governor Robert Cochran was out of the state, but the acting governor swiftly complied with the request. He declared martial law in Omaha, rushed in eighteen hundred National Guardsmen, and ordered the traction company to stop running streetcars. Cochran, a New Deal Democrat with pro-labor leanings, hurried back to Nebraska and proceeded to Omaha, where he took charge of the city. The newspapers called him the "Dictator of Omaha."

Cochran called for an "immediate settlement" and asked the union and the company to name representatives to an arbitration board. The company said it would agree to arbitrate "all but three points": the rehiring of strikers, the closed shop, and the question of seniority. Because these were fundamental points, the company really had not altered its previous stand. The governor reacted by telling the company that no streetcars would run until the company complied. At that point, the company gave in and agreed to the governor's demands. Arbitration began on June 19, the same day that the city finance commissioner released a report disclosing that the company had a net profit over the previous four years of $1.5 million, far more than its officials had claimed. There was what appeared a swift settlement, virtually dictated by the governor's representative on the arbitration panel. The strikers were to return to work at their old pay and the strikebreakers were to be fired. At an unspecified future date the arbitrators were to consider the possibility of a pay increase. A special two-man board was to decide the seniority question. Cochran ended martial law and withdrew the National Guard.

The agreement quickly disintegrated. The strikebreakers, with help from the company, obtained a court injunction preventing implementation of the understanding on the grounds that the governor had exceeded his authority. When the two-man board voted full seniority rights to all strikers, the company rejected the decision. The streetcars returned to the streets, manned as before by strikebreakers and armed guards. This time there was little violence; the union wrote the strike off as lost. Cochran claimed "the tram company broke faith immediately after the national guardsmen left Omaha." In 1938 the National Labor Relations Board cited the Omaha Traction Company for unfair labor practices over the seniority question. It represented a pyrrhic victory for the strikers who had long since gone to other jobs.

By winning the streetcar strike, the Omaha Traction Company, at a cost of $170,000 for private protective services alone, achieved what first appeared a major victory for the Omaha Business Men's Association. George R. Leighton, who wrote an interpretive history of Omaha in 1939, summed up the situation when he concluded that the cars were running and the precepts of Wattles gloriously upheld. Still, the success was only short-term; in retrospect it was more of a dramatic last stand than anything else. The Congress of Industrial Organizations made inroads in the packing houses and other industries. Surveys indicated that the vast majority of non-union laborers in Omaha wanted to organize. Federal legislation and rulings provided the basis for Omaha becoming a union town. Omaha businessmen reluctantly acquiesced, learning how to adjust to the changed conditions. Developments on the labor front in the Great Depression resulted in a lessening of the Omaha business community's power over its working force. The Wagner Labor Relations Act of 1935, which created the NLRB, became a hated entity in Omaha board rooms. Businessmen viewed it as a further indication of Roosevelt's supposed plot to "socialize America" and to centralize all power in the hands of New Deal planners in Washington. This position, of course, did not preclude accepting various forms of federal largesse. After all, a major goal had always been to lure capital into Omaha. So, after the Second World War broke out in Europe in 1939, Omaha manufacturers competed with their counterparts in other cities for government defense contracts.

It became conventional wisdom in Omaha to claim that only the war and not the New Deal got the city out of the depression. Actually, there was no abrupt departure from the New Deal philos-

Burning Streetcar in 1935 Strike, from Roy Towl Scrapbook

205

ophy of the 1930s that government spending would bring about a return to prosperity. The biggest change was that the expenditures went for the war effort rather than for WPA and PWA-type programs. Despite motives framed in patriotism and the necessity of quick action to ensure national survival, the results were the same — the pumping of massive amounts of federal money into the economy. There was more government money going daily into the economic system than any New Dealer had envisioned back in 1933. Wartime controls led to a tremendous expansion of government power in many walks of life. By the time the conflict ended, government involvement had become accepted; President Harry Truman was harshly criticized by both business and labor for moving too quickly to abolish controls. By then, the government's role in Omaha had become institutionalized. Prosperity depended upon federal funds flowing into town. Curtailment of federal activities in Omaha and its region would have had disastrous consequences. There was a price to pay to keep the money coming; and it was an ever-increasing federal say over all levels of affairs in Omaha. The dreams of Wattles for the business community to obtain a free hand in setting policy had ended.

The first war contracts won by Omaha firms had little impact on the economy. Many of the early orders, gained through competitive bidding, helped small and already established concerns. The S & L Neckware Co. received one for $1,150 to produce 10,000 field caps; the Omaha Seat Cover Co. agreed to furnish 25,000 half shelter tents for $9000. An award for $1,357 went to the Miller Cereal Mills. More substantial were two contracts for a total of $5.5 million obtained by the Omaha Steel Works to produce artillery ammunition components. These developments had little impact on the unemployment problem, and in January 1941 the Nebraska State Employment Service clearance supervisor confidentially told federal authorities that he anticipated no serious labor shortages in Omaha. Four months later, a federal study on Nebraska's economy admitted: "To date, direct defense orders have had little effect on employment. We estimate that at this time no more than 1,300 workers are being employed directly as a result of the defense program. The WPA has felt some effect; women have been hired from the sewing project in Omaha to work on tents, caps, trousers, and other army wearing apparel. One steel plant has had substantial orders for material, but employment has been held back because of a lack of machine equipment." The situation changed overnight after America went to war. Omaha, as other cities, soon needed manpower, particularly skilled workers in all industrial classifications. Relief programs ended, and the vexing problems created by wartime needs were for many persons a welcome change from the 1930s.

The expansion took different forms. Of minor value were activities encouraged by the authorities to give as many members of the general population as possible a feeling of participation in the war effort. These efforts, including the gathering of scrap iron and planting of "Victory Gardens," while self-satisfying for some people and bringing much favorable publicity, had little impact one way or another on Omaha's economy. Other developments were of more substance. During hostilities, the Omaha area gained many new factories, almost all of which owed their being to the war.

Senator George W. Norris used his prestige and Washington connections to help gain vast facilities for the Omaha area. Norris argued that not putting plants in Nebraska would be "injurious to this long-suffering part of the country" and "to the harmony and even to the patriotism of the country at large when the time of returned prosperity comes." He reached Roosevelt through Chester C. Davis, the head of the Advisory Commission to the Council on National Defense. While the primary function of Davis' section was to offer advice on farm matters, it also dealt with industrial plant locations and the expediting of war production priorities. Norris wrote Davis on November 27, 1940, calling attention to proposals for a powder plant between Lincoln and Omaha, a military cantonment south of Hastings, and an "aircraft engine research laboratory" at Omaha. The senator noted the Omaha area WPA Tricounty power project, stating that the government should "patronize one of its own children." This letter, sent on to the White House, brought a direct reply to Norris from Roosevelt in early December. The President said that one of several large midwestern aircraft plants had been recommended for Nebraska, that he hoped it was the forerunner of other developments, and that he believed further broad programs would make use of resources and manpower in the state. Other projects followed: one of the most important an ordinance plant near Wahoo, which employed thousands of commuting workers from Omaha. Norris concluded that Nebraska defense plants were a result of his long fight for public power projects. He saw cheap electricity as the key to the state's wartime prosperity.

The largest war establishment was the Glenn L. Martin-Nebraska Co. bomber plant. The concern was a subsidiary of the Glenn L.

Martin Co. of Baltimore, Maryland, one of the nation's leading producers of military aircraft. Martin leased the government-built and owned facility as part of the plan to place a large aircraft assembly plant in Nebraska. The bomber plant, located just south of Omaha near Bellevue, was at Fort Crook. This was a small post that continued to operate throughout the war primarily as a supply depot, training school, and reception center. The fort was also the site of Offutt Field, which was greatly expanded during the course of hostilities. It handled the planes produced by the Glenn L. Martin-Nebraska Co. The gigantic operation consisted of forty-eight buildings, most constructed in 1941, at a cost of close to $15 million. One of the prime contractors was Peter Kiewit Sons Co. of Omaha. The factory had over two million square feet of work space — the main building was six hundred feet by nine hundred feet — and at its peak of production employed 14,500 people. Roughly seventy-five percent of all the workers had lived prior to the war in either Omaha or Council Bluffs. In terms of numbers of employees at a single site, the bomber plant was one of the country's largest war arsenals. It modified over 1,000 planes; made 1,585 B-26 Martin Marauders, two-engine medium attack bombers; and 531 B-29 Superfortresses, four-engine planes that carried the air war to Japan. The two B-29s that dropped atomic bombs on Hiroshima and Nagasaki were both made and modified at the Martin-Nebraska plant.

Less dramatic, but of fundamental significance, were advances in areas that had long been important. Omaha's railroads prospered as a result of war traffic and booming agricultural production. Stockyard receipts rose to the greatest heights ever, and Omaha boosters again talked confidently about possibly surpassing Chicago as the world's largest livestock market. Then came the end of the war, and a flurry of telegrams terminating government contracts: Martin–Nebraska stopped production on September 30, 1945. The return of peace raised an important question. Would prosperity last?

In 1945 the Omaha City Planning Commission issued a cautiously optimistic report. Avoiding the florid language of the booster literature of the 1920s, it stressed that Omaha had gained in population during the 1930s, contending that this and wartime changes seemed to indicate future progress. The planning commission envisioned a bright future for the food processing industry and, in addition, noted that workers in defense plants had developed a variety of skills in new areas of fabrication. The prospect of increased air and barge transportation also seemed to work in favor of Omaha. The report suggested that because people had become accustomed to moving often during the war any local downturn would not result in much unemployment. It concluded by predicting a new era of sharper competition between cities in which a community's ability to provide jobs would be a determining factor: "A city is a place in which to earn a living, and a place in which to live. In our democratic society, the provision of economic opportunities depends primarily on individual courage and action; providing a better city in which to live depends primarily on the joint initiative and courage of the individuals in the city. If it is to maintain its 1940 population, Omaha must offer more opportunities for employment, it must be a better place in which to live." Hardly revolutionary at first glance — the language bordered on the bureaucratic — the statement indicated a shift in community ideology: an official document admitted that the business leadership could no longer run the city alone. There was a growing accommodation with the realities of the changes wrought by the Great Depression, the New Deal, and the Second World War. Omaha had entered a transitional period.

The electrical and traction industries reflected the changes in the wind. The Nebraska Power Company and the Omaha Traction Company had led the fight in prewar times for free enterprise and internal direction of affairs by the business community. James E. Davidson, the president of Nebraska Power, who had used advertising techniques to help achieve the same objectives that the traction line did by using strikebreakers, surrendered quietly to the public power interests, doing so adroitly and with considerable grace. Indeed, he took the lead in going public. In 1944 he helped a state-authorized Electric Committee buy Nebraska Power from its parent company, the American Light and Power Company. Two years later, the state created the Omaha Public Power District. The first head of the OPPD was Davidson; he easily made the transition from private to public power, citing changing times and conditions. His pleasing personality and public relations skills tended to cloud a fundamental change.

The Omaha Traction Company did not surrender as easily or gracefully, battling until the end of all hope to continue the policies that Wattles had articulated many years earlier. In the late 1940s and on into the 1950s, frequent strikes continued to characterize the company's labor relations. While the traction leaders gradually adopted current national practices, phasing out streetcars in favor of buses, they seemed incapable of adopting a new approach to employer-employee relations. The firm's adamant stand came when automobiles made streetcar and bus strikes more of an inconvenience to users than anything else. During the 1950s the number of Omaha Traction Company employees dropped from one thousand to four hundred; and the line lost business, resulting from a combination of the technological changes and a gradual drop in public confidence. In the middle of the 1950s a franchise change added public appointees to the company's board, paving the way for municipal control. By that time the fight against unions in Omaha had assumed different forms, as a rule not very effective. The successful passage in Nebraska of a "right to work" amendment hurt unions, but by 1960 roughly 50,000 of 150,000 gainfully employed workers in Omaha belonged to labor organizations and national unions wielded growing political power. So, for that matter, did the utilities.

In 1958 a publicist wrote in a booklet intended to attract outside business: "Public utilities in Omaha are worth 1.2 billion dollars. Therefore they play an important part in the city's economy, both as creators of payrolls and as suppliers for industry and commerce." Less than twenty years earlier the same organizations had emphasized free enterprise and the open shop. Now they talked of building a better Omaha. While many of the same people who had fought for the older goals remained in key positions, there was a different attitude. Despite continued rhetoric about the virtues of capitalism — an uninhibited kind in which entrepreneurs would have a free hand in the market place — in practice the dominant economic groups in Omaha accepted the new age.

Omaha continued to enjoy prosperity throughout most of the postwar era. The general upward economic movement came despite serious inflation in the years immediately after the war, severe drought conditions on the Great Plains in the early 1950s, and periodic recessions in 1949, 1954, and 1958. There were several contributing factors.

A meaningful aspect was federal involvement. Government money never stopped coming into Omaha and its hinterland. Irrigation projects added hundreds of thousands of acres to the agricultural base. Farm price support and commodity programs, which especially worked to the advantage of grain farmers and cattle ranchers, helped bring a much-needed element of stability to Nebraska farming. Disaster relief and farm loan legislation lessened the impact of the drought and recession times. Foreign aid programs, particularly Point 4 and the Marshall Plan, under which the United States supplied its friends and allies with great quantities of farm products, furnished ready overseas markets. Closer to home, the Veterans Administration opened a large regional hospital in Omaha, constructed between 1946 and 1951 by local contractors. In addition, the Korean War led to increased military demands for produce. The Corps of Engineers stepped up its traditional functions along the Missouri River. The Pick-Sloan engineering plan for the Missouri River Basin, which called for construction of a series of dams and other public works, added another dimension to the economic picture. Lewis A. Pick, best known for his role in building the Ledo Road in Burma during World War Two, headed the Corps' Omaha office. He had good connections in Washington, which ensured careful congressional consideration of his proposals, even though he never realized his dream of a full-scale Missouri Valley Authority. Another federal program, the Interstate Highway Act of 1956, brought millions of dollars for freeway construction. Many Omaha and other Nebraska politicians rode to power by denouncing government spending and raising the twin spectres of inflation and high taxes. Their declarations found a responsive audience, but big government played an essential role in keeping Omaha's economy healthy.

Of great importance was the moving of the headquarters of the Strategic Air Command to Offutt Air Force Base, the site of the former Glenn L. Martin-Nebraska Co. bomber plant. The massive facility had reverted to the government after the war. It had one of the few runways in the middle of the continent capable of handling fully loaded B-29s, which required over 10,000 feet to take off. Although SAC commander Curtis LeMay complained about having to operate a global air force out of an old factory building, the bringing of SAC to Omaha guaranteed a share of postwar defense spending.

The decision was a complex one that related to a combination of military and political considerations. Nebraska's two Republican senators, Hugh Butler and Kenneth Wherry, wanted postwar defense bases for the state. In 1946 Butler had sought unsuccessfully to get Fifth Army headquarters located in Omaha. A supporter of military spending programs and an opponent of New Deal measures, he was a resident of Omaha. Wherry, a World War One naval flying corps officer and Republican Senate Whip in the Eightieth Congress, exerted behind the scenes pressure. The Omaha Chamber of Commerce and other local groups also provided enthusiastic support. While this helped, congressional action loomed as far more important. No one at the local level had the power to influence events.

In July 1946 Lieutenant General Ira C. Eaker, Deputy Commander of the United States Army Air Forces, decided that SAC headquarters should be transferred from Andrews Air Force Base near Washington to "a station in the mid-West." He thought the capital too crowded with military personnel and aircraft and believed a large continued military presence undesirable. Colorado Springs was the first choice, but orders moving SAC there were countermanded after Air Force representatives determined that a serious housing shortage existed in the area. In February 1947 Lowry Field near Denver came under serious consideration. However, General Carl A. Spaatz, the commanding general of the Army Air Force, ruled that Lowry would remain an air training command base. There matters stood until December 1947, when another survey ruled SAC had to relocate in the Midwest. Early the next year, representatives of the nearly formed United States Air Force recommended four sites, including Offutt Air Force Base.

The SAC commander, George C. Kenney, strenuously objected to the first choice, Topeka Air Force Base, because he wanted SAC headquarters to stay in Washington. He cited such criteria as the need to have a command post along a "positive axis of communication" and the availability of sufficient office space. If SAC absolutely had to move, he felt it should be no further from Washington than Mitchell Field, New York. Kenney's superiors, including Hoyt S. Vandenberg, the Air Force chief of staff, and Stuart Symington, the Secretary of the Air Force, overruled him. During the deliberations, Wherry had promised Symington that Omaha business interests would provide adequate housing for base personnel. In late May 1948 Symington informed Wherry's office that SAC headquarters would move to Omaha, and a few days later on June 3 General Vandenberg signed an official order to that effect. Without much public fanfare, Omaha had obtained what had the potential to develop into a major defense installation.

Wherry's next goal was to ensure that SAC headquarters would remain permanently at Offutt Air Force Base. Omaha builders gave little sign of providing the estimated two thousand housing units that the SAC base required. Secretary Symington did not help matters when he responded to an inquiry by a prominent Omaha realtor by stating, "present Air Force plans contemplate the indefinite utilization of this base." Under the circumstances, no developer wanted to take the risk, especially when LeMay hinted that Omaha had military and administrative drawbacks. Wherry, who had promised that Omaha interests would provide housing units, sought a solution. To begin with, he blamed the military rather than Omaha builders. On December 28, 1948, he wrote Secretary of Defense James Forrestal, "I know from personal contacts that if home builders in Omaha were sure that the S.A.C. or a similar installation were to be permanently headquartered at Offutt Field, the builders would solve the housing shortage at Offutt within the year." Next, Wherry introduced legislation under which the Federal Housing Administration would guarantee mortgages for housing units built on military bases designated as "permanent." He told the Senate Banking and Currency Committee that his purpose was to keep existing military bases in Nebraska. The Wherry Housing Law, which received strong backing from the armed forces, easily passed Congress and became law in August of 1949. While it required technical changes, the legislation led to a solution of Offutt housing problems. Omaha civic leaders donated fifty acres adjacent to the base to the government; and a local builder, the Carl C. Wilson Offutt Housing Corporation, started a housing project after receiving a $5 million FHA loan. A measure designed to solve a specific problem that had national implications helped keep SAC headquarters at Offutt Air Force Base.

In its early Offutt days SAC had only a small number of B-29s modified to carry nuclear weapons. But, as the Cold War progressed, SAC became one of the West's chief weapons. In deciding how to counter the Russians, contingency planners ruled out a preemptive strike and developed a system to protect North America against a surprise attack from over the North Pole. Offutt Field was at the heart of these plans. It lay behind three lines of defense; an early warning system in the Arctic, another along the Canadian-American border, and finally short range missile batteries around population centers. If Russian bombers should come, the scheme called for SAC officers at Offutt to coordinate worldwide retaliatory strikes against targets in the Soviet Union. Large sums flowed into Offutt for runways, buildings, and underground fortifications. Omaha contracting and engineering firms received lucrative contracts. By the late 1950s the base was already a city in itself with over 20,000 servicemen and dependents. Again, outside factors —these related to the prospects of global war—had advanced Omaha's economic fortunes.

The Omaha Chamber of Commerce claimed that the postwar

progress resulted from the pluck and spirit of private enterprise, plus the attractions of the area. "Omaha has enjoyed a steady, healthy growth during the past several years," a 1958 promotional booklet indicated. "Because of its abundant water supply, natural resources, friendliness of its people, geographical location, unexcelled transportation facilities and because Omahans are united as a civic team, our community has prospered." A number of indicators buttressed the assertion. Aggressive promotion brought new industrial concerns into greater Omaha, including the Continental Can Company; the Allied Chemical and Dye Corporation; and the Omaha Production Company, a division of the Sperry Corporation. The local concern, C. A. Swanson & Sons, used production line methods to quick-freeze canned chicken and pioneered TV dinners. Manufacturing and other employment lines stabilized so that throughout the 1950s Omaha's gainful working force stood between 140,000 and 150,000, far above the levels of the depression years. Livestock receipts increased from 5.3 million in 1948 to 5.9 million ten years later, with the number of animals slaughtered locally rising from 3.3 million to 4.3 million. With the decline, owing to changing industry practices, of the Chicago and Kansas City markets, Omaha achieved the long-sought goal of becoming the nation's leading meat supplier, generating an annual business in excess of $5 billion.

Equally impressive was the rise of the insurance industry. The Fraternal Woodmen of the World started an insurance company in 1895. After changing the age of those eligible from fifty-one to forty-five, altering membership qualifications to exclude blacks, and adding a hazardous occupation clause, the Woodmen prospered. It built Omaha's first skyscraper–the Woodmen of the World Tower–and by 1933 claimed assets of more than $26 million and a membership of 134,000. The fraternal insurance society survived the depression, and in the immediate postwar era claimed to be the largest insurance organization of its kind in the country. By then another Omaha insurance company was better known and more successful. Mutual of Omaha, founded in 1909 as the Mutual Benefit Health and Accident Association, after a slow start did well over the years under the leadership of Dr. C. C. and Mabel L. Criss. The firm and a subsidiary had over six hundred employees in 1939. During the 1950s Mutual of Omaha, helped by aggressive selling and nationwide advertising, became the nation's leading accident insurance company. By 1960 Omaha was the home of thirty-eight insurance companies, many subsidiaries or spin offs of the original concerns. The industry employed eight thousand persons and had a premium income of $325 million. As other Midwest financial hubs —Chicago, Milwaukee, Kansas Citiy, and Des Moines—Omaha developed an insurance industry of impressive proportions. Because of the complexities of coverage warranties and estates, banking and insurance many times had developed in the same centers. Yet there was another reason; Nebraska had some of the most lenient insurance laws and pro-business regulatory agencies in the United States. Indeed, another Cornhusker city, Lincoln, rivaled Omaha as an insurance center.

A showdown of sorts over increased federal involvement in Omaha came over urban renewal. There was little new residential and commercial construction during the depression and World War Two, all at a time when the city experienced significant physical changes. Downtown, particularly in the blocks around the center core, showed signs of decay. Large numbers of blacks remained

Omaha Stockyards, ca. 1954

confined to a blighted district on the Near North Side; older housing predominated in South Omaha's ethnic neighborhoods. After the war, most new building was on the west side and in the growing suburban ring. In 1945 and 1946 the city responded to the situation by creating the Omaha Housing Authority to construct low cost housing and insure participation in federally leased housing programs. A Housing and Slum Area Elimination Committee identified deteriorating areas, formulated a housing plan that focused on present and future rehabilitation, and revised the original 1920 zoning ordinance. Beyond these technical matters, little more was done; the city council rejected creation of a permanent slum commission and made no attempt to take advantage of the Federal Housing Act of 1949 or its successive amendments, notably one in 1954 that provided lucrative incentives for developers. In 1956, after a lengthy court battle, the city did succeed in enforcing a minimum dwelling standard ordinance. The following year, Omaha business interests supported a comprehensive redevelopment plan under the Federal Urban Renewal Program.

The proposal was defeated at the polls in 1958, as were subsequent measures in 1965 and 1970. Opponents charged that government housing destroyed neighborhoods, raised taxes, helped special interests, and violated property rights. Organized opposition came from black groups; spokesmen noted that there were no provisions to help people displaced under the program. While loopholes led to some later limited participation in federal housing programs, Omahans, unlike their counterparts in many other cities, decided to take the primary responsibility for solving their renewal problems. There appeared limits on the extent to which Omaha voters would take federal handouts. Whatever the needs or benefits, a majority felt that the government should stay out of housing.

Omaha prospered. The population increased to more than 300,000 during the 1950s. Grain receipts rose to over sixty million bushels and shipments to fifty million bushels. Omaha remained an important wholesaling and warehouse center. From 1947 to 1957 the annual wholesale volume increased to slightly over $2 billion. In the same period retail sales jumped by fifty-one percent, with 1957 totals of $421 million. At that time, the city had an estimated thirty-five hundred retail establishments. Combined deposits in Omaha's ten major banks advanced accordingly, crossing the $500 million mark late in the decade. As had been the case for decades, Omaha continued to serve as a transportation hub. Nearly two hundred freight and over seventy passenger trains entered and left

Omaha every day. Thirty-five major truck lines and another 120 franchised motor carriers had headquarters in the city. Five airlines afforded fast national and regional transportation. More advances seemed in the offing, and under the circumstances there was a general uplift in the community spirit. In 1954, a hundred years after initial settlement, Prof. Walter H. Rawley, Jr., of the University of Nebraska history department, viewing construction activities as a unifying theme, commented on what he believed the prevailing mood in the Omaha *World-Herald.*

> Gratifying evidence of civic achievement surrounds Omahans in their Centennial Year. There is the City-Wide Planning Commission; the building of the Outer Drive, with massive reinforced concrete piers waiting to support a massive viaduct over the Union Pacific Shops along the new arterial linking the Municipal Airport with downtown Omaha; construction of a Belt Line Highway; plans for increased parking facilities in downtown Omaha; remodeled and modernized department stores; a small but firm step toward solving the city's slum problem, and the long stride toward easing the community's traffic congestion by the adoption of an engineer's report calling for a one-way street plan. . . . So post-war progress — in business, transportation, education, art and private housing — is Omaha's tribute to its founders on its one hundredth birthday.

Omahans took pride in what had been accomplished in a relatively short period. The making of the city had involved the overcoming of numerous challenges. In that context, the Great Depression was just one in a series of problems that confronted Omaha's citizens. Yet the economic disaster defied simple quantification, given its indispensable role in first raising questions about the possible boundaries of aspirations and then setting the course of events for ensuing decades. As it turned out, the questions had affirmative answers. Omaha had not reached the limits. There was no inevitable decline. "Artificial lines" continued as sources of strength. Industries stayed. The hinterland recovered faster than expected. While all this was for the good, the reasons for the return to prosperity were somewhat disturbing.

Through three decades of the New Deal, the Second World War, and the Cold War, federal money was the key element in putting Omaha back on a positive course. It came at a high price: ever greater federal interference in local affairs and a long and ominous inflationary cycle characterized by a gigantic increase in the national debt. Further questions intruded upon the Omaha scene and shadowed the rosy predictions of a bright economic future.

Air View of Omaha, ca. 1950s

The bottom line remained the same as always; there was no easy way to build a city in the United States. For every success and difficulty overcome, there were new challenges to confront. In attempting to maintain and expand the position of Omaha, its leaders would have to continue to respond to outside forces, both public and private, while developing innovative ways to counter aggressive rivals. It was a price that came with the responsibility of metropolitan advance and one that Omaha's business leaders believed worth paying. A strong spirit of enterprise continued to exist.

8

At Heart It Is Still a City in the Making

On the upper plains, many small towns that flourished at the end of the 1920s were empty shells thirty years later. They were victims of the depression, the changes in agricultural marketing patterns, and the ability of larger and more powerful rivals to hold, maintain, and expand their hinterland empires. Omaha survived because of the position it had achieved prior to the crash. Its role as a transportation, financial, and agricultural center was of such regional importance that it had to figure in plans for recovery and then in those for war and the postwar economy.

According to the Omaha Chamber of Commerce, the city made dramatic strides between 1945 and 1960. As proof, the chamber, in addition to citing all sorts of statistical evidence, called attention to the construction of freeways, the erection of large buildings, the development of numerous subdivisions, and the modernization of city government. Despite the protestations of great progress, there was much about the Omaha of 1960 that resembled the Omaha of 1930. There had been little in the way of new downtown construction; so the skyline looked the same. New buildings, such as the headquarters of Mutual of Omaha, were to the west of the business district. The Union Pacific Railroad still played a crucial role in the life of the community. As prior to the depression, the Union Pacific headquarters was in the city. The stockyards and packing plants remained important, enhanced by Omaha's advance to the nation's number one livestock center. Hinterland boundaries, set by the 1920s, were about as before. The public schools were a source of local pride; and the Joslyn Memorial afforded a sense of community. The Knights of Ak-Sar-Ben carried out a wide variety of activities. The outward changes had not been as obvious as claimed by boosters. About the best that could be said was that Omaha had succeeded in accomplishing what its business leaders had hoped for in the depths of depression which was to ride out the storm and to maintain the city's hard earned position in the American urban system.

Downtown Omaha, ca. early 1930s

There was a price to pay, and those who bore it were the people of Omaha. In the harsh realities of the moment, it was all too common to not think of them individually. Rather, taken as a whole they served as the basis for the statistical data used in the formulas that determined relief expenditures, war contracts, and urban housing programs. From the 1930s through the 1950s the faith of Omahans in the future of the city was first shattered and then gradually restored. However, restoration brought new conceptions about the nature of the city. By the 1950s many Omahans felt that they lived in an increasingly cosmopolitan community that had evolved into a rather typical American regional metropolis. This was far different from the prevailing view back during the 1930s. Works Progress Administration writers analyzing Omaha in those years caught the prevailing mood when they wrote in 1939:

> Omaha has not yet lost a sense of surprise over becoming a big town: at heart it is still a city in the making, with Saturday-night brawls, "drug-store cowboys" and packing-house workers on parade. Overalls and straw hats are not out of place in the marble lobby of the Livestock Exchange, and an occasional Indian is seen on the streets. The city has the small town's interest in local boys who made good; the front page always has space for the doings of any "former Omahan," whether he wrote a script for Hollywood or was arrested for theft in Denver. . . . Life here has more variety than is usual in Nebraska: gambling halls, dime-a-drink girls, formal banquets, a community art museum, conventions, folk festivals of European tradition, and the annual crowning of a King and Queen of Ak-Sar-Ben. . . . Notwithstanding the soot in the air and the odor of the stockyards that pervades South Omaha, the people are practically convinced that although Omaha could be improved upon, it is better than any other town within a thousand miles.

Even as the WPA writers drew their conclusions, forces of change were at work, rooted in the Great Depression, which had a fundamental effect upon community ideology.

The economic collapse had an impact on every person in Omaha. As might have been expected, the vantage points differed. The wealthy saw it mainly in terms of paper losses and the threat of a loss in social status; membership in Ak-Sar-Ben dropped markedly. Even so, the life styles of local business leaders — merchant George Brandeis, hotel owner Eugene Chase Eppley, railroad executive William M. Jeffers, and electric power official James E. Davidson — remained much as before. The prestigious Omaha Club was still a citadel of privilege and the coronation of the King and Queen of

Ak-Sar-Ben remained the major annual social event. Things were much different for the middle and lower classes of Omaha. They experienced anguish and suffering: the wage cuts, the pink slips, the loss of savings, the debilitation caused by long-term unemployment, and the sickening feeling of downward mobility. They were the unfortunates in a generation of Americans who had an unwanted rendezvous with destiny.

Omaha's black population was especially hard hit. Historically, blacks had occupied the lower economic rungs, excluded from skilled blue collar positions and white collar office work. Generally, blacks were the last hired and the first fired. They performed tasks that whites did not want to do when better alternatives existed. In 1931 major Omaha industrial firms employed 1,800 blacks out of a total working force of 16,000. A year later these same concerns had 14,750 operatives only 600 of whom were black. Opportunities for blacks dried up in direct relationship to rising white unemployment. "We have used a few Negroes as porters and in the stables but there is no opportunity open now in either place," the manager of a large dairy reported. "The men we have in these departments are sticking rather close to their jobs." Sometimes, ethnic clannishness was an employment factor. In an extreme case early in the depression, a new Bohemian foreman in a large downtown office building arbitrarily discharged thirty-two black cleaning women and replaced them with Bohemians. A pessimistic and discouraged J. Harvey Kerns, the executive secretary of the Omaha Urban League, concluded in a 1932 monograph "that the inferior economic status of the Negro in Omaha, involving as it does, irregular employment and low wages of men and women and limited opportunities for economic advancement, is one of the most serious problems confronting the race." Kerns accurately described a situation that in its worst forms was to exist the rest of the decade and throughout all of black America.

In 1941 researchers for the Federal Writers Project of the Works Progress Administration for Nebraska interviewed several dozen Omahans about their experiences during the depression. Few cared to discuss in detail the hardships that they endured. Rather, they tended to recall happy moments and to talk about their lives in general. The "Life History" project, an early experiment in oral history, was somewhat unstructured. The participants were not asked many specific questions. Instead, they were encouraged to talk about themselves. This methodology, considered imperfect by later standards, had an unintended dividend. At times rambling and ungrammatical observations provided a unique record of what average Americans thought of when they tried to recall and explain what the cruel decade had meant in human terms.

Peter Christensen, seventy-four years old at the time of his interview in his modest home, was far from bitter about his depression experiences. He had no formal schooling, but through self-study he had attained a third-grade level of competency. Born in Horsens, Denmark, in 1867, he immigrated to the United States in 1881. After living for short periods in Ohio and Massachusetts, he moved to the Great Plains. He settled in South Dakota, married, and fathered fifteen children. During most of his life he was either a farmer or grain elevator manager, but like countless others he fell victim to the depression. Forced out of work in 1932, he migrated to Omaha two years later, where he eventually eked out a meager living peddling eggs. He was six feet tall, weighed 185 pounds, had iron grey hair, a moustache, and blue eyes. Musing over his daily routine he viewed his state of affairs with a certain degree of optimism, claiming it did not bother him to have customers slam doors in his face. He placed his hopes for the future in the Townsend Plan. Referring to the controversial proposal advanced by a retired Californian, Christensen said: "It would take care of us oldsters — make us feel secure. That's about the worst trouble with getting old — the insecurity — we can't get jobs. We've put our lives into doing our share for the country, and now, when we are old, the security we'd get from the Townsend Plan would allow us to live our last days happily. The money we'd receive would have to go right back into circulation and it would leave profits to people all the way down the line, from raw material to delivery-boy. I'm for it — even though my own needs are well taken care of. Just think of being forced to spend $200 a month!"

Sam Piccinoni, born in Sicily in 1894, was of medium height, rather heavy-set, and partly bald. He had a round face, dark eyes, and a pleasant disposition. For recreation he liked to play a guitar. He had a wife and one child. Educated in common schools in Italy, he was a businessman in Omaha until ruined by the depression. He said that he had few regrets about his experiences in Omaha and America, even though he failed three times in the restaurant business in the 1930s. After that he was unemployed until his wife gave birth to a baby girl and he decided to swallow his pride and go to work for the WPA. "I thinks this WPA work is ver' good to help people without anything," he contended. "This people who work for WPA, they need money. They have to support their families.

223

Many people criticize this government, but, from my estimation, they are wrong. The people who criticize this WPA, they are the people who never had to work hard in their lives, or people who are mean and never have any love for poor people. . . . Cold weather, hot weather, rain or storm, I know mind. I am living very happy." At the time of his interview, Piccinoni was a sewer department foreman.

Another subject of a "Life History," James Breezee, born in Wisconsin in 1917, had an unpleasant childhood. His mother died and his stepfather committed him to a home for the feebleminded. Breezee escaped after completing fourth grade and became a drifter. He had no permanent address when a WPA worker asked him about his experiences as a youthful runaway. Breezee, who made a living selling trinkets on street corners, had lost a leg while trying to catch a freight train in Council Bluffs.

> I usually eat at some of those beaneries down on lower skid-row. What is skid-row? Well, in Omaha that's Douglas Street. There are some pretty rotten dumps down there too, while some of them are not so bad for the money. Sometimes I sleep at the Salvation Army but a lot of times I just sleep out doors. Last night I slept out doors all night; no it wasn't cold. Starting early in the fall, it makes one tough to stand the winters. Sometimes I sleep out doors all winter. The toughest thing is not to be able to get a bath whenever you want it. They stick you from twenty cents to thirty-five cents for a bath down there, and a fellow has got to clean up once in a while.

In a 1933 Hollywood movie, "Wild Boys of the Road," a young runaway lost a leg while riding the rails. The film was a significant social document that called attention to the hundreds of thousands of teenage Americans put on the move during the Great Depression. James Breezee was one of those persons. His story served as another stark indication of the human cost of the disaster. On the fiftieth anniversary of the Crash, in October of 1979, media accounts emphasized the excesses of the 1920s, the collapse of the stock market, the bread lines, and the start of federal programs. Somehow, none of those things seemed to have much to do with the life of James Breezee, although they did.

Of the many New Deal programs, the Tennessee Valley Authority, which sought to transform a whole region, was the most grandiose and comprehensive economic and social experiment. Arthur E. Morgan, the first chairman of the TVA board, observed, "The TVA is not primarily a dam-building job, a fertilizer job or a power-transmission job. . . . We need something more than all these." In the 1930s broad plans for a similar regional development along the Missouri River never materialized despite the interest of Senator George W. Norris, a leading supporter of TVA and friend of Franklin D. Roosevelt. However, in Omaha, as throughout the nation, the WPA tried to combine relief activities with social reconstruction. Activities, ranging from Sunday concerts in city parks to sewing bees, represented an attempt by a president of the United States to use federal agencies as a means of standardizing life in the country.

Typical of the New Deal attempts to progress beyond economic recovery were several programs in Douglas County sponsored by the WPA Division of Women's and Professional Projects. In 1938 the division employed over sixteen hundred persons on sixteen different projects, several of which had been in operation for more than four years. Usually, the sponsors were city or county agencies that sometimes had contributed money toward operational expenses. The idea was that all those employed in the programs would have something to show for their efforts. There was a conscious effort to avoid patterns set by a few of the more controversial early New Deal relief programs. In some places unemployed workers dug ditches in the morning and then refilled them in the afternoon, leaned on shovels, or raked and reraked leaves. Community action was at the core of WPA efforts in Omaha; the needy would help the needy. The objective was to develop a collective solution to community problems, far transcending immediate economic needs — a response that would break down ethnic, racial, and parochial barriers and give rise to a new and more united American society.

Working for the good of the individual and of the state took many forms. A thousand women participated in a sewing project sponsored by Douglas County which provided $2,000 for space, equipment, and materials. Pleased bureaucrats noted that after three years the WPA workers had produced 245,000 garments, repaired 2,300 pairs of shoes, and made 2,000 burlap rugs. City agencies in Omaha used WPA personnel in a number of ways. Seventy-five men enumerated over 70,000 dwellings as part of a comprehensive real property survey. The library board employed twelve people to repair and bind books. A day care nursery for children between the ages of two and six had a staff of twelve and enrolled over eighty-four hundred youngsters. Throughout the Omaha school system, twenty-four clerical assistants handled routine office tasks, allowing administrators more time for

Douglas County Sewing Center, 1935

educational duties. The health department contributed $2,200 to start a disease prevention and treatment service. Six nurses spent most of their time in a new program of home visitations and examinations. A large adult education project that initially cost $13,000 had seventy-seven teachers. WPA statistics claimed that classes had attracted 19,000 participants. A particular success was a park department recreational scheme. The department received a very good return on its contribution of $35,000, most of which went for space and equipment. In 1938 a total of 222 recreational leaders staffed twenty-six centers. During its first four years of operation, close to 950,000 persons visited the facilities. A WPA official reported, "The community cooperation with this project is wonderful."

Two cultural uplift programs highlighted the role of the WPA in the life of Omaha. These were a "Dramatic Unit and Children's Theatre" and a "Music Project." By 1938 both had been in operation for more than two years. Forty-two people worked for the theatre project which had separate departments for dramatics, marionettes, children, and vaudeville. The city of Omaha furnished stages and offices; surrounding towns requested performances.

During the first two years of operation, an estimated 70,000 people witnessed productions. More than twice that number attended symphonies conducted under the direction of the "Music Project." The Omaha Urban League helped organize sixty-five musicians into "colored and white symphonies." These units entertained in the schools, in the hospitals, in the parks, and on the radio. Sunday afternoon free park concerts received good receptions, causing WPA supervisors to write enthusiastically about the results. Audiences had totaled 178,465 over a two-year period.

Roosevelt's opponents thought the federal government wrong in getting involved in social mores. Among them was Louis B. Adams of Omaha, who in 1941 was seventy-five years old when a WPA worker interviewed him. Adams, a native of Kentucky, had spent most of his adult life in Nebraska. Married and the father of one son, he retired in 1932 after a career in business and politics. He had been a station agent, county clerk, real estate man, postmaster, and traveling auditor. A neat and well-dressed man, he explained his position on federal programs, along with those on general educational needs:

> Politics concerns me very little today. Almost anything you may say against this administration would be OK by me. The suggested doing away with the Civilian Conservation Corps and the National Youth Administration is all wrong. They are well established, have all their buildings and equipment, are doing a good work in the training of our youth and should be kept. Education in our schools extends over too long a period for many of our students. I mean that some are not interested in their school work and naturally, that is a waste of time. Practical experience is what they need. Teach them some useful trade. Do away with the Works Progress Administration — WPA — by keeping the CCC and the NYA. Of the Community Chest inner workings, I knew very little. It seems too much of the money collected goes for overhead. More people every year seem to think the same. Maybe we could do a much better job taking care of our poor and our sick through our local government. The idea that all who hold positions in industry or politics should contribute I believe is wrong. A poor man with a family knows better than anyone else what he can spare to help his fellow man.

There was little politics of relief in Omaha, unlike the situation in some other large Midwest cities. The lack of political interference in Omaha New Deal programs related directly to two deaths, those of Mayor James C. Dahlman and "Boss" Thomas Dennison. Without their dominating personalities, Omaha's commission form of government was too ineffective and divided to determine relief

Urban League Recreation Group, ca. 1930s

WPA Sponsored Orchestra at Morton Park, ca. 1938

229

policies. The business community, accustomed to dealing through Dennison, had not developed an alternative way to exercise power. The machine, its image eroded by gangland style killings in the early days of the depression—notably the unsolved murder in 1931 of businessman and reformer Harry Lapidus—disintegrated following Dennison's death.

Dahlman's two immediate predecessors Roy Towl and Dan Butler were cautious men lacking in political appeal. Both had been around city hall in other roles for over two decades. Neither had been elected directly by the people. Rather, they won the mayoralty because they got along with a majority of their fellow commissioners. During the traction strike of 1935, Towl had turned the city over to Governor Robert Cochran without making a major effort to restore order. When violence erupted around him, Towl had contented himself with pasting newspaper clippings about the strike in his scrapbook, which was hardly the response expected of a strong leader with police powers. Given the vacuum, relief agencies had a free hand in Omaha. For that matter, most decisions on New Deal programs in Nebraska were made either through the governor's office or that of the two senators, Norris and Edward R. Burke, an Omaha Democrat. This was in keeping with general political practices in Nebraska. Omaha usually was the home of a United States Senator; and the governor, nominally the chief spokesman for the state in dealing with the federal government, almost always came from elsewhere.

New Deal activities concerned with social reconstruction and betterment ended during World War Two. Assertions by bureaucrats that the relief agencies made major contributions to the war effort —the CCC claimed to prepare teenage boys for army life and the NYA contended it trained production workers—fell on deaf ears. Congress terminated both activities with little opposition. The WPA had been controversial from its inception. In Omaha, highly qualified WPA employees had worked for several years to write a comprehensive survey of the city for the American Guide Series. Their goal was to produce a descriptive history, to identify and discuss major points of interest, and to analyze the social fabric. Ethnic and religious groups received prime consideration. The "Life Histories" of Omahans were a small portion of the many cubic feet of collected and codified research material. The project died just short of publication. The Nebraska State Historical Society gained custody of the manuscript drafts and raw research, which constituted for future generations an indispensable, unique, and informative source about Omaha. It was harder to measure the impact of recreation or theater functions. However, the park programs received local funding after the federal grants expired; and the legitimate stage remained an important part of Omaha cultural life.

World War Two had roughly the same effect on Omaha as on other parts of the country. Dislocations and separations were commonplace occurrences. The great number of women drawn into manufacturing forced adjustments, as did increased shift work. Traditional commercial business habits underwent marked changes; many stores remained open throughout the evening hours. More money went for recreation than at any time since the depression. Omaha's entertainment district, its wide open tradition curtailed in the 1930s by pressure from state authorities, regained some of its former lustre. "Gin mills" located near the stations competed with the Red Cross and separate black and white United Service Organizations for the patronage of the thousands of military personnel who daily changed trains in Omaha. While a nationally imposed wartime ban on horse racing closed Ak-Sar-Ben, other gambling outlets continued to operate. Such activities constituted only a small part of the city at war. Its citizens took their home front duties seriously. They bought war bonds, endured rationing, and served in civilian defense groups.

A combination of a patriotic war supported by the vast majority of citizens, coupled with the success of New Deal programs in making people accustomed to following the lead of the federal government, helped assure a unified response to the emergency. Perhaps the New Deal and World War Two made Americans of all races and creeds more like each other and more aware than ever before that they shared a similar experience. This seemed especially true of the metropolitan components in the American urban system. Key elements tended to come closer and closer together as they were pressured by an ever more powerful national government to move in the direction of common problem solving. Cities increasingly had less local or individual authority over their own affairs.

In 1946 an extensive program report prepared by the Young Men's Christian Association and the Young Women's Christian Association analyzed the needs and problems of Omaha's youth. Compiled by private agencies, the study was another indication of the growing acceptance of social planning as an important element in solving local problems. The authors attributed the situation to rapid growth rather than to depression and war. They called

Omaha a "new city," comparing it to a youth who had to assume adult responsibilities before reaching maturity. As a result, they thought that Omaha struggled toward solutions to problems using an outmoded economic and social outlook that reflected "the essentially conservative and ultra-realistic philosophy of the men who get their living from the soil." They said that the circumstance had retarded Omaha's social development, that it trailed other cities in recreation, school, and social programs, and that the juvenile court was "under-staffed and under-served." There was a necessity to study "youth needs" and the relationship to "Omaha proper." The New Deal may have no longer been alive and well in Omaha, but important agencies continued down the path of social action.

The community survey collected data on the major "behavior problems" among youth. Indices showed that juvenile delinquency was more than just a wartime problem, as some persons had thought. The Omaha Juvenile Court had a case load of about five thousand per year and no real way to deal effectively with habitual offenders. High numbers of truants from the commercial and industrial districts were another cause of concern. Because of lax enforcement of the Nebraska child labor laws, many fourteen-year-olds, who obtained legal summer work permits, violated the conditions by continuing to work into the school year. Frequently, they found it hard to hold jobs and attend school at the same time. Juvenile deaths in street accidents added another dimension. Most occurred on service roads in black districts on the Near North Side that had few playgrounds. Just as disturbing were a series of drownings in suburban Carter Lake, attributed to poor supervision.

Teenage drinking was a serious problem. Omaha had 752 liquor stores and drinking places, far more than other cities in the same population class. Oklahoma City had 610; Syracuse 488. The report contended, "With the poverty of public recreational facilities and social programs it is not surprising that Omaha leads cities of comparable size in the number of drinking places to total stores, and in the percent of total retail sales spent in drinking places." The general conclusion was that the girls and boys of Omaha could be best served by greater public expenditures for recreation. With the curtailment of federal funding, however, voluntary agencies supported by private philanthropy were unable to meet the needs of the city. Still, there was increased public involvement in youth programs, and political considerations evolved around how much money should be spent rather than about whether it should be spent. This was another legacy of the New Deal; one not as obvious and publicized as others, but it was a legacy just the same.

The character of Omaha's population underwent significant changes between the Great Depression and the Second World War, and increased opportunities for social mobility arose as hostilities wore on. Many immigrants as well as native settlers had passed away and the city exhibited an increasing American character. The number of Omahans rose from 223,844 in 1940 to an estimated 233,500 in 1945. At the start of the 1940s there were 22,311 foreign-born, representing slightly under ten percent of the population and down by over 7,000 from ten years earlier. Census totals for the four largest nationalities — Italians (2,834), Czechoslovakians (2,816), Germans (2,756), and Swedes (2,183) — reflected the decline. Close to nine thousand of the immigrants lived in South Omaha where they continued to dominate cultural life, giving the former industrial suburb an identity and consciousness that set it apart from the city proper. Another annexed area, the old country village of Benson, had a strong sense of identity. Otherwise, Omaha, as from its beginning, remained homogeneous, except for the black community on the Near North Side. In 1940 most of Omaha's 12,015 blacks lived in the section. They constituted slightly more than five percent of all Omaha residents. During the 1930s the number of blacks rose by only 892, an indication more of a dearth of opportunities than of neighborhood stability.

In 1944 approximately seventy-eight percent of all Omahans lived in single family dwellings, making the city in the terminology of the day a "front porch town." Community spokesmen found this desirable, equating it without substantial evidence with the promise of American life. They did not emphasize that enrollment in the public schools dropped between 1930 and 1944, falling from 46,766 to 41,992. As always, religion remained difficult to quantify. The best available statistics came from the 1936 federally-conducted religious census that showed that less than fifty percent of all Omahans had a church affiliation. Of those who did, Protestants were in the majority, with Lutherans the largest body. Roman Catholic claimed in excess of 40,000 communicants. All in all the various social statistics, taken at different intervals and circumstances, provided an important insight into the Omaha of the immediate postwar years. So many changes had occurred that future social trends seemed impossible to predict. As it turned out, the 1950s in Omaha meant much the same as elsewhere: a false sense of stability.

"Little Italy" in South Omaha, 1940

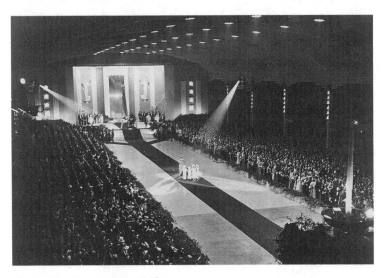

Ak-Sar-Ben Coronation, 1947

All during the 1950s a cautious hold-the-line attitude prevailed in Omaha. Despite the return of prosperity fear persisted — fostered by memories of bad times and by recurrent recessions — that good times would fade away plunging the town back into the depths of economic decline. Omahans had experienced too much adversity for an optimistic attitude to last. It was almost as if the years of depression and war had devitalized the community. Other traumas kept people on the defensive: the Korean War, the rise and fall of Senator Joseph McCarthy, the threat of hot wars in Europe and Southeast Asia, the fear of a missile gap, and the possibility of atomic attack. The horror of an apocalypse seemed very real in Omaha, given its proximity to the headquarters of the Strategic Air Command. People in Omaha avoided extremes, either the atmosphere of experimentation in the growing cities of Southern California or the morass that prevailed in the decaying industrial towns of New England. It was as if Omahans wanted a return of the 1920s. Yet any longing for the past missed a major trend. As a result of changing employment patterns, particularly in insurance as opposed to meat packing, Omaha was slowly shifting from a blue to white collar town. This would bring significant cultural and social changes in following decades.

The Knights of Ak-Sar-Ben continued to exert important influence in Omaha. Critics charged that the organization had far too much power, pointing out that for a number of years it controlled automobile and truck access into the city from the east by operating a Missouri River toll bridge. Defenders responded by pointing out that Ak-Sar-Ben purchased the link from the Street Railway Company in the depths of the depression as a public spirited venture. Ak-Sar-Ben officials worked out a speeded up schedule of paying off the bonds and lowered tolls, making it easier for Council Bluffs residents to cross over to Omaha to shop. This enhanced Ak-Sar-Ben's local image, as did the running of a gambling enterprise. The race track brought thousands of patrons into town every late spring and early summer, and some of the pari-mutuel profits went to all Nebraska counties for educational purposes. Of other Ak-Sar-Ben activities, from circuses to auto shows, none approached in prestige the annual coronation of a leading member and his choice as consort. In effect, if not in name, they became rulers of Omaha for the coming year. While groups in several American cities crowned kings and queens, there was no other place in the country where the recipients exercised social power comparable to that in Omaha. Even in a time of change, Ak-Sar-Ben provided moot indication of the role of the business community in upholding what were considered conventional standards and perhaps, in a period of Eisenhower prosperity, a growing desire to avoid sharing power with other groups, public statements to the contrary.

The image that Omaha's leaders wanted to present to the world ignored the harsher realities of life. A sanitized view in booster publications depicted Omaha as a city of homes, peaceful neighborhoods, and numerous churches. The citizens appeared as a law-abiding group dedicated to following the rule of law. Ethnic and racial harmony prevailed in a classic sense. Vibrant charitable institutions illustrated the responsible spirit of Omahans to work together to build an even more stable community than already existed.

The happy picture of an idyllic city that was a good place to raise children in and where hardly anything unpleasant ever happened came under sharp criticism in a 1952 expose, *U.S.A. Confidential.* The authors, Jack Lait and Lee Mortimer, followed in the tradition of the sensation seekers who produced "Sins of the City" literature in the late nineteenth century. Together, Lait and Mortimer had co-authored "confidential" studies of the underworld in New York, Chicago, and Washington. Lait had a number of other literary credits including *The Big House* and *Gangster Girl.* Mortimer had written *New York Behind the Scenes.* They gathered material on Omaha during a short visit. According to them, they almost left immediately upon arrival when they noticed that all the taxicabs carried advertisements on the rear reading, "Visit your church on Sunday." They stayed after a "hackman" asked them, "Whatta you wanna do? Places to bet? Just go to Chet's cigar store across the street from the Burlington bus terminal. Or try the Rocket on Farnam St." The result was a highly uncomplimentary short section in *U.S.A. Confidential* entitled "Omaha — Beef and Bookies" which raised questions about the extent that some aspects of life in Omaha had changed since its days as a wide open town.

Lait and Mortimer offered little new about supposed conditions in Omaha beyond undocumented comments, derogatory statements, and a few street addresses. They demonstrated no knowledge about the history of the city, and their information about geography and sectional mores appeared muddled. They placed Nebraska in a "Bible Belt" that included such diverse jurisdictions as western Virginia, Mississippi, Alabama, and Iowa. According to their analysis frontier Methodists in the North and hard shell Baptists in the South provided a common denominator by fighting hard to preserve the Sabbath. The two authors said that Nebraska was "pickled in alcohol." They noted, "Other than that it hasn't much to speak of." That set the tone for their discussion of Omaha, the conclusions foregone. They claimed that provincial headquarters of the "International Mafia" in Chicago, Kansas City, Denver, and Minneapolis surrounded Omaha on all sides; and that Omaha was a "common ground" where "hot-money boys" met to transact interstate affairs, rubbing shoulders with local politicians in South Omaha steak houses.

Lait and Mortimer claimed that bookmaking was a major business in Omaha, except during infrequent crackdowns usually made during the racing season at Ak-Sar-Ben. With no supporting evidence, they contended that on one hand the Knights of Ak-Sar-Ben "bleed the public white" through pari-mutuel machines and on the other dispensed some race track profits back in the form of charitable relief. The authors went on to make the unsubstantiated accusation that the Senate Kefauver Committee, which investigated organized crime in America during the 1950s, "pulled out fast" in Omaha when faced with the possibility that "embarrassing testimony might have shown how Big Mob money is laid off at Ak-Sar-Ben." The authors found other things they deplored or pretended to ignore: "dope" at Central High School, prostitutes in major hotels, black bars open after hours, "fags" at the YMCA, Indians on "skidrow," poor security at the Douglas County Jail, with corrupt lawyers and judges thrown in for good measure. Omaha, they crowed, "is so typically a dirty-minded Bible Belt town." The reaction in Omaha was one of rage, a response that was part of an attempt to create new images and to articulate different goals. A history of Omaha published in 1954 to celebrate the hundredth anniversary of the city in the *World-Herald* made little mention of crime or vice. Rather, it concentrated on other aspects of community building.

The major issue of the 1950s was not corruption, but reform in city government. The loosely-knit system that evolved under Dennison and Dahlman suited the purposes of the way they controlled the levers of government. Since their deaths in the early 1930s, an obvious drift had set in that hurt orderly administration. The mayors of the 1940s faced similar difficulties as those of the 1930s; without a boss cast in the same mold as Dennison, there was no way to really govern. In 1947 Mayor Charles Leeman and leaders of the business community tried to move the city ahead through a plan that *Life* called a "blueprint for progress." It involved such proposals as better sanitation systems, airport improvements, and river-rail terminals. In short, it followed a traditional route toward economic progress. The voters approved some of the plans and rejected others. More importantly, the seven commissioners went their way, constructing their own bases of support. They showed little interest in cooperating with business interests in a broad sense. By the 1950s the fragmentation of services was such that it could no longer be ignored. The situation had degenerated to such an extent that the commissioners sometimes drew straws to see who would get the controversial job as police commissioner and tried in general to avoid responsibility for unpopular acts. Many boards and committees had overlapping or ambiguous authority. There was an obvious need for structural improvements in the machinery of government. There was an obvious drift in city government. Too many people operated at cross-purposes and there was a need for a means to formulate a clear and consistent policy. Hence arose a movement for a new charter, touted as making the city administration more attuned to people's concerns.

Change did not come easily; in 1950 voters defeated a proposed city manager plan. While people in many walks of life fought for reform, two prominent leaders of the movement were John A. Rosenblatt and A. V. Sorensen. Rosenblatt, a businessman and World War Two veteran, was mayor of Omaha all during the 1950s. Popular and energetic, he felt frustrated by the constraints imposed by the old cumbersome system. Sorensen, a self-made man who had amassed a considerable fortune selling electrical equipment, was president of the Omaha Chamber of Commerce. Rosenblatt furnished the political clout and Sorensen the backing of the business community. In the spring of 1956 Omaha voters, choosing from among sixty candidates, selected fifteen delegates to a Charter Convention. Most were men and the vast majority middle-aged business leaders. They received no pay and met through the ensuing summer in a room without air conditioning on the top floor of the city hall. Sorensen, the chairman of the convention, recalled: "It was the worst job I ever had. The law said we had only 120 days to complete the job. Fifteen people had to come to a meeting of the minds, and we finished on the 119th day. It was a very difficult assignment. We worked morning, noon and night sometimes. We just rolled up our sleeves and got wet." Another member remembered: "The convention never was dull. But it was one of the busiest times I've ever spent."

The resulting eighty-three page document separated the legislative and administrative branches, established a full-time planning department, cleaned up housekeeping details, and called for a return to a mayor and council form of government. By design, it placed day-by-day administrative responsibility in the hands of the mayor. "We put the mayor up like a sitting duck," a convention delegate told a group, "so that he'll have to answer to the people at the polls." The plan, which required majority approval, was submitted to the voters in the fall of 1956. Despite a drive mounted by John J. Cavanaugh, the only convention delegate to vote against the proposed charter, who argued that a change would hurt South Omaha, fifty-five percent of the voters approved the document. It went into operation the following year. Civic leaders proclaimed that the new government would cope with change and that it had the necessary machinery to deal successfully with social needs. Many thought the dawning of an age of harmony at hand. The National Municipal League gave Omaha a 1957 All America Cities Award, along with such places as Ketchikan, Alaska, and Philadelphia, Pennsylvania.

Omaha had entered the 1930s searching for an identity. The events of the decade dashed immediate hopes, overturning illusions about how individuals could cope with bad times. Necessity spawned changed attitudes; the New Deal saw the promotion of a spirit of joint action that carried into the 1940s. By the conclusion of hostilities, Omahans assumed that government at all levels would continue to exert control over the lives of everyone in order to bring about better conditions for all. In the 1950s the goal was security. As memories of depression faded, the business community prepared to assume its traditional role in Omaha affairs. Serious social imperfections were largely overlooked; technical changes in the structure of government would solve the problems. The general belief was that Omaha had come of age; its citizenry had melded into a homogeneous group that would accept direction, either from private or public quarters, as long as it meant peace, progress, and prosperity.

Part Five

1960-1980

9

The Dynamics of Quality

An elaborate brochure issued in the middle of the 1960s by the Omaha Chamber of Commerce contained the usual rosy predictions. It called Omaha "a vital and growing city," citing census return, a traditional measurement of progress. And there was no doubt that Omaha had added a great many people as part of a trend that would continue on into the 1970s. The statistics were such as to make leaders forget about the fears of depopulation in the depression years. Omaha had 251,117 residents in 1950 and 301,598 in 1960. Ten years later, 347,328 persons lived inside the expanded city limits. Even more dramatic was the advance of the Omaha metropolitan area that included all of Omaha's Douglas County; Sarpy County, the jurisdiction directly to the south of it in Nebraska; and Pottawattamie County, the location of Council Bluffs, on the Iowa side of the Missouri River. Between 1950 and 1970, the populations of Douglas, Sarpy, and Pottawattamie counties rose from 310,249 to 542,646. Because of postwar urban sprawl, it was no longer possible to consider the extent of an urbanized area purely in terms of the central city. Despite different governmental structures, they were part of a whole. The Omaha Standard Metropolitan Statistical Area, which ranked sixty-ninth nationally at the start of the 1970s, continued to grow at a moderate rate. In 1976, according to an overly optimistic estimate, the SMSA had 575,000 residents, up six percent in six years. Its growth rate ranked in the upper third of the seventy largest metropolitan areas and above the average 3.4 percent increase for the nation's 259 SMSAs. On the surface, all this appeared very impressive; but there was not unqualified approval. For the first time in the history of Omaha observers questioned the need and the desirability of further urban growth.

In 1966 thoughtful critics argued that continued rapid expansion might adversely affect the quality of urban life. They stood aghast at Omaha Chamber of Commerce predictions of over one million people in the SMSA by the year 2000. The prospect of adding an additional ten thousand persons every year held little appeal, although several experts gave qualified approval to some future population increase. They saw it as desirable if newcomers were not unskilled laborers, elderly "non-producers," or individuals with little earning power. H. W. Reynolds, director of the Urban Studies Center at the University of Omaha, said: "I don't think the City of Omaha should grow appreciably bigger than it is. Any city that gets to be over a half a million in population begins to get into increasingly insoluble situations – in traffic, health, welfare, for instance." Reynolds believed population growth would be good "provided it doesn't take out more than it puts in in terms of net worth of the economy." A colleague, sociologist Phil Vogt, stressed the quality of life rather than any financial factors as a reason to support population limits. Vogt believed that cities had "become unmanageable, unfit for human habitation," and that in Omaha, "There's no sign of our social disorganization reducing."

Advocates of rapid enlargement, somewhat taken aback by any attack upon an established and generally accepted way to determine urban success in America, responded by claiming that Omaha must move ahead. Alden Aust, city planning director, argued that when a city stopped growing it started to die. He contended that while rapid growth brought problems, it also brought the resources necessary to reach solutions. Jason Rouby of the Chamber of Commerce raised the possibility that a "fat-cat feeling" might cause Omaha to become a "shadow city" falling far behind Denver, Kansas City, and other "headquarters cities." Far from calling for a stop, he wanted Omaha to do more to attract people. Others thought the same. E. J. Steele, chairman of the University of Omaha Economics Department, claimed that a city would lose population if it made no effort to advance. A county planning consultant, Robert J. Selander, observed: "With a city, you either have to go one way or the other. You grow or decline. In my opinion, a growth is better than a decline, even with the problems you have." He saw current problems as "stemming from way back." Selander cautioned that growth would bring increased civic responsibilities, resulting in greater tax expenditures. None of the growth advocates agreed with the critic who remarked, "If quantity would do it, China would be the place to go." Such a rationalization begged the question.

Arguments over how many people should live in the Omaha area continued into the 1970s. Early in the decade private voluntary organizations, especially the Quality Environmental Council and Zero Population Growth, along with concerned citizens, stressed that Omaha's quality of life declined with every passing day, sometimes perceptibly, sometimes imperceptibly. The realities related to more cars, crowds, and pollution; rapid movements of people into Nebraska, more than counterbalancing a lower birth rate; increasing incidences of mental and emotional stress due to the strains of everyday living; failure to make comprehensive future plans; and a rise in noise levels, coupled with a decrease in natural open spaces. James Malkowski, director of the nearby small public Fontenelle Forest, raised the spectre of radiation from nuclear power plants. He sought a systematic study on Omaha's size and attacked the business community observing: "We seem to be entrenched in the philosophy that bigger is better. The Chamber of Commerce attitude prevails—let's get more and more." He cited problems with sewage treatment, pollution, and mass transit as the start of permanent growing pains. This kind of thinking continued to puzzle advocates of upward population progression.

At first there was a routine counterattack. City planning director Aust responded: "Suppose we build a big wall around Omaha; that wouldn't improve the quality of life a bit. I'm not impressed with the arguments that at a certain size, a city's costs go up or that it's bad to be big. We certainly haven't reached that point. When you study urban areas of all sizes you find small communities which have a great paucity of quality and large cities that have a great deal of quality of life." Contending that advocates of restricting growth were usually "ins" rather than "outs," he emphasized, "That's not very democratic." He went on to discuss the cultural and economic advantages of large urban centers. "Another thought you should explore," he declared, "is that urban areas, in order to provide

245

ample opportunities for employment, recreation and cultural employment, have to have a certain critical mass to sustain such activities. There's no playhouse in Weeping Water." He reflected that Omaha had avoided the problem of suburbs draining off the tax base because of Nebraska's liberal annexation laws. Land use, rather than more people, seemed the most serious matter of concern. However James Monroe, the manager of economic development for the Omaha Chamber of Commerce, in defending growth, indicated that his organization was not adverse to studying possible limits. While another chamber official remarked that anti-growth arguments "didn't make a ripple around here," there was a growing recognition that simply encouraging more and more people to come to Omaha might not be the answer to concerns facing the city. It was all part of a natural transition; without realizing it at the time business and environmentalists, for different reasons, had common ground.

In 1976 the Omaha Planning Department proposed a new policy designed to stop "urban sprawl" and "leapfrog" developments. Strongly backed by Mayor Edward Zorinsky, the plan at first glance seemed a dramatic departure from previous positions; several environmental and inner city groups expressed support. On closer examination the proposal seemed somewhat self-serving, motivated by economic considerations. The plan called for dividing Omaha and its suburban fringe into urban development zones. Three embraced Omaha proper and the south limits. In these "in-city zones" authorities would encourage residential upgrading through such incentives as improved urban services, favorable consideration of apartments and condominiums, and waivers on fees for building permits. The other sectors, designated as a "present development zone" and an "agricultural zone," were on the rapidly growing west and northwest sides. Here was the catch. A belt varying in width from one to three miles and extending for many miles would have the effect of acting as a sort of wall against further expansion. Within the "present development zone" the city would control growth by creating economic "disincentives." In the closer-in portion, authorities would at the time of any annexations refuse to assume public improvement debts, impose strict environmental standards, and require builders to help finance needed urban services. On the western edge, the plan called for giving a tax break to landowners who used the state greenbelt law to rezone their property to an agricultural classification. Proponents claimed that twenty-five percent of every tax dollar spent in Omaha went to expand city services and utilities into new western neighborhoods, and that seventeen percent of land in recently developed areas remained overlooked for residential purposes. They concluded that putting a damper on west and north side development would lead to better community-wide services, raise the tax base in the inner city, and revitalize the older parts of town.

In a lead editorial, "Where, and How Much, Should Omaha Grow?," the Omaha *World-Herald* raised a series of questions about the impact of the plan on the texture of urban life. Did the city have the means to make it attractive to build closer in? Would builders find a better economic climate in nearby communities, hemming Omaha in by suburban towns too large to annex? How would restricted developments affect the tax base? Would the policy make it more difficult to attract business and industry? To what extent could the government tell people where or where not to live? Might the "natural functioning of the marketplace" set limits on geographical expansion? "There is a critical difference between limiting growth reasonably and intelligently and strangling needed expansion," the *World-Herald* explained. "We hope that Omahans will familiarize themselves with the issues so that the crucial choices involving urban growth will be made with the knowledge and consent of those affected."

Even though the city government adopted the urban development policy in April 1977, the basic issues remained unresolved. The debate over growth continued into the 1980s. Opponents charged that Zorinsky had supported a short-run policy designed to hold down taxes in order to promote his own immediate political fortunes, leaving later administrations to face problems that in the middle 1970s were unpopular with many Omaha voters. What Zorinsky did was to halt annexations. Under Nebraska's incorporation laws, among the most liberal in the United States, many kinds of areas could be annexed by an order of a city council. On the outskirts of Omaha, real estate interests had become accustomed to creating legal entities called Sanitary Improvement Districts. While these districts had full government authority except for police powers, they usually were covers for either housing developments or apartment complexes.

After a SID incurred ballooning debts for such items as sewer lines, sidewalks, streets, parks, and in some cases even apartment swimming pools, annexation by Omaha had followed as a matter of course, hurting the overall debt ratio. This was a practice that Zorinsky ended on the grounds that it discriminated against Omaha taxpayers and led to unsavory relations between realtors and politicians. Unfortunately the 1977 development procedures, updated in March 1980, did not solve the fundamental reality of how to control growth in Omaha. The city continued to expand to parts of the "zone of present development," particularly southwest into Millard, an old country town annexed prior to the Zorinsky administration; and outside the Omaha city limits new SIDs went unannexed. This had the effect of leaving mill levies in Omaha artificially depressed and at the same time keeping valuable land off the tax rolls. Projections showed that growth would continue in the "zone of present development;" so at some point a change in policy appeared inevitable. A direct impact of curtailing annexations was a rather dramatic population loss. The 1980 census showed Omaha with 311,681 people, down over 36,000 from 1970. In the same period the SMSA as a whole added over 27,000 inhabitants, for a total population of 570,399. Omaha badly needed a comprehensive growth development plan.

View of Downtown Omaha, 14 September 1979

The circumstances that brought about a prolonged debate over the texture of the urban experience in Omaha and the creation of a development plan was a general economic advance of the 1960s and 1970s. The railroads, rivers of rust during the Great Depression, again served as avenues of commerce. Despite the phasing out of passenger business and the advent of Amtrak, the Union Pacific continued as it had for over a century, to lead the way over the plains and on to the West Coast. The road's media advertisements—emphasizing its role in building the West, its status as a "great big rolling railroad," and its future—served as indication of its continued important position in the life of Omaha. A survey by *Fortune* magazine showed that in 1975 the Union Pacific, with sales of $1.7 billion, ranked as the nation's fourth largest transportation company. The railroad's spacious headquarters building in downtown Omaha was an obvious symbol of its role in constructing the city.

Trucks and planes further enhanced Omaha's position as a transportation hub. It was a center of long-haul truck business, functioning both as a national and regional terminal. This activity had roots in the overland freighting of the 1850s that during the gold rush in Colorado had brought Omaha its first prosperity. Air transport added another element. The municipal airport renamed Eppley Airfield in honor of Eugene C. Eppley, a prominent Omaha aviation pioneer, philanthropist, and hotel owner, underwent a major expansion. During the 1960s approximately $10 million went toward such major projects as a new terminal and improved runways. The Omaha Airport Authority raised money from a number of sources: the Eppley Foundation, federal grants and matching funds, state appropriations, and revenue bonds. Moreover, Omaha's two major carriers, United Airlines and Braniff International, both added to their terminal facilities. Passenger traffic increased markedly in the decade, but there were disturbing aspects. No major airline had established headquarters in Omaha; there was no direct overseas service; and with the advent of long-range jets, few transcontinental flights stopped in the city. Even so, future progress seemed assured.

In contrast to transportation was what happened in the meat packing industry. Neither the promise of incentives by the city government nor appeals to tradition by South Omaha leaders prevented the major companies from pulling important operations out of Omaha; they came for callous reasons and left the same way. Three of the "Big Four" moved away within two years of each other in the late sixties: Cudahy in 1967, Armour in 1968, and Swift in 1969. Wilson held on a little longer, curtailing operations in 1976. These dreaded developments cost Omaha more than 10,000 jobs, plus an estimated $500 million annually in wages, services, purchases, and taxes. Several causes led to the closings. The largest were age and obsolescence. The major components of the Omaha plants had all been built prior to World War One and some dated back to the previous century. By 1966 seventeen modern slaughterhouses operated in small towns and rural areas in eastern Nebraska and western Iowa. A plant in Dakota City, Nebraska, which had fewer than five hundred employees, slaughtered 25,000 head of cattle a week. An Omaha establishment required the services of two thousand men to kill the same number of cows in a similar period. The owners had experienced frequent labor problems in the late 1950s and 1960s, when they tried to introduce automated systems. Union officials claimed the companies deliberately made impossible demands that they used as excuses to close down. Federal directives designed to stop the pollution of the Missouri River were another irritant to the packers. They spent time and money on solid waste disposal systems which never worked properly.

Direct stock buying was the final blow to Omaha's chances of remaining a packing house center. Buyers went directly to producers, bypassing terminal markets; and small towns offered inducements to packers to build plants much as Omaha interests had done decades earlier. The "Big Four" left not only Omaha but Chicago and Kansas City, diversifying operations throughout the central states, bringing an abrupt halt to a colorful and important period in metropolitan industrial development.

As the plants pulled out, a livestock spokesman in Omaha tried to put as happy a face as possible on what was, after all, a very depressing situation. In 1968 Robert B. McCreight, the new president of the Omaha Union Stockyards Co., said he saw "no reason for dismal gloom" and predicted that Omaha would grow as a livestock marketing center. McCreight noted that some of the small decentralized plants had already become good customers and maintained that he had a success formula to turn things around in Omaha, claiming: "An aggressive market can render services to both buyers and sellers. Here again it's a job that takes team effort." His rosy assessment failed to halt the decline. Omaha lost its number one positon as a livestock market; and in 1973 a New York firm bought the stockyards company, ending ninety years of local ownership. Statistics illustrated the downward course. In 1960 the yard handled 6.2 million cattle, calves, hogs, and sheep. The number dropped to 5.2 million in 1965; and as plants closed, it fell to 3.3 million in 1970. Five years later receipts amounted to 2.5 million, mostly for 1.2 million cattle and 1.2 million hogs. By then, after being the world's largest livestock market from 1955 until 1973, Omaha had fallen to third. While the stockyards remained important, the glory days had, at least temporarily, ended.

Dire warnings that the curtailment of "Big Four" operations would bring an economic catastrophe failed to materialize. Cheery predictions by Omaha politicians that turning the old packing house area into an industrial park—demolition experts flattened the huge Armour plant in eight seconds in 1971—had little impact. The attracting of new business to the park, such as the Mid-Continent Refrigerated Service Co. that employed less than thirty persons, was cosmetic. What was important was that the general prosperity of the American economy in the 1970s overrode the closing of obsolete facilities. Most of the senior unskilled workers in the packing houses were old and close to retirement. Younger men moved into other jobs with little effort. Retirement benefits and unemployment insurance softened the blow as did other employment opportunities. National recessions in 1971 and 1974-75 had only a short-term impact on Omaha. By then, the packing house workers had retired or been absorbed into the greater local economy. Throughout the boom years that characterized the 1970s, Omaha continued to add to its industrial work force. In 1979 over 25,000 people, more than double the number engaged at the end of the Great Depression, worked in Omaha industry. Meat packing still occupied the services of almost four thousand. Added to that were another sixty-nine hundred individuals in general food processing. While more than 14,000 employees held additional manufacturing positions—3,000 in metals, 3,250 in printing, and 8,400 in a host of other classifications—food stuffs continued basic to the Omaha employment market. Such was the potential and demand that a few local experts expected Omaha to escape easily the ravages of a sharp downturn of the American economy in 1980. The comparative ease with which the city absorbed those thrown out of work by "Big Four" closings tended to buttress that assumption.

The further rise of Omaha as an insurance center was another reason why experts believed continued good times lay ahead. In the 1960s and 1970s Omaha emerged as a possible rival to such older established northeastern insurance centers as Hartford, Boston, and Philadelphia. By 1967 Omaha insurance companies employed over eighty-five hundred men and women in white collar jobs with an annual payroll of $34 million. In seventeen years, yearly premiums had increased from $190 million to $600 million. The Omaha-based companies dealt in three broad kinds of insurance: life, casualty and liability, and accident and health. During the 1970s, new construction by the leading businesses gave evidence of progress. The Woodmen of the World built a huge skyscraper in the heart of downtown. Given its location high on a bluff, the imposing clean-lined structure could be seen from many miles away, serving for many motorists as the first indication that they neared Omaha. Mutual of Omaha, the best known nationally of the city's insurance concerns, twice added to its gigantic office complex, located several blocks west of the business district. Even though Omaha had not become "the Midwest Hartford," as proclaimed in booster brochures, excellent management and aggressive advertising had combined to create a growing, profitable and formidable insurance industry. The future appeared bright, like a rising star.

The federal government continued to play a very visible role in Omaha's economy. City officials, battling mountains of paper work required by authorities in Washington and inundated with overly detailed and in many cases incomprehensive directives, voiced bitter frustration. They opposed federally financed urban renewal projects and violently attacked the government in general. (What they wanted was federal money with few strings attached.) It made little difference who was president – John Kennedy, Lyndon Johnson, Richard Nixon, Gerald Ford, or James Carter – the message was the same. The coincidence that Ford had been born in Omaha was of no consequence; it was one thing to honor the man by building a monument at his birth site and another to support his urban policies. Republican Ford's strictures against New York may have impressed some people, but it failed to change things in Omaha. Despite his desire to curtail government intervention in the cities of America, Ford followed policies designed to further federal involvement. The course was set earlier in the century, in the middle of economic calamity; and there seemed no turning back. Although Ronald Reagan hoped to drastically cut federal aid to cities, his emphasis on defense spending ensured a continuing flow of money from Washington.

Many federal activities helped Omaha. Offutt Air Force Base continued to pump great sums of money into the local economy.

Old Woodmen of the World Building, March 1977

Several Strategic Air Command bases closed in the 1960s, but there was never any question of that happening to Offutt which remained SAC headquarters. SAC's role changed and broadened in accordance with the development of new weapons delivery systems; and with the advent of guided missiles with nuclear warheads, Offutt remained a major American defense component. In 1968, at the height of the war in Vietnam, the installations' population numbered 36,000 airmen and their dependents; and an additional 2,000 civilians worked there.

Offutt Air Force Base, 1963

Another military organization, the United States Army Corps of Engineers, continued to develop plans for flood control-recreation projects in the Omaha area. During the middle 1970s the Corps ran into major criticism from citizens' groups when it proposed the construction of a whole series of dams around the environs of Omaha as part of the Papillion Millard project. The opposition was part of a general adverse national reaction to corps policies; countless critics claimed it had become a bureaucratic monster that had lost all sense of direction and built dams for the sake of building dams. In Omaha, following political pressure and revelations of what appeared inflated payments for land at dam sites, the corps backed down, dropping plans for several dams. Even so the corps' Omaha office, as it had for a long time, spent considerable money every year in the city and its environs. Most of the funds went for Missouri River improvements, and by the end of the 1970s river traffic was greater than at any time in the days of steamboating.

More spectacular was the tremendous amount of money expended under the Interstate Highway Act of 1956, the poverty programs of the Lyndon Johnson administration, and revenue sharing. Two great links in the interstate system passed through the Omaha SMSA: east-west I-80 and, on the Iowa side, north-south I-29. Another two roads completed the local net. I-680 was a belt route that semi-circled Omaha to the west and north; I-480 ran through the center of town. The total cost came to over $140 million; ninety percent was from the federal government. Much of the money came without a great deal of fanfare, granted in routine bid openings that received little publicity. Other projects received more notice. Great Society programs, reminiscent of the New Deal and designed to bring sudden social equality for blacks and the urban poor in general, brought in millions. So did allocations in the 1970s; first and second round appropriations to help the concentrated jobless under a public works act amounted to $20 million. No one wanted to admit it, but without such monies Omaha might have returned to a state of depression. The city's ability to gain government favors, plus more equitable distribution under revenue sharing and other measures, served well, although the programs were not always welcome. The expressway system broke up or destroyed old neighborhoods. The placing of a job corps center in a former downtown hotel frightened shoppers. Too much revenue sharing money went for projects where it was hard to see a tangible return. In particular, however, critics attacked Great Society measures, noting that the Omaha programs failed to prevent the racial trouble that divided the city in the 1960s.

Events that led to an increased dependency on the federal government had complicated the local impact on the Omaha power structure. Even though the Knights of Ak-Sar-Ben installed a king, queen, and other potentates every year, regardless of depression or war, no individual or set of individuals inside Omaha dictated the course of community policy; those decisions seemed to lie elsewhere. The times were not right for another Dennison, Dahlman, or Wattles. There seemed no way for the city's traditional leadership to reassert itself. After suffering decisive defeats in a couple of elections–especially one in 1958 calling for an economic plan that opponents charged would help "the silk-stocking crowd"–wealthy people tended to move into the background. Contrary to what some of the farmers had envisioned in 1956, the successful battle for a charter change had not resulted in a return to a government run by the business interests. A major and unintended result was to help define a new coalition of voters from moderate and low income areas who tended to vote against the big interests. The result was a further business withdrawal. In 1966 Paul Williams, the former managing editor of the Omaha *Sun* publications, made an influential study of the city's leadership. He focused in on the problem by stating in his first sentence, "There is a gap about twenty years wide and three elections deep in Omaha's power structure." He found the most powerful men in town, those who had "the money, prestige, time and a desire to do good works," had stopped trying to frame a comprehensive community policy. Instead, they continued to serve on each others' boards and to raise funds for each others' pet cultural and welfare projects without much thought to a larger policy. What happened was what one source, experienced in both civic and political leadership, called "a sort of power vacuum."

Noting endless variations within the power structure, Williams identified "Twenty Influentials," all business leaders. Insiders claimed that physicians and lawyers were primarily important only in their fields. Medical doctors had numerous divisions of their own between different hospitals and specialties; and as a source said, "They know too much." Lawyers functioned as paid consultants for influential interests and had to operate along lines dictated by the needs of their clients. It went without saying that labor leaders were excluded from the upper levels of community affairs, except when their presence could not be ignored, or when they accepted invitations to support bipartisan projects, such as charter reform. The wealthy women in Omaha showed little inclination to exercise community power on a grand scale or to play major philanthropic roles. No new Sarah Joslyn came to the fore.

Williams believed that little more than 1/20th of 1 percent of Omaha's population had the desire, the skills, and the resources to move the city ahead. He thought part of the problem was that many of the "Twenty Influentials" had been in command positions for too long a time, some for as many as thirty years. It made little difference if they held considerable power, if they had no inclination or way to use it effectively. Moreover, new men, either from inside or outside Omaha, found it much more difficult to gain entrance than had been the case prior to the 1930s. Under the selection process that prevailed in the 1960s, aspiring civic leaders were at least ten years away from entering the inner power structure. Newcomers were expected as a first step to win the support of the hierarchy for a "good" community project, one that would be measured against prevailing conservative business standards. "Even if a young aspirant 'makes it' as a campaign fund-raiser and moves up to general chairmanship of a charitable group, he may not consider himself an insider until the majority of 'power elite' people nod at mention of his name, or insist on his presence on their boards and committees," Williams asserted. "The senior executives continuously test the aspirant for willingness to work hard at recruiting and organizing people, for recognition and protection of the diverse interests of persons involved, for ability to 'put together' a project."

Those desiring to advance into the upper strata of the power structure accepted the long and tough screening process as a necessity. Was it worth it, given the virtual impossibility of exercising real leadership and the endless possibilities for criticism? What difference did it make when federal regional administrators were usually faceless political appointees and bureaucrats from the outside who remained for a short time before moving on, exercised greater power over individuals, controlled huge monetary resources, ducked criticism by hiding behind difficult-to-understand policy directives, and cloaked stupid decisions in the common good? An elderly member of the elite in Omaha, admitting that the process of gaining entrance to the leadership group was disappointing and frustrating at times, thought that if a person believed in the community it was necessary to simply keep plugging away. Sounding an optimistic note, he stressed the need for involvement: "I'd encourage anyone who wants to make a better community to join and really be active in organizations that are open to him. There are very satisfying roles open for anyone who wants to work, and I feel it's important to any of us to be able to make a positive contribution." The somewhat idealistic statement ignored reality; the power group in Omaha was in many ways a closed society. And, it ignored the ultimate social reward: election and coronation as King of Ak-Sar-Ben.

The "Twenty Influentials," as was only to be expected, had impressive credentials. They carried the titles associated with power in American commercial and industrial life; among them were presidents, chairmen and executive vice-presidents, and secretary-treasurers. Some exercised influence as a result of family connections; others had climbed up the corporate ladder in the city's major commercial, industrial, and financial enterprises. Omaha *World-Herald* owner, philanthropist Peter Kiewit, was president of Peter Kiewit Sons Co., the large construction firm. Frank P. Fogarty served as executive vice-president of Meredith Broadcasting. Bankers included John F. Davis, president of the First National Bank, and Edward W. Lyman, president of the United States National Bank. Leo A. Daly headed the Leo A. Daly Co., an architectural concern. Richard W. Walker directed the Byron Reed Co., a real estate and investment corporation. A. W. Gordon was chairman of the Omaha Loan and Building Association. Two members came from the flourishing insurance industry: V. J. Skutt of Mutual of Omaha and Clarence L. Landen of the Central Insurance Group. From food processing came Gilbert C. Swanson, the president of Swanson Enterprises, and Erhard D. Edquist, the chairman of Fairmont Foods Co. There were two officials of the Northern Natural Gas Co., the chairman of the board, John F. Merriam, and the president, Willis A. Strauss. Another utility executive was President A. F. Jacobson of Northwestern Bell. Vice-President Willard D. Hosford, Jr., of the John Deer Plow Co., had an industrial background. So did Kenneth C. Holland, the former president of Carpenter Paper. John F. Diesing was secretary-treasurer of J. L. Brandeis & Sons, and Morris E. Jacobs served Bozell & Jacobs Advertising as chairman of the board.

It was arguable whether all these men belonged to a "power elite." They were not the only leaders in Omaha with impeccable credentials; and some of them doubtless felt their inclusion unfair, feeling they had been singled out as responsible for an alleged lack of community leadership. Yet there was no argument about one other name. That was that of Edd H. Bailey, president of the Union

Pacific. As had been the case for over a hundred years, the chief operating officer of the Union Pacific automatically wielded power in Omaha. Of course, the question in 1966 was just how much of a force, given the drastic changes over the previous twenty-five years.

Local politicians hovered on the edge of the power structure, heeded or ignored in direct relationship to the extent that their policies and actions pleased the business community. Members of the city council had small power bases, usually associated with neighborhood needs or a specific interest group, and only in rare instances access to large amounts of private money. Given the constraints, about all they could do was to concentrate on winning support for pet issues, serve the needs of constituents, and keep making an occasional headline to remain in the public eye. This was a predictable result of a return to a mayor and council system. So was the switch to an elected mayor. Despite the aims of the framers of the new charter, the holder of the office was not in a position to chart a course for Omaha. Getting elected and maintaining a political base required the building of support throughout town. This necessitated the making of various commitments which by their nature acted as restraints. Holding the mayor accountable for day-by-day administration did not help much either. The natural inclination was to force the mayor to pay attention to a great deal of minor matters, if only for protection against possible charges of official misconduct. The biggest problem of all was money. No mayor had the kind of economic power necessary to exercise wide control over events.

The mayors were either from outside the power structure or on the fringes. None—even A. V. Sorensen who helped write the document—fulfilled the expectations of the charter framers. They had hoped for an all-powerful executive capable of charting and implementing a community policy. As critics claimed, the changes were cosmetic, relating to modernizing the structure of government but not at giving a mayor significant new power. The second mayor elected under the new charter was James Dworak. He was a thirty-five year mortician and two-term member of the city council. Charges of corruption tarnished his administration; he suffered an overwhelming defeat when he ran for reelection. A Chicago builder, John Coleman, claimed that Dworak and others had solicited bribes from him in return for the rezoning of land for town houses. Ultimately, two city councilmen and a real estate man were convicted for accepting bribes; a member of the planning board pleaded no contest to a misdemeanor charge of malfeasance in public office, and Dworak won an acquittal after an eight-day jury trial. To say the least, this was inauspicious for charter government. Embittered by his experiences, Dworak left Omaha and moved to California. In a 1975 interview he lashed out at one of Omaha's most prestigious institutions, stating: "If the people of Omaha think Chicago has a political machine, they should try to look at the internal workings of the governors of Ak-Sar-Ben. They control millions of dollars that no one has authority to investigate." Dworak claimed that his administration had many accomplishments: housing for the aged, golf course construction, revamping of the police communications system, and "cooling" of racial unrest. He failed to mention that during his term many Omaha leaders severed connections with City Hall.

None of the mayors who followed Dworak over the next fifteen years had to face a jury. However, they did have to restore the prestige of the office in the eyes of the business community, and that was not easily accomplished. A. V. Sorensen, AVS for short, served ably as mayor in the last half of the 1960s, declining to seek reelection. Sorensen, as a result of his contribution as head of the charter convention, had emerged as a civic leader, following the traditional path into the inner circles of Omaha society. His quest for mayor hurt his chances. He had trouble attracting establishment support when he considered running for mayor in 1961 and received strong business backing four years later only after he won a primary election. Although he did much to improve relations between the city government and influential citizens, Sorensen freely admitted that he was not part of the power structure and that he had abandoned his aspirations to become mayor. When he became mayor he resigned from the board of the Omaha National Bank. An "insider" of "means and influence" said, "He does not have the power in terms of dollars or people of his own to put on a project." Another person acquainted with the ways of power in Omaha explained: "He can deal with them, but he doesn't get entangled with them. He stays apart." AVS had to pay a price. That was to accept the views of senior business leaders and to resist dramatic changes. He summed up his own term when he said: "When I took office, we had an administration which was . . . well, less than the people had a right to expect. My job was building a good staff, fostering a favorable climate for new industry and developing pride of people in their community. I think we got that done."

Omaha had four mayors in the decade after AVS left office. Eugene Leahy, first in line, was a former Iowa farm boy and Marine Corps staff sergeant. After leaving service, he worked his way through Creighton University, graduating from law school in 1960. He entered politics with the help of a political power broker and soon became a presiding municipal judge. Displaying a dynamic personality, he gave hundreds of speeches in which he attacked drug abuse and "dirty books." Gaining the support of over four hundred different groups, he won a surprisingly easy victory in 1969. As mayor he rode elephants, read Sunday funnies on television, gave several hundred speeches in one four-month period, and delivered tirades against the city council. He gained a reputation as a "people's mayor," a "City Hall jester," and as "Omaha's Harry Truman." He stressed a traditional version of "progress"—a larger city through annexation, an increase in public services made possible by a rise in the federal funding and a broader local tax base, and a stepping-up of efforts to attract new industry. In the first three years of his administration the city budget rose from $42 million to $70 million, primarily at his urging; and he obtained a $4.8 million grant from the Economic Development Administration to help develop the South Omaha Industrial Park. Leahy was hard to classify from an ideological standpoint. At times he sounded like a Barry Goldwater Republican, at others like a George McGovern Democrat. He had no establishment credentials but in general followed policies favorable to the business community.

Leahy's immediate successors were Edward Zorinsky, Robert Cunningham, and Al Veys. All three faced rising inflation, taxpayer hostility, and post-Watergate morality. Zorinsky was forty-three years old at his election in 1973. A chemistry and zoology major in college, he had run the H. Z. Vending Co. for over twenty years and had served for fourteen years in the military police reserve. He had gained stature as a member of the board of directors of the Omaha Public Power District by questioning the method of distributing engineering contracts without competitive bidding. As mayor, he established a controversial Office of Management and Budget to keep track of what was going on in city departments. Even though he sometimes criticized the business community—he said the Union Pacific had unloaded a "white elephant" on the city when the railroad donated its Omaha station for a museum—he took credit for projects designed to further historical preservation, extend freeways, and build libraries. He followed an "open door" policy and tried to broaden his political base. In 1976, after a sudden switch of party allegiance, he was elected as a Democrat to the United States Senate; and Cunningham filled out his term, acting as interim mayor. He allowed the OMB to fall into disuse and ran a caretaker administration.

Veys, who won election as a write-in candidate to a full four-year term in the spring of 1977, operated Veys Foodland grocery store in South Omaha. One of his early moves was to abolish the OMB. "I don't need a middle man to go between me and my department heads," he explained. Veys liked to meet in an informal gathering at the end of every working day with his top advisors to discuss policy and thrash out differences. His whole approach was less frenetic than that of either Leahy or Zorinsky. An assistant allowed: "A lot of people look at style rather than substance. Al's not a flashy guy. Al's not a spell-binding public speaker. Al's just a helluva administrator." Mayor Veys sought to hold down spending, while at the same time promoting the growth of Omaha. So, no matter what his style, he followed traditional policies.

A major goal of the city government and important segments of the business community during this era was to obtain funds to revitalize downtown and the river front. Leahy, when he had declined to seek reelection, had become the chief executive officer of the Riverfront Development Foundation. He had helped to establish the RDF, founded by business interests in 1971, as a vehicle obstensibly intended to secure private and public funding to revitalize a roughly two-hundred-square mile "project area" along the river, mostly in the Omaha vicinity. Critics charged that it had the broader purpose of creating a "shadow government" headed by Leahy that would circumvent the electoral process to exercise broad authority over decision-making in the Omaha SMSA, despite disclaimers to the contrary. Willis Strauss, one of the "Twenty Influentials" and chairman of the RDF board, said, "Gene was under pressure to announce something . . . you know this was a quiet little foundation until the mayor announced his intentions." Yet the involvement of important people and the sources of money seemed to negate that observation. It fit into the overall Riverfront Development Program.

Funding for RDP planning and construction flowed from four different sources: federal grants for specific park and recreation programs, matching local and federal monies, state contributions, and private assets. B. P. Pendergrass, the director of the RDP staff and a retired Corps of Engineers officer, said: "I would be very surprised if we weren't asked to comment on any major housing or park project development in this area. . . . We can get input and reaction from a broader constituency than any other entity." Hopes for RDP were very high during the administration of Richard Nixon; local leaders talked of great federal grants and the spending of countless billions of dollars. By 1980, while some significant results had been achieved, the broader designs of RDP had yet to reach realization; and RDF had fallen far short of becoming a metropolitan government.

The RDP had an important part in getting downtown development off of dead center. A major feature involved a Riverfront Land Use Plan that called for dramatic changes in the Omaha Central Business District. Fundamental to success was a widely-heralded "Return to the River" concept, representing an attempt to connect the center of the business district with the Missouri River. The plan called for a great green mall a block wide and close to a mile long running through the heart of the CBD, west to east, to the bluffs overlooking the Missouri River. Below, in the river valley, would be a housing development of over a thousand units called Marina City. The project was very popular with business interests that owned property within the proposed mall. Dozens of buildings inside the limits were old and dilapidated structures that had long since outlived their usefulness. In 1975 the scheme, designated the Central Park Mall, started to become a reality. A year later most of the site had been cleared at an estimated cost of $15 million, almost entirely in federal funds. By decade's end, the great mounds of dirt and the signs of destruction that marked progress puzzled visitors, calling to mind havoc wrought by World War Two bombing raids on urban areas. The mall, originally scheduled for completion in 1981, promised to provide Omaha with a central core park, a small version of Central Park in New York. The Omaha Central Park Mall gave evidence of fulfilling its designers' fondest expectations: to afford Omaha with a unique urban symbol, one of historical significance cut from the city's original design.

There were other indications of functional change in and around downtown Omaha. Gary Carlson, an economic coordinator for housing and community development for downtown interests, wrote in 1976: "What we don't need is a 'Status Quo' feeling about Downtown. What we should look for is how can we help to eliminate the existing functional obsolete and promote economic stability and vitality. To do this we must have a vocal public support as well as commitment by private business and government to provide the atmosphere for redevelopment and change."

Heart of Old Market District, 13 September 1979

Scene in Old Market District, May 1976

265

Starting in the middle 1960s Samuel Mercer, who owned several of the buildings, led the way in turning a four-block section of the then declining wholesale and jobbing district into a fashionable and quaint shopping and restaurant area. The efforts met with considerable success, demonstrating the possibilities for rejuvenating older structures by changing their original functions; in one instance a tenant converted the loft of a former banana warehouse into a stylish apartment. In another, a narrow alley became a skylighted arcade lined with specialty shops. By the 1980s the Old Market District had become a tourist attraction, nominated as a national historic district. It was complemented by a significant preservation project. A city-sponsored non-profit organization, the Omaha Performing Arts Center Corporation, restored the Orpheum Theater to the splendor it had enjoyed in 1927 when it opened as one of the nation's leading "movie palaces." Gala ceremonies in 1975 transcended many controversies over the structure. In a short time, the former movie theater attained eminence as Omaha's performing arts center, drawing renewed attention to the CBD. Despite the razing of many buildings, including in 1977 the city's original skyscraper, the Woodmen of the World Building, Omaha did much better than many other American metropolises in preserving its architectural heritage.

During the 1970s, the construction of gigantic edifices was a crucial element in the rejuvenation of Omaha's business district. A multi-million dollar public library graced the western edge of the Central Park Mall. The city and county shifted many administrative offices to the new Omaha Douglas Civic Center, partly financed by a grant from the Eppley Foundation. Both private and public funds contributed to the building of a downtown educational center for the University of Nebraska at Omaha. The Union Pacific Railroad added a large addition to its headquarters, and the Northwestern Bell Telephone Co. spent $25 million for an office building. The new Woodmen Tower was the tallest building on the upper plains. A campaign for a new first-class hotel culminated in the erection of the Hilton Hotel. Just to the northeast of downtown, Creighton University added a number of buildings. The largest was the gigantic new St. Joseph Hospital, a 784,000-square-foot facility that cost in excess of $65 million. "For several years now, people have been reading and hearing about the redevelopment plans for downtown Omaha and wondering when it was going to happen," a booster article proclaimed. "Guess What? It's happening now." However, there was a major setback. In the fall of 1980 J. L. Brandeis and Sons, Inc., despite promises of a long-

The Omaha Theater, September 1975

Downtown Redevelopment, November 1975

standing commitment, closed its downtown store. And, in another unexpected development the Hilton became the Red Lion Inn.

A few observers questioned the need for massive downtown redevelopment, or the motives that lay behind some of the activities. The large amounts of public money spent in the district caused concern. People wondered if it might have gone for better purposes; and there was a suspicion that while malls, preservation projects, and up-to-date public buildings were all to the good, a main result was to line the pockets of powerful Omaha businessmen. Even the Hilton Hotel had controversial overtones. Within a short time after it opened the Fontenelle Hotel closed its doors, raising the possibility that Omaha had not needed two large hotels and that the existing one could have been renovated for a lot less money than it cost to build a new one. In addition, environmentalists worried about erecting large hotels and offices in an already congested part of town. Other groups deplored the destruction of older buildings. The old Woodmen of the World Building became a symbol; the UNO educational center built on the location had a smaller amount of square footage. To some, there was a sinister conspiracy of architects and builders. The Leo A. Daly Co. designed many of the new structures and the Peter Kiewit Sons Co. erected several of them Of course, there were those who just did not think the buildings looked very good. Leo A. Daly, when asked about that in 1977, observed: "Some feel that our architecture in Omaha lacks the appeal . . . of other parts of the country. It might be a shade more conservative than, say architecture in Los Angeles, Las Vegas or Florida, but, all in all, I would think we have a good quality of architecture in Nebraska and I would hope it continues to be good." No one denied that, for better or for worse, there had been a great deal of major construction in Omaha.

The 1960s and 1970s saw a questioning of cherished values in the Omaha business community. The objections raised to continued growth caught leaders off guard. Although few restraints resulted, careful planning seemed a necessity. Unfortunately, the sudden demise of meat packing showed the pitfalls of planning. At the end of World War Two, no one in a policy position in Omaha had considered that a possibility. Another imponderable was federal involvement. The amount of federal money varied from administration to administration, and upon conditions. In the 1920s no one could have predicted the programs of the 1930s. In 1980 it was impossible, given skyrocketing inflation, high interest rates, the

Downtown Redevelopment, 14 September 1979

world situation, and the election of Ronald Reagan, to know what would happen next.

And there was still the issue of leadership in Omaha. The charter change had not strengthened the office of mayor in the way originally envisioned. Internal authority now seemed to rest in the hands of a small group. Knowledgeable sources called them "The Big Five." Three had been members of the "Twenty Influentials" of 1966: architect Daly, insurance executive V. J. Skutt, and Northern Natural Gas board chairman Willis Strauss. Two newcomers were John C. Kenefick, president of the Union Pacific, and Jack McAllister, president of Northwestern Bell Telephone. Although it was wrong to assume that these men formed a cabal that manipulated Ak-Sar-Ben and ran the city over lunch at the Omaha Club, they did represent a rationalizing of community decision-making. They all had interests far beyond Omaha; they all had experience dealing with the federal government, and they all had ideas of what was best for Omaha. Despite talk in the immediate postwar era of involving all Omahans in the administration of the city, a few business leaders continued to predominate. The successful pushing of downtown redevelopment served as evidence. Early in the 1980s, over fifty years after the start of the Great Depression, men such as those who comprised the "Big Five," following in the tradition of earlier city builders, appeared to have control over affairs.

10

I Sensed a Restlessness

During the 1960s the cities of America came under severe attack. Presidential aspirants spent campaign time talking about sick cities and how they intended to heal them. No previous candidates of the major parties, with the possible exception of Franklin D. Roosevelt in 1932 and 1936 when he cloaked matters in terms of relief and recovery, had even discussed what they would do about the urban parts of the country in such direct ways. By the 1960s, however, cities not only mirrored the society, they were the society. Any major problem, domestic or foreign, either had an impact or roots in urban centers. Time-honored agrarian values of Jeffersonian democracy no longer seemed relevant. The United States had become a nation of cities.

The urban crisis came to Omaha in the form of racial unrest. In 1960, according to the census, the city had 25,212 blacks: 12,332 males and 12,880 females. By 1970 there were 34,431 blacks, with the increase coming primarily as a result of the last stages of the general black migration from the South to northern cities. Although there were fewer blacks in Omaha than in many other metropolises, the grievances of the city's black community were much the same as elsewhere. The 1964 Civil Rights Act had little local impact, except for ending covert discrimination in certain public accommodations. Omaha never had a formal segregation system; denial of rights took subtle forms. The vast majority of Omaha blacks lived in a jammed-in district on the Near North Side. Few black youths went to college or for that matter finished high school. Job opportunities had not improved measurably since the Great Depression. A 1965 report by a Creighton University political science professor, Rene Beauchesne, concluded that for Omaha blacks educational levels had little effect on upward employment. "Being a Negro," Beauchesne's report contended, "in a white man's society apparently disqualified many people and made the 'American Dream' hardly more than something for the 'white folks.' " Militancy spread among blacks in Omaha. Ernest Chambers, a Creighton graduate, barber shop operator, and emerging black leader, gained a following and received media coverage for his anti-establishment views. He headed a committee of the Near North Side Police-Community Relations Council which presented to city officials a long list of complaints against Omaha police practices. All this was somewhat puzzling to whites, used to having the Omaha Urban League and the local chapter of the National Association for the Advancement of Colored People claim to speak for blacks at large.

Mayor A. V. Sorensen said that he felt that blacks would make more rapid progress if they got together and agreed upon what they wanted. In what he intended as a well-meaning comment, Sorensen pointed out that Omaha blacks needed a "leadership which can speak in a united voice for the Negro community like the Chamber of Commerce does for the business community or B'nai Brith does for the Jewish community." He indicated his respect for several Omaha black leaders including Lawrence W. M. McVoy, president of the NAACP, and Douglas Stewart, Urban League executive director. Sorensen said he had met with Chambers, "although he has heaped a lot of abuse on me." The mayor indicated that he would "be perfectly glad" to call a top level conference to discuss minority complaints against policemen. This was in March 1966, eight months after the bloody Watts civil disorder in Los Angeles had focused national attention on the plight of urban blacks. Few whites in Omaha envisioned such a thing happening in their city. After all, Nebraska was not California; and unusual things always seemed to happen on the West Coast. Omaha blacks were reasonable, so whites thought when Sorensen claimed his administration was "maintaining communication" on race matters. It turned out that was not enough.

The first of two disturbances that broke out in Omaha in the summer of 1966 occurred during an early July heat wave. For three straight nights there were confrontations between black teenagers and the police. Trouble developed after youths gathered late at night in food store parking lots; as one observer said, they were the places to go, in lieu of recreational facilities. Rioters threw rocks and bottles, smashed windows, and looted several stores. The owner of a hardware store reported the loss of six guns and twelve television sets. A few vehicles were damaged. Most of the action occurred along North Twenty-fourth Street. The police made sixty arrests, concentrating on containing the mobs and holding down violence. On the third night the police had trouble with a milling and rock-throwing crowd of around 150 people and authorities called in a small contingent of steel-helmeted Nebraska National Guardsmen to restore order. They cleared the streets without violence as those involved quickly dispersed. It was one thing to taunt the police and another to face troops carrying guns and bayonets. That ended the first wave of racial trouble in Omaha. Injuries were few and minor. Damage was minimal. There were no fires or sniping. The only gunfire came when police fired a couple of warning shots into the air. At another time the affair might have been written off as a product of teenagers letting off steam during a period of very hot weather, but times were not "normal" in 1966. Any clash involving urban blacks assumed grave implications.

A general consensus that the rioters acted spontaneously and received no direction failed to prevent instant sociological observations about the causes. Chambers and young blacks who met with Mayor Sorensen on the last day of the disorders attacked the police response, giving no specific reasons beyond suggesting that arrests the first two nights inflamed the crowd. In addition, they complained about unemployment and a lack of recreational opportunities. Sorensen said, "I can't say that they were happy with me but they had a good chance to tell their grievances." He did not believe the incidents racial in character. Asked what role the City Human Relations Board should assume, he replied: "I don't agree this is a problem of human relations. That implies racial relations. Nothing I saw suggested that this had a racial impact." A member of the board tended to disagree, claiming that both police and blacks involved in the fracas appeared "edgy" and that lawmen ordered "people around like animals." Governor Frank Morrison of

Nebraska, in the middle of an unsuccessful bid for a seat in the United States Senate, was in Los Angeles attending a governors' conference during the Omaha disturbances. In a telephone interview with a *World-Herald* reporter he blamed "an environment that is unfit for human habitation in many areas," rejected force as a solution, and expressed faith in the ability of Sorensen and "the Negro leadership of Omaha."

The Omaha black ghetto exploded again for three nights in a row in early August. The outbreak was in many ways similar to that of the previous month. Again, there was no special pattern, although a safety official blamed events on "a number of hoodlums out for looting." As before, groups of black teenagers milled around on North Twenty-fourth Street in the late evening and early hours of the morning. Rocks were thrown and there were several arrests. Roving groups smashed windows and looted stores. There were a number of fire bombings as unidentified individuals, responding to two dozen shotgun blasts fired skyward by police to scatter a crowd of 150, hurled Molotov cocktails through several display windows. While few of the fires caused extensive damage, one destroyed the interior of a cleaning establishment burning a large quantity of clothing. Several places hit during the July rioting were targets a second time. Sorensen visited businessmen in the stricken area. He discounted rumors that there was any relationship between the violence and the shooting death a few days earlier by the police of a suspected young black burglar. Taking a hard line, he indicated, "We simply are not going to tolerate this lawlessness, whether it is teenagers or young adults." Urging black parents to keep closer track of their children, he warned, "Many whites wish to help the Negro achieve first-class citizenship, but this lawlessness stiffens attitudes and makes it difficult to help." The vandalism ended and conditions on the Near North Side returned to normal.

There was no rush to social revolution. The City Council responded by cutting the budget of the Human Relations Board from $5,000 to $1,750. An aide to Mayor Sorensen confided: "This city is conservative in any case, and there seems to be a lot of suggestions that someone stirred up trouble. For some of these men in the Council it is a natural conclusion that any trouble stirred up would be stirred up by those fellows from the Federal government and the Human Relations Board." Right or wrong, this was not an approach calculated to bring racial progress. Obviously, two steps taken after the July riots, the opening of two ghetto recreational centers and the promotion of job opportunities for black youths, had not been enough to prevent more violence. There were still thousands of unemployed black teenagers, all part of a larger problem. In addition to a lack of opportunity, black Omahans complained about the drabness of their surroundings, the failure of authorities to enact open housing legislation, the virtually segregated nature of the school system, and the consequence of police brutality. None of these points of dispute appeared ripe for early change, and the same was true of prevailing racial attitudes. "We must remember," the chairman of the Human Relations Board reminded city officials, "that no man, black or white, can truly believe he is equal unless the majority of society around him treats him as an equal. And, as long as the majority persists in treating the Negro as a second-class citizen, we will have angry outbursts against the double standards of American democracy."

Predictions that further trouble might come at any moment proved wrong, and there was no further rioting in the summer of 1966. Nor did any serious disturbances happen the following year. A variety of social programs seemed to improve matters to the point that the head of the Human Relations Board thought Omaha on the road to racial harmony. A few black militants and white social activists pointed out that all the fundamental problems remained, but no one took them very seriously. Despite some inflammatory "black power" rhetoric, serious racial turmoil appeared over in the city. Unfortunately, it was a lull.

In March 1968 a week of assaults, vandalism, fire bombings, and fear followed a disturbance at a rally for presidential hopeful George Wallace, former governor of Alabama, in the City Auditorium. When the controversial Wallace appeared to address a crowd of fifty-four hundred persons a group of less than forty sign-carrying black and white demonstrators, strategically situated in front of the podium, booed and jeered, throwing sticks and pieces of wood at him. The obviously agitated Wallace denounced his tormentors, bellowing: "These are the free-speech folks you know. And these are the kind of folks the people of this country are sick and tired of." When many of the blacks sat down after being asked to clear the aisles, Wallace continued, "Those responsible for a breakdown of law and order are not the majority of American people, but a group of activists, militants, and communists." There was renewed disorder—more jeering and thrown sticks—and Wallace stood back, asking the police to clear the aisles. Officers, who had quickly lined up in front of the speakers' stand, did just that, forming a flying wedge after a black youth apparently swung

275

a fist at a police captain. The lawmen swept the dissenters from the building. A journalist for the *World-Herald* described the scene. "Folding chairs flew," he reported, "nightsticks cracked down on heads, and some police used a chemical spray designed for crowd control. Some of the audience jumped in with fists and boots. . . . It was over inside the hall within five minutes. But outside, nine windows were broken and here and there a fight between opposing forces." Comments made afterward were predictable. Black leaders charged that the police used excessive force and that the demonstrators had in effect been led into a trap, guided by Wallace's supporters to a conspicuous place in front of the hall. Mayor Sorensen contended the police acted "superbly" in what he called a clash in an "emotional environment" between "black power advocates and white bigots." He added that he hoped Wallace would not return to Omaha.

The days of black rage that followed the Wallace disturbances caused less destruction than those of 1966. An off-duty policeman armed with a riot gun shot and killed a sixteen-year-old black male after he refused to halt on command, but it was unclear whether his death was related to an attempted jewelry store robbery or to racial strife. Only a few other persons required hospitalization and there were not many arrests. Yet the trouble had a more direct impact on white Omahans, because it spilled out of the ghetto. There were numerous incidents at Omaha schools, including the large downtown Central High School. Black students chanted "Black Power" slogans in the study halls and frightened teachers and white pupils. Black teenagers broke windows at several schools; and at predominantly black North High School, there was trouble in the parking lot as roving gangs of blacks taunted the police. Fear swept through the white community. People temporarily kept their children at home. At almost entirely white schools, there were disruptions caused by rumors that "they" — meaning blacks — were on the way to spark violence. As quickly as it had come, the trouble passed. There was no new outbreak, even after the murder of Martin Luther King, Jr. which touched off severe civil disorders in many large American cities.

The primary result of the Omaha disturbances was to at least temporarily polarize sides. Ghetto opinion crystalized around charges of "unresponsiveness." City officials warned of the consequences of violent acts by members of both races. "Why don't they do what every minority did?" a white housewife from the west side of town asked. "Why don't they pick themselves up by their bootstraps?" A black laborer in the ghetto, informed of the remark, replied: "They tell me to pick myself up by my bootstraps. Why, hell, they've taken away my boots."

Throughout the 1970s race continued in the forefront as an Omaha problem. In 1970 three nights of rioting and burning swept over the Near North Side in response to the shooting and killing of a fourteen-year-old black girl by a police officer. Other disturbances followed, but no major outbreaks occurred in the ghetto during the rest of the decade. In a sense, the riots served a purpose; they conclusively demonstrated the gulf that existed between blacks and whites. As an outgrowth, there were genuine efforts to open lines of communication and to solve ghetto problems. Upon detailed examination, the gap between the West Omaha matron and the black laborer did not appear imsurmountable. In addition to being a matter of race, it was one of understanding one another.

There were other reasons for the relative calm. The police became more skilled at riot control and came under pressure to be fairer in dealings with blacks. Militants lost favor ("black rage" could only go so far as a policy) and either moderated their stands or gave way to others with a milder message. Chambers went into politics and became a state senator. While much diversity remained in the black community—certainly, one thing whites learned from the confrontations was that blacks did not speak with one voice—there was a reestablishment of Urban League and NAACP leadership, along with that of the black churches. Of paramount importance was the channeling of money into the ghetto for jobs and social action programs. Increased efforts to aid black teenagers in the summer months helped prevent a recurrence of what happened in 1966. While some of the funds came from city, county, and state sources, the greatest amounts flowed from the largesse of the federal government, even under Republican administrations. Any opposition stemmed from charges of waste and corruption in the running of specific projects; the influx of Washington monies was taken for granted. So was government involvement in the school system. A shrill but limited outcry was heard in the fall of 1976, when the Omaha Public Schools started busing students as mandated by the United States Eighth Circuit Court of Appeals. The school board worked closely with the court to work out a plan. An interracial committee, Concerned Citizens for Omaha, which had strong business backing, helped to prepare citizens for the transition, as did the local media. Even though there had been no millenium, the Omaha racial climate appeared better on the surface in 1980 than in 1970.

Related to racial disharmony was a quickening of white movement to the suburbs. This process, which started after World War Two with the building of the first tract subdivisions in Omaha, had a dramatic impact on housing patterns. Many older neighborhoods underwent fundamental changes. South Omaha progressively deteriorated. By the 1970s Omaha had less than five thousand immigrants. While many of the older foreign-born continued to live in the old "Magic City," it had lost much of its old ethnic flavor. However, most of the members of Omaha's Hispanic community lived in South Omaha. There was little in the way of new construction; many houses had fallen into varying states of disrepair; I-80 divided the community; and the commercial district had badly decayed. Although many second and third generation Omahans, usually of modest means, resided in South Omaha, many other people had moved away. "We don't visit South Omaha much, partly because it isn't the same," a former resident wrote. "Oh from time to time a group of us will drive into near-downtown South Omaha for lunch in the original steakhouse territory, and I still get a kick out of negotiating those narrow, steep hills and admiring those small, peak-roof houses. South Omaha has character." South Omaha's problems mirrored those of other older parts of town.

An area of West Omaha called New Rockbrook, roughly covering 1970 Census Tract 69.02, which contained many winding roads and numerous stylish homes, served as a prime example of the kind of new neighborhood in which Omahans aspired to live. Census statistics indicated the medium house valuation was $43,752, and that eighty percent had been built since 1960. Of the 8,854 residents, forty-four percent were under eighteen years of age and two percent more than sixty-five years old. Over ninety-nine percent of the people were white, and fifty-eight percent had attended college. The median income of $16,638 was higher than other parts of town. By the 1980s there was a great deal of talk, much of it related to the energy crisis and rising housing costs, about a return of the middle class to the inner city. However, statistics showed that the outward march had not stopped, and that its racial character remained unchanged. Suburban blacks remained few in number.

Omaha benefited from other major developments that went a long way toward solving long-standing problems in higher education. At the start of the 1960s, college educational opportunities for

Omaha high school graduates were somewhat limited. The closest major public institution was the University of Nebraska at Lincoln. Well-known nationally for its consistently fine football teams, which had a large and enthusiastic following in Omaha, it had evolved over many decades into a respectable university, with a broad range of undergraduate and graduate programs. Of special note was its agricultural school, an important component of Nebraska's, and hence Omaha's, economy. Renowned for contributions to basic agricultural science, the agricultural school's course of study held little attraction for Omahans who numbered roughly half the students on campus. They tended to major in the liberal arts, business, and engineering, all fields that could be taught just as well and effectively at other locations. The University of Nebraska as a whole had an active extension division, but its most obvious presence in Omaha was the University of Nebraska College of Medicine. This large health science center brought an ever-increasing amount of money into the community. Even so, it was more of a hospital than a school; and its educational components had small numbers of students. It was inaccessible to all except a few fortunate and talented Omaha students.

That left two local choices, one private and the other public. Jesuit-operated Creighton University had a large endowment, impressive property holdings, rigorous entrance requirements, and relatively high tuition. In addition to a liberal arts college, Creighton had several professional schools including those in medicine, pharmacy, dentistry, and law. The nationally recognized Roman Catholic university had an excellent community image. It was the alma mater of many of Omaha's leaders. In the 1960s school officials began a modernization program, building new dormitories, classrooms, a library, and massive medical facilities. Creighton, which had under five thousand students, was a selective undergraduate and graduate institution. It was not designed to serve the educational needs of all segments of Omaha life.

The other alternative was the University of Omaha, in the early 1960s one of the few remaining municipal universities in the United States. Established by local Protestant leaders as a private institution in 1908, it gained municipal status—and much-needed governmental financial backing—in 1931 after a close election and a court challenge. The university eventually erected a large administration building with money authorized under the Public Works Administration. The school attracted many fine young faculty, but was unable to keep most of them. There was no emphasis on research at

OU; critics considered it a glorified high school—"West Dodge High"—that served as a sort of tax-supported trade school for the business community. The library was very small. Faculty members had heavy teaching loads and little time for research and writing. By the middle of the 1960s, when OU had six thousand students, Omaha had as poor public higher education as any city of its size in the United States. There was a crisis, albeit not an obvious one; there were no riots or shrill statements.

Affairs at the University of Omaha reached a critical stage in 1965, when Milo Bail left after sixteen years as president. He had resisted major changes. "Bail was a tyrant," Paul Beck, a respected and influential faculty member, recalled. "He held everything in his own hands." Bail's successor, Leland Traywick, assumed office when colleges throughout the country were upgrading their roles and scopes. Students were plentiful and leading graduate schools accordingly increased production of Ph.D.s in almost all fields; under the right direction "instant Harvards" appeared within reach. Traywick wanted to change the intellectual atmosphere at OU and to allow more faculty participation in decisions. He moved too slowly for the faculty and too quickly for the regents, who forced him out after less than two years in office. His contribution was to call attention to deteriorating circumstances, complicated by the rejection by the voters of tax levies designed to increase OU support. In an age of educational plenty, the institution lost students and money. The solution was the same as in other states—a merger, almost always with a larger university in a smaller town, and the creation of a "system." After a publicity campaign, lengthy negotiations, and legislative action, in late 1967 the Omaha electorate approved merging OU with the University of Nebraska. While much remained to be done, for the first time the opportunity and resources appeared at hand to build a fine public higher educational institution in Omaha.

The new University of Nebraska at Omaha aspired to become an "urban university." This apparently meant that it hoped to offer quality education and to marshal the necessary resources to solve a wide range of urban concerns. President Kirk Naylor, who had a major role in engineering the merger, said: "We're virtually building a new university. It is a great challenge and a great opportunity. We are changing the image of the university to that of a great urban institution. We hope to have the same relationship to the city that land grant universities have had historically to the agricultural areas." He planned to measure success in terms of the impact of UNO on the community, rather than in regard to scholarly papers written or doctoral degrees awarded. "The time has passed when we can simply issue a report on something so pressing," he indicated, referring to a proposed technical education center in Omaha. "What is necessary now is to make definite decisions about what has to be done, and push for the changes. In other words, the university has to cease always proclaiming neutrality, and once in a while, stand up to say 'This is right, and it should be done. . . .' When we are interviewing a prospective new faculty member these days, that's one of the first questions we ask him — Does he want to get involved in community problems and is he willing to take the time to help the university in its goal of addressing itself to urban problems."

Over the next decade the university underwent an impressive expansion, adding several hundred faculty members and a number of programs. By the end of the 1970s, the campus boasted 15,000 students, a sizable number by national measurements. The "urban university" concept took different turns than expected. Development followed rather traditional lines. Most research tended to be basic rather than practical. No matter how well intentioned the motives, few faculty had the expertise or the training to solve urban problems. There was also a great deal of strife. Powerful forces on the Lincoln campus fought a desperate delaying action to prevent UNO from gaining equal status, by keeping control of all graduate programs. Naylor resigned in 1971 over internal matters. One clash after another between the administration and faculty over prerogatives followed, culminating in unionization. Despite the significant improvement in quality at UNO, the severity of the conflicts prevented the university from attaining its full potential.

Other Omaha cultural agencies experienced vicissitudes. Many of the difficulties related to the change of Omaha into a white collar town. For the first time in the city's history there was a broad interest in cultural pursuits. However, this had not as yet translated into a more comprehensive funding of institutions. The Joslyn Art Museum, long considered the city's most prestigious institution, had a succession of problems with conditions reaching serious proportions in the 1970s. Lagging contributions and rising costs forced financial retrenchment and public requests for funds. The museum cut back on educational programs and drastically curtailed art purchases. Before anonymous donors came to the rescue, it appeared at one point that the Joslyn would have to sell off around $1 million in art works from its collections as a temporary

Joslyn Art Museum Interior Court, April 1977

282

measure to solve a growing deficit. Some critics contended that the troubles were a direct result of the Joslyn's elitist orientation. They argued that the building had a "stuffy" atmosphere, that it rejected twentieth century art, and that its permanent exhibits, especially the parts that emphasized nineteenth century Americana, had little general appeal. One gallery had a series of display cases filled with varied materials intended to illustrate the history of the Omaha region; a number of old covered wagons of the kind used in Nebraska settlement ringed the center court. Less than 150,000 persons visited the museum annually; and many of those came to view special temporary shows — the art of Norman Rockwell, the photographs of Lord Snowdon, and paintings of University of Nebraska "Big Red" football players. A Jamie Wyeth exhibition drew six thousand patrons in a week; the rock group Chicago attracted eleven thousand people in a single night concert in Omaha. Creighton University's basketball team, which played in the Missouri Valley Conference, had over nine thousand spectators for many games. The Kansas City Kings of the National Basketball Association drew well for the games they played in Omaha during much of the 1970s. A minor league American Association baseball team, the Omaha Royals, averaged over 200,000 fans annually during the course of the decade. The art gallery appeared stagnant by contrast.

In 1975 the Joslyn management tried to generate interest through an energetic advertising campaign. It featured such slogans as "Joslyn — Your Friendly Neighborhood Art Museum" and "A Little Culture Never Hurt Anybody." The effort, which temporarily sharply increased attendance and attracted some new members, alienated the Joslyn's traditional constituents, the advocates of art for art's sake and the affluent contributors. The former scorned what they considered "baby talk" and attacked the concept of featuring celebrities rather than leaders in the art field. "Public relations is all right," said a critic, "but the Joslyn needs to do more for art." The latter felt the "selling" of the Joslyn undignified and uncalled for, cheapening the end product. In response, the director claimed that museums throughout the country were all trying similar methods to curry favor. Manya Nogg, chairman of the drive, said: "A lot of people are intimidated by the Joslyn before they ever go in. My big crusade is to let people know we're not that stuffy and we do care. But every time we try something kinky like 'a little culture never hurt nobody' we get all kinds of people on our backs telling us we're too facetious." Even though all those directly involved believed the Joslyn important to community life, there were no easy solutions. Wishful thinking about the possibility of solving everything through a $5 million gift that never materialized proved just that. Changes in directors accomplished little. By 1980 hopes for a renaissance rested upon a change in policy that would see to a phasing out of the covered wagons and some of the other Americana that seemed to have little relationship to art. Whether the changes would help remained to be seen.

Raising operating money was the biggest problem faced by Omaha's many and varied cultural institutions. One reason for the Joslyn's troubles was that inflation forced it to look for additional finances; its endowment, which had seemed large fifty years earlier, was no longer enough. By the 1970s Omaha had a number of small performing arts companies that added to the richness of community life. Most lived hand-to-mouth existences, hoping that someday a benefactor would come along and put them on their feet. In addition, there were such larger and better-publicized organizations as the Omaha Symphony Orchestra, the Omaha Civic Opera, the Omaha Community Playhouse, the Henry Doorly Zoo, the Orpheum Theater, and the Western Heritage Museum. Their funds came from several sources. The orchestra and opera relied on ticket sales, foundation grants, a close working relationship with UNO, and federal aid. The zoo, operated by a non-profit organization, received several hundred thousand dollars annually from city coffers. The Orpheum Theater, donated by Ak-Sar-Ben to the city, received an annual public appropriation. The Western Heritage Museum, founded in 1973 by a non-profit organization, had its headquarters in the former Union Station, given to Omaha by the Union Pacific Railroad. A proliferation of cultural institutions was a relatively recent phonomenon. Few had roots more than a decade old. Even the symphony, by local standards a long established institution, had evolved from the Omaha Civic Orchestra, a WPA project of the depression years. In effect, the city had few cultural traditions.

Although there seemed general agreement that the Western Heritage Museum, which planned to emphasize area history, was a good idea, its establishment illustrated the difficulties. The building needed work and it would take several years to develop exhibits that would make the operation self-supporting. Mayor Zorinsky, after he had alienated the biggest potential donor, the Union Pacific, by raising questions about why it gave the building to the city in the first place, tried to cut off a direct cash subsidy by the

Interior of Western Heritage Museum, 14 September 1979

city to the museum. He explained: "You have to have priorities. I think there would be a greater outcry if we closed the Orpheum than if the Western Heritage Museum folded. If I had the tax dollars to fund a museum, I'd rather spend them on a well-established one like the Joslyn, rather than one that hasn't proved itself, like Western Heritage. . . . The key to a AAA credit rating isn't to say yes to everyone who asks for money." The museum managed to survive the 1970s, mainly as a result of effective fund raising. Director Michael Kinzel sought to demonstrate that there were many people in Omaha with the means to do so who had never until approached contributed a dime to anything, except maybe the University of Nebraska football team. For one reason or another they were not interested in the Joslyn or the Omaha Symphony but in a regional history museum. By 1980 there seemed a growing recognition by civic leaders, the city government, and the public that a city the size of Omaha needed a well-rounded cultural mix. There were grounds for optimism about the future.

Another venerable Omaha institution, Boys Town, came in for criticism for supposedly having too much money. From a modest start in 1917 in an old Omaha mansion that housed twenty-five wayward boys, it became by the 1970s the best-known child care home in the country. Boys Town's fifteen-hundred-acre campus just west of Omaha was an incorporated village with its own mailing address. The seven hundred boys, who lived in what a publicity brochure called a "home-school-city," received an education through high school and learned vocational skills. The founder of Boys Town was Father Edward J. Flanagan, an Irish born Roman Catholic priest. When he had first visited Omaha in 1912 on his way to an assignment in rural Nebraska, he became so concerned about the plight of the poor that he soon returned to the city. "It was as if Heaven kept drawing him back to this city," his official biographers wrote, "as if some special job awaited him there." Under his leadership Boys Town, originally named Father Flanagan's Boys' Home, struggled along for many years, narrowly overcoming recurrent financial adversities. An excellent publicist, Flanagan had little financial talent, although he tended to think in grandiose terms. Before his sudden death in 1948, while on a mission to Europe to study youth problems for the White House, he believed his dream of a "city of little men" approached realization.

The turning point had come in 1937 when a Hollywood studio produced the immensely popular film "Boys Town," featuring Spencer Tracy as Father Flanagan and Mickey Rooney as a homeless youth. Through ingenious direct mail campaigns, Boys Town accumulated an ever-larger amount of money, most of which went into profitable investments. The managing board, under the jurisdiction of the Archbishop of Omaha, included many leading local business leaders and a few social workers. As the years passed, there was a nagging feeling that Boys Town had lost a sense of purpose; that it had not kept up with the times; and that business considerations superceded helping boys. On March 30, 1972, a special report that was to win a Pulitzer prize in journalism for the Omaha *Sun* newspapers showed that Boys Town had a net worth of $200 million and that the amount increased every year by around $25 million. The "liquid endowment" of $176 million was larger than that of any other of the nation's Roman Catholic schools. By way of comparison, Creighton's was $6.8 million and the University of Notre Dame's was $64.8 million. Boys Town had twice as much capital as the three top Omaha banks, and much more than any Nebraska industrial firm. Even though the endowment had risen to approximately $250,000 per boy, aggressive fund raising continued. A downtown Omaha office operated by Boys Town solicited donations by sending out 34 million letters annually, which contained heartrending appeals. The editor of *Sun* newspapers charged:

> Though millions of Americans have sent in checks and cash — most of widow's mite proportions — Boys Town has never felt it necessary to tell them where the money was going. Rather than relating its successes and reporting its accumulation of stocks, bonds, and mortgages, Boys Town has continued to plead as if it had the sheriff at the door and an empty coal bin. This approach bordered on institutional arrogance. . . . These are hard words, we realize. They are hard for us to write, and they will be an embarrassment to those in the Boys Town establishment who have continued to play the game of institutional safety.

In response, the directors made changes and initiated new programs. The money continued to roll in, and Boys Town became richer and richer.

Omaha continued to have trouble living down its old reputation as a prostitution center. By the middle 1970s there was no longer a clearly marked red light district, as there had been back in the heyday of the old First Ward. Prostitutes — one told a reporter that she and her colleagues preferred to be called "leisure ladies" — worked throughout the Omaha area. The lowest-priced "hookers," many of whom were on drugs, operated out of the dives in South Omaha.

Younger harlots frequented downtown go-go clubs and the vicinity of the Hilton Hotel. By general agreement, they considered Mondays through Thursdays the most profitable nights, because of the presence of visiting businessmen. "We can't do anything about them coming in here unless they are trying to hustle a guest," a security man at the Hilton indicated. "If they are wandering the halls, we escort them out, but if they aren't bothering the people, we don't do anything." Prostitutes could also be found in West Omaha. About thirty-five women, many of whom "moonlighted" in cover jobs, formed the hard core of the trade. An undercover officer noted, "They appear to be unorganized, though they do often know each other. A few work out of their homes, but most make the motel and bar scene." An added feature of the vice scene were outsiders who came in on special assignments, usually to entertain at parties or to solicit conventioneers, and then moved on after a couple of days. Omaha had few regular call girls.

Authorities, professing to deplore prostitution, claimed that they could do little about it. Mayor Eugene Leahy, a frequent opponent of vice when he served on the municipal court, launched no campaign. During 1970, the first full year of his administration, there were only forty-three arrests for pandering or prostitution. When asked, after a prostitution-related murder of a retired Army officer visiting from Florida, if he thought prostitution helped Omaha become a convention center, Leahy replied: "Absolutely not. The things that really lend to the image of a convention center are clean streets, a reduction in crime, being a safe place for men, women and children, day-time or night-time. When you have street walkers and pimps on the streets people are going to be set up." In reply, a vice officer scoffed: "This city is wide open for prostitution. All kind of riff-raff is coming in. There are women from Kansas City, Denver, California, and Texas. And they just couldn't operate without some kind of protection." Six years later, in the winter and spring of 1977, Robert Cunningham devoted part of his short tenure as acting mayor to a "crackdown" on what he called the "skin trade." The results were inconclusive. For a short time, the women left the streets and gravitated to truck stops on the urban fringe, returning after conditions quieted down.

During its first 140 years, Omaha had experienced only a few natural disasters. The great Nebraska droughts and grasshopper plagues of the nineteenth century, devastating to the economy, had no effect on local lives and property. Long hot summers and cold winters were a matter of course on the edge of the Great Plains. A

Tornado Damaged Motel, May 1975

Missouri River flood in 1881, considered "great" in retrospect, hurt
Council Bluffs more than Omaha. Another flood in 1952 caused a
few permanent relocations. Of more consequence was the terrible
tornado of 1913. People could only hope that similar storms would
miss Omaha. A favored theory held that tornadoes tended to go
around or jump over densely populated urban areas, even though
one smashed the Kansas City suburb of Ruskin Heights in 1957 and
another tore through Topeka in 1966. Omaha's turn came in 1975, a
year of unsettled weather that started when a blizzard, called the
"Century Storm," swept across the city for two days in January. It
had hardly been forgotten when very early in the tornado season, a
mammoth tornado with three tails struck the west side of Omaha
just before 5:00 P.M. on May 6.

The worst impact area was along Seventy-second Street, a main commercial thoroughfare. Instead of jumping or remaining aloof a great finger of the storm, which materialized out of the southwest, touched down and stayed on the ground for several miles, racing south to north along the street, smashing buildings in all directions before eventually rising and vanishing forever into the atmosphere. A stunned survivor recounted, "It was like being in a rainstorm of bottles, plaster, and everything else." Several persons died—many more would have if there had not been some advance warning—and property damage amounted to an estimated $100 million. A large motel complex was almost completely flattened. In the aftermath of the disaster rebuilding proceeded quickly, helped by federal funds. By 1980 few scars remained; parking lots, vacant spaces, or new construction covered the affected areas. No beautification or comprehensive renewal projects resulted. A disaster survey prepared by the Omaha City Planning Department indicated that survivors wanted to forget what happened as soon as possible.

Tornado Damage, May 1975

Aftermath of the Tornado, June 1975

   In the 1960s and 1970s Omahans worried more than ever before
in the history of the city about the quality of life. When they compared themselves to people in other parts of the country they
tended to feel inferior. Joseph Levine, conductor of the Omaha
Symphony Orchestra, noted this in a 1960 article, "Omaha, I Love
You," which appeared in the *Saturday Evening Post.* The maestro,
an easterner tired of world-wide touring, wrote: "It seemed to me
that Midwesterners wavered between intense pride in their
accomplishments and a feeling of deep inferiority. They took an
almost masochistic delight in running themselves down in front of
me, perhaps to watch me defend the considerable strides I thought
were being made. . . . I sensed a restlessness, an invigorating sense
of excitement in the air, where good music and art are still adven-
tures. It was a marked change from the East, where there is a sur-

feit of artistic events. There was no apathy, no boredom here." A decade later, Kenneth Woodward, the religious editor of *Newsweek* and a former Omahan, claimed the city suffered from a massive inferiority complex. As the 1970s progressed, Omahans remained defensive about their community. The attitude was, as a resident observed, "What in the hell ever happened in Omaha?" However, a 1974 study in *Harper's* by Arthur M. Lewis concluded that Omaha ranked tenth in quality among large places in which to live in the United States. Chicago, St. Louis, Kansas City, Denver, and Minneapolis-St. Paul were larger; but that did not dim the accomplishments on the edge of the Nebraska plains. Entrepreneurial leadership, outside decisions, and government aid, combined with geography and agriculture, built Omaha. Thousands of promotions failed; it prospered.

In the fall of 1980, viewed from the restaurant on the top of the Woodmen Tower, the Omaha Standard Metropolitan Statistical Area spread in all directions. To the north was Florence, the old Winter Quarters, the resting ground of many of the earliest whites to set foot in the area. South lay South Omaha, the erstwhile "Magic City," plus Bellevue and Plattsmouth. The headquarters of the Strategic Air Command occupied land once intended for city buildings. Council Bluffs was directly to the east. A place of hills, old buildings, twisting streets, and railroad yards, it essentially had ceased to exist as an independent community in-and-of itself. West from downtown Omaha beyond the Mutual of Omaha headquarters, block after block of structures built along gridiron streets numbered north to south and extensions of older roads with names such as Douglas, Leavenworth, and Dodge, sprawled over the Nebraska prairie. There was much to speculate about in the building of Omaha.

Sometime in 1853 an obscure ferry operator and small-time promoter, William Brown, stood on the Iowa side of the Missouri River and gazed across to the bluffs that would soon be part of Nebraska Territory. He decided it a good place for a town; and, as events proved, he was right.

Woodmen Tower, March 1977

View to the Southeast from Top of Woodmen Tower, 14 September 1979

Conclusion

1980-1997

11

We Don't Want a Bull on a Pedestal

Harl A. Dalstrom

In the period 1980 to 1990 Omaha's population grew from 313,989 to 335,795 and by 1994 to an estimated 342,862. Subsequent annexations brought the total to an estimated 348,894 in 1996. During the 1980s, Bellevue grew 42 percent, and its 1990 population of 30,982 made it Nebraska's fourth largest city. By 1994, Bellevue had an estimated population of 41,274, slightly higher than the figure for Grand Island, for many years the state's third-largest community. The Omaha metro area was then home to an estimated 662,801 persons, making it the nation's sixtieth largest urban center.

Omaha's transition from a blue-collar to a white-collar community, which started in the 1950s, continued through the late twentieth century to bring about a "new Omaha." In 1968, with the packing industry in decline and this new Omaha emerging, Mayor A. V. Sorensen asked the public to propose a symbol for the city. Just as the Arch had become the hallmark of St. Louis, Omaha needed a symbol to proclaim its role as "Nebraska's largest city, the gateway to the West." But Sorensen looked away from Omaha's past when he said, "We don't want a bull on a pedestal."

Although no official symbol for the city emerged, by the mid-1980s the Central Park Mall, the fulfillment of the much more grandiose Riverfront

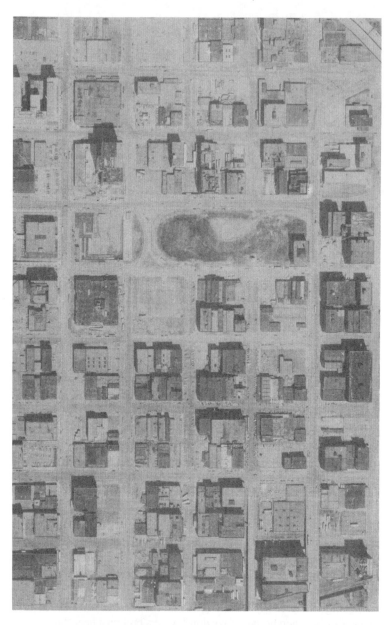

Aerial view of eastern downtown Omaha and riverfront, April 19, 1980. The cleared area that became Leahy Mall is visible.

Aerial view of eastern downtown Omaha and riverfront, April 15, 1995, showing the Leahy Mall and lagoon extending from just west of Thirteenth Street east to Eight Street. The Heartland of America Park, ConAgra campus, and lake show the redevelopment of the riverfront and warehouse area.

301

Development Program of the early 1970s, was the unofficial icon of the new Omaha. The Mall, a park at the eastern edge of the central business district, was largely funded from federal grants, and in 1982 its first major segment was completed from Fourteenth to Tenth Street between Douglas and Farnam Streets. Its main features included plazas, a landscaped embankment, and a lagoon that symbolized Omaha's ties to the Missouri River. In 1992, Central Park Mall was renamed the Gene Leahy Mall in honor of the mayor who had promoted riverfront development. A city bond issue funded the completion of the Mall from Tenth to Eighth Street in 1994.

The mall project reflected an emerging approach to city planning that emphasized making downtown areas livable as opposed to merely serving the needs of business. In Omaha, this approach prevailed after 1966 and reflected the city's reorientation from manufacturing and transportation to a service economy. Planning initiatives recognized that, because of the great territorial spread of the city and the attending changes in retailing and other activities, the downtown area no longer served the same functions as it had through the 1950s. In 1970 some 46,800 persons were employed downtown, but by 1996 only about 25,000 people worked there.

Although the Mall was basic to a new planning vision to make downtown a center of "people-oriented amenities," it also fostered redevelopment of the surrounding area. In 1982, a Chamber of Commerce representative, speaking of the nearby area, noted that "The Central Park Mall has stimulated $3.77 of private investment for each dollar spent." This construction was part of a pattern that between the mid-1970s and mid-1980s brought some $470 million in redevelopment expenditures to downtown.

The "Return to the River" theme of the early 1970s came closer to reality with the completion in 1990 of the Heartland of America Park. Adjoining the east end of Leahy Mall, this Douglas County project, linked to the new headquarters of food industry conglomerate ConAgra, Inc., was basic to the new image for downtown. The centerpieces of the Heartland of America Park/ConAgra campus were computer-controlled fountains and a lake. Early plans for a "Marina City" were too expensive to implement, but Omaha had a "new front door" that County Board Chairman Mike Albert likened to St. Louis's Gateway Arch.

Behind the completion of the ConAgra campus in October 1990 were events that challenged Omaha's ability to maintain its economic vitality and that demonstrated the power of the private sector in the city's decision-making process. The story began in 1985 with the plight of Omaha-based InterNorth, Inc. (formerly Northern Natural Gas Co.), a civic leader and local employer of 2,200 persons.

Operating in Omaha since 1930, Northern Natural Gas emerged under the leadership of John Merriam in the 1950s as a major pipeline and gas marketing firm. Merriam was strongly committed to Omaha's cultural life and was a vigorous advocate of the quality of life in the Northern Plains. Northern Natural's civic leadership continued under Merriam's successor, Willis Strauss.

In early 1985, the price of InterNorth stock rose sharply as a result of purchases by a corporate raider. A calculated expansion of InterNorth's debt could dissuade a takeover; accordingly, the firm determined to pursue a major acquisition that also would be an appropriate business addition. InterNorth thus acquired Houston Natural Gas, a major energy company. The $2.4 billion transaction placed a premium price upon Houston Natural Gas stock and assured HNG a strong position on the InterNorth board of directors. Particularly noteworthy was the agreement that Kenneth Lay, HNG's chief executive officer, would ultimately become CEO at InterNorth.

The details of the acquisition, especially the arrangements with Kenneth Lay, brought an estranged relationship between some InterNorth board members and chief executive officer Sam F. Segnar. As a result, Lay became CEO in November, 1985 – well before the previously arranged time. Because Houston was the premier city in the oil and gas industry, a shift to a Houston-oriented HNG/InterNorth operation was in motion. Although InterNorth had just built a $36 million headquarters on the western edge of downtown, Omaha's champions on the board of directors could not prevent this redirection. In November 1985, the board decided that Omaha would remain the firm's corporate headquarters while Houston would become the operational center. However, in May 1986, the HNG/InterNorth board voted to move the headquarters of the company – renamed Enron Corp. – to Houston. By 1991, Enron had only 250 employees in Omaha and its corporate donations to local charities fell from $2 million in 1985 to $484,000 in 1990. InterNorth's acquisition of Houston Natural Gas led to a serious blow to the city, and as a *World-Herald* headline put it, "Tail Wagged Dog, And Omaha Lost."

The loss of the Enron headquarters and its many well-paid professionals was a challenge to Omaha's civic leaders not soon forgotten. In retrospect, Omaha attorney and former legislator Vard Johnson said, "There was a genuine erosion of the spirit." Indeed, a *New York Times* article called Omaha "a city desperate for development." Incentives for economic development seemed essential, and as 1987 began, the administration of Nebraska's newly-elected governor, Kay Orr, would take vigorous action. The principal result was the legislature's passage that year of LB 775, a business incentive statute that strongly reflected the wishes of Charles M. ("Mike") Harper, CEO of ConAgra.

ConAgra symbolized the emergence of the new Omaha. Known as Nebraska Consolidated Mills until 1971, the company's enterprises had evolved from milling into a cornucopia of livestock feed and grocery products. But for a time ConAgra struggled with debt and commodity market setbacks, and new leadership was essential. The new leader would be Mike Harper, who came to ConAgra from Pillsbury Co. and brought ConAgra from an $11.4 million loss in 1974 to a $4.1 million profit in 1975. Over the next six years, ConAgra became an ever-bigger presence in the food industry and Harper rose to the chairmanship of the board. By 1985 ConAgra's earnings exceeded $90 million and the following year the company began to consider a new headquarters. Particularly ominous for Omaha was ConAgra's discovery that eighteen cities might be cheaper in terms of corporate overhead.

Given the Orr administration's desire to stimulate economic growth in view of the farm crisis of the 1980s and Omaha's anxiety after Enron's departure, Mike Harper and ConAgra did much to shape a revision of state law to favor corporate investment. At the heart of this 1987 revision were the Employment and Investment Growth Act, commonly known by its bill number, LB 775, and LB 270, the Employment Expansion and Investment Incentive Act. This legislation granted tax concessions to companies that invested in the state and expanded employment. When the Legislature balked at making corporate aircraft and computers tax-exempt, ConAgra said that it would relocate elsewhere. Hence, the tax package that became law reflected ConAgra's wishes. Although Kay Orr and her administration saw the business incentives as partly their handiwork, Mike Harper was the moving force in the tax revision.

The new tax laws assured that ConAgra would stay in Omaha, but the company had a prospective site on the northern outskirts of the city that did not square with the downtown redevelopment thrust. To get ConAgra to build downtown required that the city permit the demolition of Jobbers' Canyon, the buildings of Omaha's traditional wholesale district. These structures at the eastern edge of downtown had been nominated for the National Historic Register of Places in 1986, but Mike Harper saw the "big, ugly, red brick buildings" as an impediment to building a riverfront ConAgra headquarters. It would not have been necessary to raze the majority of the Jobbers' Canyon structures to make way for the ConAgra headquarters, but when civic leaders saw that ConAgra would not yield on the issue, Mayor Bernie Simon's administration fell into line to satisfy the company. In 1988, demolition in Jobbers' Canyon began and ground was broken for ConAgra's campus, an eighty-million-dollar project completed in 1990. Although ConAgra funded development of its thirty-acre campus, the city contributed to street and sewer redevelopment and the project received tax subsidization.

Just south of Leahy Mall and its rejuvenated surroundings was the Old

Market area of shops and restaurants that had emerged since the late 1960s as an entertainment area, drawing over 1,200,000 visitors annually. The new Embassy Suites Hotel on South Tenth Street adjacent to the Old Market and ConAgra was another mark of the vitality of the eastern downtown area. But with some exceptions, such as the Orpheum Theater and the Westin Aquila Hotel, downtown west of Thirteenth Street lacked vitality. Sixteenth Street had a pleasing appearance, but its heated bus stop shelters attracted panhandlers and other street people whose presence gave this part of downtown a bad image. As the *World-Herald*'s Kenneth Freed wrote in mid-1996, "Downtown Omaha is full of 'vacancy' and 'for rent' signs. Empty or barely occupied buildings abound, and there is no major convention center, a feature experts agree would attract other significant development."

Despite these problems, there were positive signs for the heart of downtown, such as land clearance for a new U.S. courthouse between Dodge and Douglas and Seventeenth and Nineteenth Streets. The future for northeastern downtown was also beginning to brighten, for in the autumn of 1996, First National Bank of Omaha, the Omaha World-Herald Co., and the city government announced projects that would begin the redevelopment of the area from Eighth to Seventeenth Streets and from Douglas Street to I-480. The scheme soon took clearer form with the announcement of plans for the conversion into a hotel of two warehouses between Ninth and Tenth Streets and Douglas and Dodge Streets.

The completion in 1991 of U.S. West's data processing facility and Landmark Center office building on the south side of Leahy Mall typified the redevelopment of eastern downtown and the city's adaptation to corporate change. U.S. West originated in the court-ordered reorganization of the Bell Telephone System in the 1980s and became the parent of Omaha-based Northwestern Bell Telephone Company, the principal provider of telephone service in a five-state region. Although U.S. West established its headquarters in the Denver area and eliminated Northwestern Bell, the firm remained one of Omaha's major employers.

Indeed, Omaha embraced the rapid change in the telecommunications industry and information age technology. The new competitive era in telecommunications brought the rise of MCI as a major name in long-distance telephone service and in the mid-1990s the company built a $100 million World Communications Park in northwest Omaha. A leader in building Omaha's position in telecommunications was MFS Communications Co., founded by Peter Kiewit Sons construction company in 1986. The value of MFS skyrocketed, and in a $14.2-billion stock transaction in December 1996 the company became a subsidiary of WorldCom, Inc., a Jackson, Mississippi, firm.

Omaha became the nation's chief center for telemarketing, and by 1991 over twice the number of people worked in telecommunications as in the packing industry. In 1995 the *New York Times* noted, "There are at least 30 telemarketing companies currently operating in this former corn-and-cattle town, and 20,000 or so Omahans – about 5 percent of the resident population – work for them dialing out more than one million quality calls per week."

A great telecommunications capacity arising from the presence of the Strategic Air Command at nearby Offutt Air Force Base, early availability of fiber optic telephone lines, and excellent service from Northwestern Bell contributed to Omaha's leap to primacy as a telemarketing center in the 1980s. Phone marketing from the Central Time Zone was an advantage as were the relatively unaccented speech of the telephone sales representatives, the Midwestern work ethic, and reasonable real estate and operating expenses.

Telemarketing was often stressful with scant chance of career development, yet it served the needs of many, particularly those wishing temporary employment with flexible working hours. However, other telecommunications jobs mushroomed as Omaha became the reservations center for a number of hotel chains and other firms using long-distance telephone service to reach a customer base.

The linkage between telecommunications, information age technology, and the service sector of the economy was demonstrated in the dramatic rise of Omaha-based First Data Resources. In 1969, some local banks cooperatively established the non-profit Mid-America Bank Card Association to process their credit card business. The non-profit status of Mid-America Bank Card ended in 1971 with its transformation into First Data Resources. Through the 1970s First Data grew, and in 1980 was purchased by American Express. The business later reemerged as a separate firm, First Data Corporation, which grew into an Atlanta-based Fortune 500 firm with many subsidiaries. Omaha was headquarters for a major unit, First Data Resources, which in 1996 employed some 6,250 persons in the city and was the metro area's largest private employer. By then, FDR electronically processed one-third of the nation's credit card business and handled other credit card functions. FDR generated 35 percent of the first-class mail in metropolitan Omaha.

Whatever the apprehensions about the local economy in the mid-1980s, the following decade brought economic growth. From 1988 to 1994, employment in Omaha rose 15 percent in contrast to 7.8 percent nationally. Although the service sector provided the highest employment growth rate in the country during these years, service sector growth in the Omaha area outpaced the national percentage increase. The service sector was the leading source of employment in the Omaha metro area in 1994, providing 31 percent of the jobs, in contrast to 16 percent in 1970. Data processing was a major component of this sector in 1994 as were health-related positions, the latter showing Omaha's continuing prominence as a medical center. The finance, insurance, and real estate category grew modestly in its portion of the local work force from 1970 to 1994.

During this time, construction jobs in the metro area rose 35 percent, compared to a national decline of 5 percent. Indeed, by the mid-1990s Omaha had a building boom. Transportation, communication, and utilities employed 7 percent of the local work force in 1994, in contrast to 5.2 percent nationally. Thus, Omaha retained part of its traditional identity, for more persons were employed in transportation, communication, and utilities in 1993 than in 1955, but the percentage of local people employed in this sector was well below mid-century levels. Trucking and warehouse work loomed large in the transport area in the 1990s. Omaha's Werner Enterprises, founded in Council Bluffs in 1956, benefitted from deregulation in the 1980s to become a major trucking firm.

The number of Omaha area jobs in manufacturing rose slightly in the years 1988 through 1994, while falling nationally. However, the average number of persons in the Omaha metro area employed in manufacturing in 1994 was below the 1970 figure. This trend, together with the relative decline of transportation and the growth of the service sector, indicated the long-term transition from a blue-collar to a white-collar economy.

Although transportation no longer occupied its old prominence in Omaha's economy, the Union Pacific Railroad remained a major force in the city. The 1980s witnessed the incorporation of the Western Pacific and the Missouri Pacific into the Union Pacific system. Through the Missouri Pacific, the Union Pacific acquired the KATY system and the Chicago and North Western gradually became part of the UP. In 1996, federal regulators approved the merger of the Union Pacific and Southern Pacific lines, thereby fulfilling Edward H. Harriman's early twentieth-century ambition.

The tremendous changes that made the Union Pacific the nation's largest railroad in route-miles had a mixed impact upon Omaha. Just south of the ConAgra campus, the railroad renovated its 1891 freight house into the Harriman Dispatching Center, which upon its opening in 1989 the company heralded as the world's most advanced rail control system. This operation centralized dispatching in Omaha and fit in well with the revitalization of the riverfront area and the city's emergence as an information technology center. By contrast, system expansion, particularly the acquisition of the Missouri Pacific, led to a 1988 decision to close the UP shops just north of downtown and handle shop work at North Little Rock. Accompanying the loss of the shops that employed some 800 persons was the pulling up of most of the adjoining tracks. Soon, much of the area where the Union Pacific's ground-breaking ceremony had taken place in 1863 was a weed-strewn expanse of unused land adjoining the highway between downtown and the airport.

Unemployment in Omaha, as in Nebraska as a whole, remained low, averaging under 3 percent. Through the mid-1990s, Nebraska had the nation's best figures on unemployment, but this fact had a negative aspect. With a small population and some out-migration of persons between ages eighteen and forty-four, Nebraska in the mid-1990s had a labor shortage which tended to force up entry-level wages. In the mid-1990s, some one thousand new jobs were being added in Omaha each month. The small labor pool may have contributed to Omaha's failure to induce Micron, an electronic technology corporation, and motorcycle manufacturer Harley-Davidson to establish operations in the city.

Overall employment figures obscured economic problems for some racial and ethnic minorities. From 1980 to 1990, Omaha's black population rose from 37,864 to 43,989, an increase from 12 to 13.1 percent of the city's population. In these years, Omaha's Hispanic population grew from 7,319 to 10,288 while the number of American Indians increased from 1,796 to 2,274. Omaha had a population of 1,769 persons of Asian background in 1980 and 3,412 in 1990. By the 1990s minorities composed some sixteen percent of the city's population. In 1990, the unemployment level was 22 percent for the city's American Indians, 13.4 percent for blacks, 5.9 percent for Hispanics, 3.5 percent for whites, and 3.1 percent for Asians.

Although some blacks attained managerial positions and the number of black-owned local firms rose markedly, the economic plight of many African Americans, including some entrepreneurs, remained bleak. In 1996 Omaha's black male unemployment was fourfold greater than that of the whole work force while black female unemployment was twice the overall rate.

In the 1960s, the black population had expanded westward from its Near North Side core east of North Thirtieth Street, and from 1970 to 1985 advanced well to the north and northwest of Ames Avenue. A primary pattern of northwestward expansion continued, but by 1995 black families were dispersed through the newer areas of the western and southwestern parts of the city as well. Nevertheless, according to 1996 data 41,951 black persons lived east of Seventy-second Street, but only 2,415 resided to the west.

In the meantime, the Near North Side – from Cuming Street to Ames Avenue and Sixteenth to Thirtieth Streets – steadily lost residents and business. Between 1960 and 1990, the population of this area fell from 29,655 to 9,190. Memories of the rioting of the late 1960s and a continuing perception that the Near North Side was a hotbed of crime undoubtedly hindered revitalization. The completion of the controlled access North Freeway in the late 1980s meant uprooted families and neighborhood disruption – an experience for black Omahans reminiscent of the impact of the building of I-480 through a working class white neighborhood a generation earlier.

By the late 1980s gangs and drugs were a major problem in Omaha as in other cities. Violence accompanying gangs and drug-dealing became a particular burden for the Near North Side and adjoining areas. Gang rivalry and drug-related crime continued through the mid-1990s and a *World-Herald* article headlined "Bullets Rain As Gangs Duel; Two Men Hurt" symbolized the worst social problems of Omaha and urban America.

This situation led to the formation in 1989 of a group known as "Mad Dads," which sought to create a strong presence on the streets of adult black men in order to counteract gang influence. The organization spread to other cities and won praise from President George Bush. Despite some early financial management problems, Omaha Mad Dads grew to one thousand members by 1996.

In the 1990s, as in the 1960s, police relations with the black community were controversial. Although black persons made up about 13 percent of Omaha's population, blacks numbered 43.3 percent of arrests made by Omaha police in 1994. According to State Senator Ernie Chambers, this was evidence of "out-and-out racism and discrimination." An approach to crime prevention known as "community policing," which emphasized youth programs and other elements of police-community liaison, did not find favor with officers and other persons who held to a more traditional view of police work. In any event, law enforcement was on the cusp of major social problems and a study indicated that white and non-white persons tended to have significantly different attitudes toward the police.

Deteriorated housing remained a severe problem in areas of North Omaha and a common answer was city-imposed demolition. In 1986, City Planning Director Marty Shukert said that there were between three thousand and five thousand vacant lots in the Near North Side. However, the administrations of Mayor Al Veys and his successor in 1981, Michael Boyle, shifted toward an "urban homestead" program by which federal block grant money was used to renovate deteriorated dwellings and to assist eligible individuals in purchasing these houses. Such funds came to be used for programs for home renovation, repair, and, in conjunction with private investment, expanding the supply of rental dwellings. Between 1986 and 1991, $21 million in federal money was channeled into housing redevelopment in Omaha.

The 1980s brought a move away from large public housing projects as the Omaha Housing Authority adopted a "scattered site" approach. Between 1991 and 1995 the units of OHA's Logan Fontenelle project, which dated from the New Deal era, were razed and in 1996 two other North Side OHA housing projects were demolished. Giving a refreshed look to the Logan Fontenelle area were the single-family units of Conestoga Place, erected by the non-profit Greater Omaha Corp. Persons displaced from OHA projects either went to scattered site dwellings or received subsidies to lease housing. As OHA Director Armstrong put it, "Social problems are magnified when you have large concentrations of low-income people in a small geographic area." Dispersion, he felt, "allows people to move into neighborhoods and not be identified as poor because of where they live." Although implementation of the scattered site program occasionally aroused racism, it is noteworthy that in 1995 twenty-two percent of the heads of household in scattered site dwellings were white.

The Omaha Public Schools retained a key role in shaping race relations, but court-mandated busing of white and black children to achieve racial integration remained controversial. White enrollment in the Omaha Public Schools plummeted in the 1970s and, largely because of this decline, black enrollment rose from 21 to 30 percent of the OPS total in the two decades after the start of busing in 1976. Although 10.4 percent of the Bellevue Public School students in 1995-96 were black, no other suburban district in the Nebraska portion of metro Omaha had a black enrollment exceeding 3.5 percent. The extent to which "white flight" contributed to this disparity could not be measured, but clearly the burdens and benefits of racial integration through busing were unevenly distributed through the metro area.

Whatever the impact of twenty years of busing on improving race relations and learning opportunities, passing time and demographic changes brought calls for modification or elimination of the program. Reappraisal of busing would be complicated by the fact that, as a group, black students in the mid-1990s – as a decade earlier – trailed white students in the reading, language, and mathematics scores of the California Achievement Test. The social and economic implications of this disparity were a formidable challenge to Omahans in the closing years of the twentieth century.

This era brought institutional changes that did much to give blacks political influence. The key figure in bringing about these changes was Senator Chambers, who since 1971 had been the outspoken voice of blacks at the state level. Because of the configuration of legislative districts, Omaha blacks had often served in the legislature, but blacks had never been able to build political bases large enough to win at-large elections for county and local offices. Through Chambers's efforts, the mode of selecting the Omaha Board of Education was changed from at-large to district elections in 1975. Four years later, he secured legislation requiring that Omaha City Council members, chosen at-large since 1912, be elected by district. In 1991, he brought about district election of the Douglas County Board of Commissioners. In 1981, computer programmer Fred Conley became the first black elected to the City Council; in the subsequent decade and a half, other blacks won election to offices chosen by district.

The substantial increase in Hispanic population was concentrated in the southeastern part of the city. Traditionally Czech, Polish, and Lithuanian areas that had given an East European image to South Omaha were now home to many Mexican-Americans or persons newly arrived from Mexico. This was also true of the census tract including "Little Italy." Jobs in Omaha's remaining packing plants drew many of the newcomers who faced hardships reminiscent of the experiences of immigrants generations earlier.

The latter years of the twentieth century witnessed an increase in the employment of women from 33.28 percent of the work force of Douglas, Sarpy, and Pottawattamie counties in 1960 to 43.40 percent in 1980 and 47.22 percent in 1990. Although women as a group continued to earn less than men, they were increasingly evident in professional and managerial positions. Women were ever more prominent as entrepreneurs, for in 1992 the Omaha metro area had 16,448 businesses owned by women, of which 2,452 had paid employees. The National Foundation for Women Business Owners estimated that between 1987 and 1996 the number of Nebraska businesses owned by women had risen 63 percent with a corresponding employment increase of 229 percent and a sales growth of 359 percent.

In 1978, the City of Omaha had an area of 91.54 square miles, but with a return to a more active annexation policy in 1982 grew to 111.56 square miles by 1996. As Omaha physically expanded, the city's population density fell from 5,933 persons per square mile in 1960 to 3,179 in 1996. Omaha continued its westward growth, which was only partly revealed in annexations. By 1990, more Omaha-Douglas County people resided west of 120th Street than in old Omaha east of Forty-second Street. During the 1990s the countryside west of I-680 between West Dodge and West Maple and northward was the prime area of upscale residential development.

In the 1980s the construction of new houses outpaced population growth in Douglas and Sarpy counties by nearly a two-to-one margin. A *World-Herald* headline, "Who's Buying Those Fancy New Houses?", undoubtedly posed a question in the minds of many Omahans. The City Planning Department noted in 1993 that "This increase in sales activity is primarily due to low interest rates which make it more affordable to buy a home. Homeowners are also taking advantage of low interest rates to 'trade up', enabling them to buy more house for the same amount of money." Part of the answer to the newspaper's question lay in trends in late-twentieth-century American life. Omahans of the post–World War II "baby boom" gen-

Suburban growth of the 1980s and 1990s: aerial views of area bounded on the north and south by Maple and Blondo Streets and on the east and west by 132nd and 144th Streets, April 15, 1980, and December 21, 1994. In the later photo, Eagle Run golf course is visible south of Maple Street.

eration composed a significant part of the new home market. Fewer children per household, more divorce, and increased longevity contributed to a housing market boom. Corporate executives moving to the city and affluent professionals comprised a market for expensive houses. A diversified, prosperous local economy undergirded this impressive growth.

Although expansion was a boon to the economy, it devoured farmland and cast a shadow over the future of older parts of the city. Between 1960 and 1990, Omaha's population east of Forty-second Street fell from almost 200,000 to 113,000. In the area from Forty-second Street to Seventy-second Street, population reached 105,000 by 1970, but by 1990 only about 90,000 persons dwelt in this mid-city area. As the western areas came to

symbolize newness and affluence in contrast to the image of a large part of the older section C. David Kotok of the *World-Herald* noted that "Omaha may be becoming, in effect, two cities – one east of 72nd Street and one west." The newspaper clearly showed in a 1997 series of feature stories that incomes and housing values in the newer, western sections of the city were on the whole much higher than those in Omaha's older, eastern districts. Moreover, new employment was heavily concentrated in the west. Although suburban growth meant more tax revenue, it brought added demands for municipal services. The increasing distance and the sharp social and economic differences between the newer and older parts of the city had disturbing implications for the future.

Urban sprawl eroded Omaha's 1970s-era status as a "20-minute city" – the normal time needed for driving between home and work or most crosstown trips. Increasing traffic volume – the result of social and economic trends – brought congestion, and arterial street and highway construction inevitably produced bottlenecks. Efforts such as the 1989-94 project to extend the Kennedy Freeway to Bellevue, eased the situation. Paradoxically,

Aerial views of the University of Nebraska at Omaha in 1971 and 1996, looking west. When the Municipal University of Omaha moved to its Dodge Street
location in 1938, the campus was at the western edge of the city; by the 1990s
the campus was slightly east of Omaha's center.

314

the completion of the Kennedy Freeway contributed to major suburban growth in Bellevue. More auto traffic brought declining use of public transportation; between 1988 and 1996 passenger volume on Metro Area Transit buses fell by about thirty percent. From the frontier era through the Cold War, military spending had contributed to the economic well-being of the Omaha area. Reorganization of the command structure of United States nuclear forces following the Cold War brought the abolition in 1992 of the Strategic Air Command, whose headquarters had been at Offutt Air Force Base since 1948, and the establishment of U.S. Strategic Command (StratCom). This and other changes brought a significant decline in personnel at Offutt, but the base remained a major Air Force installation. Moreover, the prospect that defense restructuring would deal a hard blow to Bellevue did not materialize.

The period 1977 to 1994 was an exceptional time in Omaha politics. Following his write-in success in the 1977 mayoral primary, South Omaha grocer Al Veys defeated veteran city council member Betty Abbott in an election that showed that some Omahans were "not ready for a woman" as mayor. In 1981, Veys, seeking reelection, lost to Michael Boyle, a lawyer and former Douglas County Election Commissioner. Differences on issues were minimal, but the thirty-seven-year-old Boyle gave a more dynamic, "progressive" image than the sixty-two-year-old Veys. Mike Boyle and his wife, Anne, had strong family ties to the Democratic Party, and his bright political future was illustrated as he easily won reelection in 1985.

But in 1986 Mayor Boyle's fortunes plummeted and by year's end he faced a recall vote. Police problems – often nettlesome for Omaha's political leaders – were central to Boyle's difficulty. As early as 1981 Boyle and the police clashed when the mayor objected to the 1:00 A.M. presence of off-duty officers outside a bar. In October 1985, Boyle's brother-in-law, John Howell, was charged with driving while intoxicated. The significance of the incident escalated following allegations that Howell's arrest resulted from improper police surveillance. An investigation led to discharge or other penalties for four police officers, but Chief Robert Wadman refused to approve the sanctions against three of them. In October 1986, the mayor fired Wadman, contending that the chief had sought to block the probe in the Howell affair. Boyle had also objected to traffic and other citations against his sons and had reportedly told a deputy police chief that no parking tickets were to be given to his family.

Boyle's firing of Wadman convinced many Omahans that the mayor was unfit to remain in office. By November a group known as Citizens for Mature Leadership had enough signatures to bring about a recall election, later scheduled for January 13, 1987. Although Boyle admitted to "excesses," he did not retreat from his dismissal of Wadman. The Boyle-

Wadman episode revealed the tensions within the Police Division, for the Omaha Police Union and Fraternal Order of Police vigorously backed the mayor.

"Whirlwind From West Blew Boyle Away" read a *World-Herald* headline following the recall vote, which by a margin of fifty-six to forty-four percent expelled the mayor from office. Omaha's western areas strongly supported recall while eastern areas generally gave strong support to Boyle. Although the recall was unprecedented in Omaha's history and a political oddity for an American city, the vote reflected a longstanding east-west political split. As the city expanded westward, upwardly mobile people – typically Republicans – established the socio-economic norms of newer neighborhoods while the older and less affluent areas, particularly South Omaha, became Democratic bastions. Partisanship did not seem crucial in the recall vote, but Boyle's well-publicized difficulties may have been particularly offensive to the city's more elite areas. Yet the recall defies easy explanation, for Boyle's public policies and the services of city government during his tenure were not issues. Perhaps a Boyle loyalist, labor leader Terry Moore, best explained the mayor's plight, saying, "Here in Omaha there is a real sense of a need for politeness and respect for others."

The City Council elected one of its members, Bernie Simon, to complete Boyle's term. Simon, a retired Northwestern Bell marketing manager, had been on the Council since 1981. Soon after taking office, the popular Simon began a struggle with cancer that ended in his death in April 1988. From its own membership the Council chose former university professor Walt Calinger, who finished the term Boyle had started in 1985.

In the 1989 mayoral primary election, a resurgent Mike Boyle finished first among six major candidates. Facing him in the run-off election was P. J. Morgan, who operated a major real estate management business and had been a state legislator and county commissioner. Morgan, a Republican, had backed Democrat Boyle in the 1981 mayoral campaign.

For Mike Boyle, the pattern of balloting in the run-off election in May replicated the east-west split in the 1987 recall vote. "W. Omaha Boyle's Downfall" read the headline of the story relating Morgan's triumph over Boyle. This contest brought the highest number of votes cast in a mayoral election, and in defeat Boyle won more ballots than he had in any previous race.

Mayor Morgan established a solid record and in 1993 was easily re-elected. Like Boyle a decade earlier, P. J. Morgan appeared upward-bound in politics, but in September 1994 Morgan resigned to take the presidency of Lincoln's Duncan Aviation Co. Councilman Subby Anzaldo became interim mayor and was a candidate in a special mayoral election held in

November, 1994. In a three-way race, attorney and former Republican Congressman Hal Daub came out on top with Democrat Brenda Council, a Union Pacific attorney and City Council member, in second place, and Anzaldo third. The run-off contest between Council and Daub the following month symbolized two sharply different perspectives on urban America in the 1990s.

In 1992, after eleven years on the Omaha Public School Board, Brenda Council won election as the first black woman to serve on the City Council. But 1994 was a year of conservative political resurgence, which favored Daub's candidacy. A tragedy also had a bearing on the campaign when a woman was accidently killed by a police car engaged in a chase. The incident led to a debate over police chases between Hal Daub, a hard-line law-and-order advocate, and Senator Ernie Chambers, often a critic of the police. Some voters may have perceived Council's critical view of chases as too akin to those of Chambers, who was anathema to conservative voters. Indeed, a recent poll showed that local voters saw crime as the state's top issue, and Daub portrayed himself as a tougher foe of criminals than his opponent. On an issue of dubious relevance to municipal policy, he vigorously supported the death penalty, which Council opposed. Not surprisingly, Daub had the support of the Police Union.

Issues and images aside, Hal Daub may have had the advantage in campaign finesse. On election day, he won by a 56.5 to 43.2 percent margin, carrying six City Council districts. Whatever the role of race and gender in this special mayoral election, *World-Herald* columnist Michael Kelly quoted an older female as having said, "I ain't ready for a woman." Kelly added: "A few probably ain't ready for a black."

The 1990s brought advances in Omaha's cultural life. Long-contemplated expansion of the Joslyn Art Museum became a reality with the completion of a new building, designed by Sir Norman Foster and Partners of London, north of the existing structure, which was renovated. The Western Heritage Museum – old Union Station – was extensively refurbished and the exhibit area greatly expanded, including the addition of trackside exhibit capacity. To help recreate the atmosphere in the waiting room during the heyday of rail travel, Omaha sculptor John Lajba produced lifelike figures of travelers and station personnel that contained audio presentation devices. Adding to the distinction of the renowned Henry Doorly Zoo were the Lied Jungle, the Durham Tree Top Restaurant and educational center, the Walter and Suzanne Scott Kingdoms of the Sea Aquarium, and an IMAX theater. A renovated building at Twentieth and Howard Streets became the Omaha Children's Museum and the long unused Astro Theater found new life as the Rose Blumkin Performing Arts Center. This renovated 1927 structure of architectural prominence housed the Omaha

Theater Company for Young People. These projects, finished between 1992 and 1997, represented an outlay of some $93.7 million. Most of this sum came from local donors, and Omaha's civic leaders continued to provide the organizational talent as well as the money for cultural development.

On Friday, May 3, 1996, residents of the Ak-Sar-Ben neighborhood in south central Omaha did not hear a familiar sound: the bugle call to the post at the Ak-Sar-Ben race track. This rainy spring day would have opened the racing season, but for the first time in fifty-two years there would be no horse racing at Ak-Sar-Ben. In 1978, daily attendance at the track had averaged 16,018 persons and in 1984, Ak-Sar-Ben recorded the sixth highest patronage of any horse track in the nation. But in 1986, the Bluffs Run dog track opened in Council Bluffs, and Ak-Sar-Ben's attendance plummeted. Race tracks were established in other cities and two Indian-owned casinos opened in Iowa, north of Omaha. In 1992, the Knights of Ak-Sar-Ben sold the 350-acre Ak-Sar-Ben property to Douglas County, but the tracks's decline continued. The many buses filled with racing fans from around the region no longer pulled into the Ak-Sar-Ben parking lot and local people had other wagering options, particularly with the addition of slot machines at Bluffs Run in 1995. That season, Ak-Sar-Ben's daily attendance averaged only 3,524. The financial survival of the track seemed to require the addition of casino gambling at Ak-Sar-Ben, but Nebraska had not followed Iowa in allowing a massive expansion of gaming. With two riverboat casinos with their lodging and dining facilities about to open at Council Bluffs, the Douglas County Racing Board canceled the 1996 Ak-Sar-Ben racing meet.

The plight of the race track was a symbol of changing times, for First Data Resources, Ak-Sar-Ben's neighbor to the west, soon announced a plan to convert the northern part of the Ak-Sar-Ben property into an information technology center that would employ about two thousand persons. FDR would purchase 140 acres from Douglas County and donate part of this former Ak-Sar-Ben property to the University of Nebraska at Omaha, which would develop a south campus to house information science, technology, and engineering programs. In keeping with existing practice, the engineering curriculum would be administered by the University of Nebraska–Lincoln. The adjoining business and educational facilties would have a cooperative relationship, which would enchance Omaha's emergence as an information technology center. The FDR-UNO proposal quickly won the support of Omaha's civic leadership, and despite the efforts of racing interests to revive the Ak-Sar-Ben track, the Douglas County Commissioners approved the plan.

Yet as the twentieth century ended, Omaha remained a Gate City with vital regional ties. About one-fourth of the local work force was in agribusiness; horses still clopped through downtown streets each September in celebration of River City Roundup, and by its very name the Western Heritage Museum suggested how Omahans saw their tradition. The Union Pacific's Platte Valley route and I-80 were heavily traveled transcontinental thoroughfares that symbolized Omaha as a Gate City. Just a few hours' drive to the northwest were Nebraska's Sandhills, one of the nation's finest ranching areas. A bucolic stereotype of Omaha persisted: a 1995 *Money* magazine article on multi-billionaire Warren Buffett, who ran his Berkshire Hathaway investment firm from Kiewit Plaza on Farnam Street, included a fanciful image of Buffett holding an ear of corn with a cornfield and barn in the background.

Yet much of old Omaha was gone. Although 4,700 persons worked in meat processing in the metropolitan area, the once busy Livestock Exchange was nearly as quiet as a mausoleum, and the stockyards were much reduced in extent. By 1983, Omaha's packing industry had experienced its principal decline, but between 1983 and 1993, receipts of salable livestock fell from 1,245,300 head to 469,500. Clearly, a "bull on a pedestal" was not a fit symbol for the new Omaha. On the river just north of downtown, the Asarco smelter, once the world's biggest lead refinery and symbolic of Omaha's links to the Rocky Mountain West reaching back to the 1870s, would probably give way to a park, its presence an environmental hazard. Omaha was still a Gate City, but the Union Pacific Railroad now had a rail network extending from Chicago to Los Angeles and Seattle and from Duluth to Laredo. Omaha was no longer the great jumping-off point to the West. The Gate City was giving way to a new Omaha, a city of the information age with national and global ties, but with no new identity to distinguish it from other urban centers. The new Omaha with all the paraphernalia of the information age seemed unrelated to its historical roots.

Or was it? Omaha was born amid the technology of the telegraph – the first thrust of the electronic age – and steam power. The technological and capitalistic synergies of the nineteenth century produced what one person of that age termed "almost an annihilation of distance." Historian James C. Malin observed that the opening to settlement of the region from the Missouri River to the Rockies occurred within a global context of transportation and communication. Far-sighted promoters of the settlement of the plains, he noted, contemplated building a railroad that would be not only a gateway to America's Far West, but would serve the nation's interests in the Pacific basin. Technology linked to a "global perspective" influenced creative thought in the mid-nineteenth century. Omaha was born in a restless age, and as a western Missouri editor said in January 1854, "Old things, old ideas, old ways are giving way, and nothing will satisfy the people but rapidity." As Senator Stephen Douglas said, "No man can keep up with the spirit of this age who travels on anything slower than the locomotive, and fails to receive intelligence by lightning [telegraph]." Douglas, whose name would grace a major Omaha street, clearly saw the role of technology in freeing humanity from the constraints of space and time.

As the twentieth century ended, Omaha was in the vanguard of the electronic information age which had begun with the telegraph and was part of a national and global infrastructure that had fulfilled the vision of Stephen Douglas. In helping to shape a new era, Omahans retained the ambitious, creative, and restless spirit that marked their city's birth.

Beyond the bright indicators of progress was the challenge of whether Omahans would alleviate the social and economic disparities polarizing their city. Omaha's problems, like its achievements, made it a representative American community. Although distant forces and massive trends had shaped the city's development, its people had done much to mold their own destiny.

For Further Reading

There is a great variety of different kinds of material available on Omaha. This bibliography is not intended to be exhaustive. While it does indicate the sources used in writing this book, a primary purpose is to call attention to items that should be available and useful to students who wish to pursue further study of Omaha's history.

General Suggestions

A number of local histories explore the Omaha experience. They vary greatly in content and quality. These books, some of which have accompanying biographical volumes commonly called "Mug Books," are unstructured, unanalytical, and uncritical. Most of the authors were local residents who, despite no formal training in historical methodology, did thorough jobs of collecting data. They borrowed from each other without attribution; so a user has to be careful and start with the earliest work that deals with a particular subject. The same pattern holds for local histories done on other American cities. Some are very long, and few have ever been read from cover-to-cover. However, they contain information not readily available elsewhere on dominant groups, urban services, industrial progress, and social life. Used judiciously and with care, they become valuable research tools.

Some Omaha local histories are old enough to be considered primary sources in their own right. Others are typical of their kind. Alfred Sorenson, a local journalist, wrote *Early History of Omaha, or Walks and Talks Among the Old Settlers* (1876), *Omaha Illustrated: A History of the Pioneer Period and the Omaha of Today*

(1888), and *History of Omaha from the Pioneer Days to the Present Time* (1889). The latter is among the best summaries of early Omaha. Sorenson moved away for several decades, but returned to write his valedictory, *The Story of Omaha from the Pioneer Days to the Present Time* (1923). There is a long section on Omaha and Douglas County in A. T. Andreas, *History of the State of Nebraska,* vol. 1 (1882, reprinted 1975). Two long and very detailed tomes were authored by James W. Savage and John T. Bell, *History of the City of Omaha Nebraska and South Omaha* (1894); and Arthur C. Wakely, sup. ed., *Omaha: The Gate City and Douglas County Nebraska: A Record of Settlement, Organization, Progress and Achievement,* 2 volumes (1917). A combination history and reminiscence, Edward F. Morearty, *Omaha Memories: Recollections of Events, Men and Affairs in Omaha, Nebraska, from 1879 to 1917* (1917), contains excellent economic, political, and promotional material. Pioneer days are covered in Frank J. Burkley, *The Faded Frontier* (1935). Of much less value are two old settlers' accounts: John T. Bell, *Omaha and Omaha Men: Reminiscences* (1917); John Rush, *A Pioneer's Reminiscences* (1928). Potboilers include Fred Carey, *Romance of Omaha* (1929); Byron Reed Co., *The Story of Omaha* (1946); Richard Hewitt, *The History of Omaha, 1854-1954* (1954); and Margaret Killian, *Born Rich: A Historical Book of Omaha* (1978). The *Omaha World-Herald* commissioned a centennial history of Omaha by Walter H. Rawley, Jr., of the University of Nebraska, published in the paper in eight parts from April 18 through June 6, 1954. The most recent local history of Omaha is a "coffee table" book, Dorothy Devereux Dustin, *Omaha and Douglas County: A Panoramic History* (1980). It emphasizes nineteenth century developments, has many pictures, and an extensive bibliography.

Several accounts, compilations, and indexes deal with themes of Omaha and Nebraska history. These include Arvid E. Nelson, Jr., *The Ak-Sar-Ben Story: A Seventy-Year History of the Knights of Ak-Sar-Ben* (1967); Nebraska Press Association, *Who's Who in Nebraska* (1940); Carol Gendler, comp., *Index to the Jewish Press (1920-1977) Including Omaha Jewish Bulletin (1919-1927)* (1978); Raymond Wilson, comp., "Nebraska History in Graduate Theses at the University of Nebraska-Omaha," *Nebraska History 56,* summer 1975; "One Hundred Years of Growing: An Omaha Bibliography, 1854-1954," found in the Omaha Public Library; Garneth Oldenkamp Peterson, "The Omaha City Council and Commission: A Profile, 1858-1930," M. A. thesis, U. of Nebraska at Omaha, 1980; Landmark Heritage Preservation Commission, Garneth Oldenkamp Peterson, *Comprehensive Program for Historical Preservation in Omaha* (1980).

Three books, plus several unpublished drafts and working papers, are essential to the study of Omaha. The Federal Writers Project of the Works Progress Administration in Nebraska planned to publish a general history of Omaha, along with studies on specialized subjects. Following the termination of the WPA in 1943, the Nebraska State Historical Society gained custody of the Omaha FWP records. They cover many aspects of the life of the city up to World War Two. The collection is complimented by one of the best volumes in the American Guide Series, FWP, *Nebraska: A Guide to the Cornhusker State* (1939). It has excellent material on Omaha. Another valuable source is James C. Olson, *History of Nebraska* (1966). This standard history of the Cornhusker State provides the framework for studying the economic, social, and political development of Omaha and its hinterland. While there are other histories of Nebraska, Olson's is analytical and comprehensive. In a class by itself is the chapter on Omaha in George Leighton, *Five Cities: The Story of Their Youth and Old Age* (1939). This material appeared originally as "Omaha, Nebraska: The Glory has Departed," *Harper's Magazine* 177, July and August, 1938 and was reprinted in condensed form in *Nebraska History* 19, October-December, 1938. Leighton produced a thematic history that emphasized a clash of wills between labor and management. His unflattering portraits of leading civic leaders made his work controversial in Omaha.

There is a wealth of information about Omaha in local newspapers. The most extensive holdings, much of which are on microfilm, are in the Nebraska State Historical Society. See Anne P. Diffendal, comp., *A Guide to the Newspaper Collection of the State Archives: Nebraska State Historical Society* (1977). The *Bee,* published from 1872 to 1927, is of special value during its first decades, when editor and publisher Edward Rosewater took a direct interest in all aspects of the paper's operation. The *News,* in print from 1899 to 1927, tended toward sensationalism. The amalgamation of the two papers, the *Bee-News,* lasted from 1927 to 1937. The *World-Herald,* created by a merger in 1889, has the longest continuous publication record of any Omaha paper. In many ways the *World-Herald* is the "manuscript of the city," and its use is essential for important events. The *Sun* publications, after 1951, are especially valuable for the 1960s because of excellent investigative reporting. Early papers—most short-lived, but easy to run—include the *Arrow* (actually published in Council Bluffs), the *Nebraskian,* the *Tri-Weekly Nebraska Republican,* the *Times,* the *Nebraskian and Times,* the *Weekly Herald,* the *Telegram,* the *Union,* and the *Dispatch.* Among South Omaha journals were the *Globe-Citizen,* the *Tribune,* the *Nebraska Daily Democrat,* the *Daily Stockman,* and the *Magic City Hoof and Horn.* The *Examiner* covered Omaha Society from 1884 to 1921. The leading black journal, the *Star,* started publication in 1938. There have been few other black papers: the *New Era,* the *Guide,* the *Afro-American Sentinel,* and the *Monitor.* The *Jewish Bulletin* is available for two years after World War One. Since then the primary Jewish paper has been the *Jewish Press.* Omaha has had a rich ethnic press; *Den Danske Pioneer, Denni Pokrok, Freie Presse and Wochenhtliche Tribune, Gwiazda Zachodu, Narodni Pokrok, Nova Doba, Posten, Osveta Americke, Pokrok Zapadu, Volkszeitung-Tribune,* and *Public Ledger* (Italian). These publications sought regional audiences and did not concentrate on local news developments. Taken collectively and used selectively, the papers of Omaha, both big and small, mirror the life of the city and its people.

The Decennial Census of the United States is the foundation for writing an urban biography of an American city. The census is more tedious and difficult to use than many other sources. In particular, confusing tables and indexes, coupled with small print, vex scholars. Still, while much of the data extracted is by necessity background information that does not show up directly in final published form, it is absolutely necessary to gain a firm grasp of demographic, social, and economic characteristics. There is an ever increasing amount of data on Omaha from the 1860 census onward. For example, the 1860 census has no information on housing; the 1970 census has an entire volume on the subject.

Chapter 1

This chapter covers early prospects, the settlement of Omaha, the capital fight, the outfitting trade, the formation of the business community, and the construction of the Union Pacific Railroad. These subjects are discussed in detail in the local histories. Indeed, some of them emphasize origins at the expense of later developments. Many of the quotations and antedotes originally appeared in Sorenson, *History of Omaha.*

Olson, *History of Nebraska,* covers the geographical features and has excellent material on early town promotion and politics in Nebraska Territory. Ella Bartlett Knight, "Geographic Influence in the Location and Growth of Omaha," M.A. thesis, Municipal University of Omaha, 1924, argues that Omaha defeated its immediate rivals for geographic reasons. John W. Reps, *Cities of the American West: A History of Frontier Urban Planning* (1979), has a section on Omaha. For data on surrounding settlements see Jerold L. Simmons, ed., *"La Belle Vue": Studies in the History of Bellevue, Nebraska* (1976); Niel M. Johnson, ed., *Portal to the Plains: A History of Washington County, Nebraska* (1974); Robert Trennert, Jr., "The Mormons and the Office of Indian Affairs: The Conflict over Winter Quarters, 1846-1848," *Nebraska History* 53, fall, 1972; E. Widtsoe Sumway, "Winter Quarters, 1846-1948," *Nebraska History* 35, June, 1954, and 36 March, 1955; Norman Graebner, "Nebraska's Missouri River Frontier, 1854-1860," *Nebraska History* 42, December, 1961. Dorothy Devereux Dustin, "Plotting and Platting North of the Platte," *Omaha* 3, August, 1978, is a short popular account of promotional activities. The general subject of promoters and their methods is developed in Charles N. Glaab and A. Theodore Brown (rev. by Charles N. Glaab), *A History of Urban America* (1976).

There are a number of valuable studies on Omaha's initial economic development. The best dissertation on the subject is Bertie Bennett Hoag, "The Early History of Omaha from 1853 to 1873," M.A. thesis, Municipal University of Omaha, 1939. Two articles in *Nebraska History* deal with freighting: Walker Wyman, "Omaha: Frontier Depot and Prodigy of Council Bluffs," 17, July-September, 1936; Carol Gendler, "Territorial Omaha as a Staging and Freighting Center," 49, summer, 1968. There is considerable information that touches on Omaha in two books by William E. Lass. They are *A History of Steamboating on the Upper Missouri River* (1962); *From the Missouri to the Great Salt Lake: An Account of Overland Freighting* (1972). Clarence Bagley, "Nebraska in 1852," *Nebraska History* 5, January-March, 1922, recalled crossing the Missouri on the steam ferry. Burkley, *The Faded Frontier,* has some interesting material on the issuance of scrip by the city government, as does an article in the *Sunday World-Herald,* May 9, 1954. Unfortunately, the Thomas Barnes Cuming Papers at the Nebraska State Historical Society shed little light on Cuming's political moves that made Omaha the territorial capital. There are bibliographical sketches of Kountze and Creighton family members in the local histories. The activities of the Kountze family in Denver are analyzed in Lyle W. Dorsett, *The Queen City: A History of Denver* (1977). For bibliographical sketches of the Creightons see P. A. Mullens, *Creighton* (1901).

The decision-making process that led to Omaha becoming the eastern terminal for the first transcontinental railroad was complex. Because of political and economic machinations, students of the subject have been forced to piece the story together from many different places. Two monographs, both done many years ago, are still essential: John P. Davis, *The Union Pacific Railway: A Study in Railway Politics, History, and Economics* (1894); Nelson Trottman, *History of the Union Pacific: A Financial and Economic Survey* (1966). A more recent study is Charles Edgar Ames, *Pioneering the Union Pacific: A Reappraisal of the Builders of the Railroad* (1969). It has an excellent bibliography. The author, a direct descendant of Union Pacific railroad builder Oakes Ames, applied the skills of a professional investment analyst to the question of the railroad's financing and its corporate structure. He reached conclusions somewhat similar to those in Robert W. Fogel, *The Union Pacific Railroad — A Case in Premature Enterprise* (1960). A very helpful book on an operational level is Grenville Dodge, *How We Built the Union Pacific Railway and Other Railway Papers and Addresses* (1910). Of major value is Wallace D. Farnham, "The Pacific Railroad Act of 1862," *Nebraska History* 43, September, 1962. The congressional investigation of the Union Pacific in the 1870s concentrated on larger questions than the terminal selection. The voluminous Union Pacific Railroad Papers at the Nebraska State Historical Society deal with later railroad operations and policies. The railroad builders are viewed in a harsh light in Leighton, *Five Cities.*

George Francis Train was among the most colorful of Omaha promoters. There is an interesting character analysis of Train in Sorenson, *History of Omaha.* Train's 1863 speech on the destiny of Omaha is printed in full in the *Nebraska Republican,* December 4, 1863, an issue that covered the Union Pacific ground breaking ceremony in elaborate detail. Train praised himself in his autobiography, *My Life in Many States and Foreign Lands* (1902). For a concise summary of his uncommon and controversial life see the *Dictionary of American Biography,* s.v. "Train, George Francis."

326

Chapter 2

In this chapter the people of Omaha engage in community building, found a claim association, move toward law and order, and establish social and religious institutions. All the local histories contain material on the subjects covered. Short biographies of settlers who left or stayed can be found in Sorenson, *History of Omaha,* Wakely, *The Gate City,* and Andreas, *Nebraska.* Of the discussions of the claim associations, Sorenson's is the easiest to follow. He has a readable account of the fight for law and order, although there is more detailed information about the same incidents in Wakely. His book is also valuable for its data on the formation of institutions. Burkley, *The Faded Frontier,* discusses Abraham Lincoln's trip to Council Bluffs, the experiences of the Burkley family, and the establishment of the claim association. Olson, *History of Nebraska,* has a good quotation by J. Sterling Morton on the expectations of the pioneers, plus information on land policy. See Roy Robbins, *Our Landed Heritage: The Public Domain, 1776-1936* (1942), for a standard account of American land policy. What happened in Nebraska is sketched in Addison Sheldon, *Land Systems and Land Policies in Nebraska* (1936).

A number of sources treat Omaha's social development. The impressions of Omaha by one of the community's first ministers are in Charles W. Martin, ed., "Omaha in 1868-1869: Selections from the Letters of Joseph Barker," *Nebraska History* 59, winter, 1978. A woman who grew up in pioneer Omaha wrote what she called "scrappy notes," published in Josie McCagne McCulloch, "Memories of Omaha: A Reminiscence," *Nebraska History* 35, December, 1954. Extra legal attempts at bringing law and order are analyzed in Olive Goss, "Vigilantes of Eastern Nebraska," *Nebraska History* 13, January-March, 1932. The punishment for horse stealing in Nebraska Territory is codified in the territorial statutes, adopted from Iowa's criminal code. Philip A. Kalisch, "High Culture on the Frontier: The Omaha Library Association," *Nebraska History* 52, winter, 1971, is a valuable account of an early attempt at bringing social niceties. See also Robert D. Harper, "Theatrical Entertainment in Early Omaha," *Nebraska History* 36, June, 1955. R. McLaren Sawyer, "Samuel Dewitt Beals: Frontier Educator," *Nebraska History* 50, summer, 1969, explores the career of an influential Omaha educational figure. The best material on early city government is in Irene Zika, "Some Aspects of Territorial and State Legislative Control of the Municipal

Government of Omaha (1857-1875)," M.A. thesis, U. of Omaha, 1946.

Chapter 3

Here, the leaders of Omaha seek a solid economic base. Subjects dealt with include the city's position in the nation's urban system, the problems created by Union Pacific policies, the fortunes of Nebraska, the gaining of stockyards and packing plants, the founding of South Omaha, the expansion of trade and commerce, the growth of the railroad net, the depression of the 1890s, the Populist crusade, and the Trans-Mississippi Exposition. While the local histories have a great deal of information on Omaha's economy, there is uncritical acceptance of the doctrine of progress, with the Panic of 1893 viewed as a temporary setback. The building of a hinterland is a key element in the Omaha story for this period, and Olson, *History of Nebraska,* provides much information on the subject.

By 1900 Omaha had become an American regional center. The tendency of people to live in cities and the construction of interior urban systems in the last half of the century was noted by many observers. A classic account is Adna Weber, *The Growth of Cities in the Nineteenth Century* (1899, reprinted 1963). Arthur Schlesinger, *The Rise of the City* (1933), saw urbanization as a central theme in the late nineteenth century United States. Lawrence H. Larsen, *The Urban West at the End of the Frontier* (1978), places Omaha within the context of an urban system that served the Great Plains. He summarizes the reasons why Chicago won the battle for economic domination of the Midwest in "Chicago's Midwest Rivals: Cincinnati, St. Louis, and Milwaukee," *Chicago History,* fall, 1976. See also James Neal Primm, *Lion of the Valley: St. Louis, Missouri* (1981). The appropriate sections of three surveys are helpful starting points in understanding urban geopolitical relationships: Glaab and Brown, *Urban America;* Bayrd Still, *Urban America: A History with Documents* (1974); Blake McKelvey, *The Urbanization of America: 1860-1915* (1963). The policies followed by two of Omaha's rivals are examined in Dorsett, *The Queen City;* A. Theodore Brown and Lyle W. Dorsett, *K.C.: A History of Kansas City, Missouri* (1978).

Railroad building and policy remained central to the Omaha experience. Wakely, *The Gate City,* Savage and Bell, *City of Omaha,* and Sorenson, *The Story of Omaha,* all hailed the obtaining of the "High Bridge" as a community triumph. The bridge opened in 1872, fell during a tornado in 1877, was rebuilt and used until a new bridge opened nearby in 1887. That bridge remained in operation until the present span was completed in 1916. See the *Sunday World-Herald Magazine of the Midlands,* October 9, 1977. The books by Davis, Trottman, and Ames on the Union Pacific all stress the road's management problems and deteriorating financial position. Gene R. Pugh, "The Consolidation of the Union Pacific and Kansas Pacific Railroads in 1880," M.A. thesis, U. of Omaha, 1963, examines a short run success that caused long run problems. For the Chicago, Burlington and Quincy Railroad, see Richard C. Overton, *Burlington Route* (1965); Thomas M. Davis, "Building the Burlington Through Nebraska—A Summary View," *Nebraska History* 30, December, 1949. Leighton, *Five Cities,* called the railroads Omaha's "glory." Larsen, *The Urban West,* contains information on the extent of Omaha's railroad net in 1880.

The advantages of Nebraska are extolled in L. D. Burch, *Nebraska as it is: A Comprehensive Summary of the Resources, Advantages and Drawbacks of the Great Prairie State* (1878). Everett Dick, *The Sod House Frontier* (1937), contains valuable data on Nebraska settlement patterns. So does Olson, *History of Nebraska;* Richard C. Overton, *Burlington West: A Colonization History of the Burlington Railroad* (1941). Herbert L. Glyne, "The Urban Real Estate Boom in Nebraska during the '80's," M.A. thesis, U. of Nebraska, 1927, examines the economic aspects of the settlement boom. Samuel Aughey, *Sketches of the Physical Geography and Geology of Nebraska* (1880), and C.D. Wilber, *The Great Valleys and Prairies of Nebraska* (1881), claimed that Nebraska's annual rainfall was increasing. The promotional activities of an important Nebraska leader are discussed in James C. Olson, *J. Sterling Morton* (1942). For a problem not mentioned by the promoters see Gary D. Olson, ed., "Relief for Nebraska Grasshopper Victims: The Official Journal of Lt. Theodore E. True," *Nebraska History* 48, summer, 1967.

Basic to the rise of the packing industry are the Omaha Livestock Market, Inc., Papers, Nebraska State Historical Society. Of special value are the incorporation papers, the corporate minutes, and the financial statements. See also an undated document in the papers, "Extracts from the 'History of the City of Omaha' by James W. Savage and John T. Bell, published, October 21, 1893." John A. McShane's account of how he convinced packers to move to South Omaha is in Sorenson, *The Story of Omaha.* This book also has good material on William Paxton. *South Omaha Stock Yards and Packing House Interests Illustrated* (1898) is an informative promotional pamphlet. The *World-Herald,* April 23, 1976, ran a "Special Report" on South Omaha. There is considerable information on the rise of the cattle industry in Nebraska in Louis Atherton, *The Cattle Kings* (1961); Edward Everett Dale, *The Range Cattle Industry* (1930); Mari Sandoz, *The Cattlemen* (1958).

Omaha's commercial and industrial life won approval in G. H. Brown, *The Industries of Omaha, Nebraska* (1887); *Omaha Illustrated: A History of the Pioneer Period and the Omaha of Today* (1888); *Historical and Descriptive Review of Omaha: Her Leading Business Houses and Enterprising Men* (1892). Conditions in Omaha after the economic collapse are elaborated upon in Morearty, *Omaha Memories.* Much usable data is contained in W. N. Nason, *Fifteenth Annual Report of the Trade and Commerce of Omaha for the Fiscal Year Ending December 31, 1891* (1892). Omaha newspapers gave extensive coverage to the 1892 Populist convention, printing the texts of many speeches. Gurdon W. Wattles explained the tactics he used to enter Omaha society in *Autobiography of Gurdon W. Wattles: Genealogy* (1922). Kenneth G. Alders, "Triumph of the West: The Trans-Mississippi Exposition," *Nebraska History* 53, fall, 1972, covers the events associated with the exposition.

Chapter 4

Social and political developments in the last three decades of the nineteenth century dominate this chapter: vice and crime, politics, community leaders, urban services, religious institutions, voluntary associations, architectural forms, and ethnic groups. Albert Shaw equated the Trans-Mississippi Exposition to the march of civilization in "The Trans-Mississippians and their Fair at Omaha," *Century Magazine* 56, December, 1898. Sorenson, *Story of Omaha,* attributes the 1869 poem about conditions in the city to a local journalist. While his evidence appears conclusive, some other local historians claim the author was a well-known poet of the time, John G. Saxe.

All the local histories have considerable sections on Omaha as a wide open town. Burkley, *The Faded Frontier,* examines Canada Bill and his gang. Sorenson, *Story of Omaha,* contains a good narrative account of vice activities. Morearty, *Omaha Memories,* examined conditions first hand and made some perspective comments. He also has helpful data on politics, the administrative of justice, and influential leaders. Wallace Brown, "George L. Miller and the Boosting of Omaha," *Nebraska History* 50, fall, 1969, analyzes the activities of an important Omahan. There is much primary material on Edward Rosewater in the Rosewater Family Papers in the Nebraska State Historical Society.

Information on urban services and institutions is available in a number of places. Useful data can be found in Wakely, *The Gate City*, and in Dustin, *Omaha*. A number of accounts deal with street transportation: *History: Street Railways in the City of Omaha, 1867-1928* (1929); E. Bryant Phillips, "Interurban Projects In and Around Omaha," *Nebraska History* 29, March, 1948 and "Horse Car Days and Ways in Nebraska," *Nebraska History* 30, September, 1949; Dennis Thavenet, "A History of Omaha Public Transportation," M.A. thesis, U. of Omaha, 1960; Gurdon W. Wattles Papers in the University of Nebraska at Omaha Library. For other services see Metropolitan Utilities District, *Water Supply: The Story of Omaha's Municipal Water Supply* (1942); Ronald W. Hunter, "Grand Central Hotel, Three-Alarm Pyre," *Omaha* 4, June, 1979; Harry Edward Dice, "The History of the Omaha Fire Department: 1860-1960," M.A. thesis, U. of Omaha, 1965; Michael Joseph Harkins, "Public Health in Early Omaha, 1857-1900," M.A. thesis, U. of Nebraska at Omaha, 1973 and "Public Health Nuisances in Omaha, 1870-1900," *Nebraska History* 56, winter, 1975; Jacqueline Johnson, "A History of Health and Safety Conditions in the Omaha Public Schools from 1872 to 1908," M.A. thesis, U. of Nebraska at Omaha, 1968; Board of Trade, *Trade and Commerce (1892); Ninth Annual Report of the Board of Park Commissioners of Omaha, Nebraska, for the Year 1898*.

Religious surveys include Carol Gendler, "The Jews of Omaha: The First Sixty Years," M.A. thesis, U. of Omaha, 1968; Henry Casper, *History of the Catholic Church in Nebraska: The Church on the Fading Frontier, 1864-1910* (1966); Alonzo DeLarme, *History of the First Baptist Church of Omaha* (1925); Carol Gendler, "The First Synagogue in Nebraska: The Early History of the Congregation of Israel of Omaha," *Nebraska History* 58, fall, 1977; Everett Jackman, *The Nebraska Methodist Story: 1854-1954* (1954); James Robbins, "A History of The Episcopal Church in Omaha from 1856 to 1964," M.A. thesis, Municipal University of Omaha, 1965.

Three fine essays are in the FWP Papers: Anne Frank, "Metropolitan Utilities District," August 10, 1938; Carl Uhlarik,

"Education," August 30, 1939; Ellen Bishop, "Religion," August 30, 1939. See also Robert S. Kittell, "The Omaha Ice Trust, 1899-1900: An Urban Monopoly," *Nebraska History* 54, winter, 1973. Welfare activities are covered in Dustin, *Omaha*. McCulloch, "Memories," and Victor Rosewater, *School Days in Early Omaha* (1912), have information on social affairs. Howard P. Chudacoff, *Mobile Americans: Residential and Social Mobility in Omaha, 1880-1920* (1972), demonstrates that Omahans moved around a great deal. Census statistics are questioned in Edgar Z. Palmer, "The Correctness of the 1890 Census of Population for Nebraska Cities," *Nebraska History* 32, December, 1951.

In recent years, there has been a growing interest in late nineteenth century Omaha architecture. There is excellent data in *Standard Blue Presents Buildings of the 80's in Omaha* (1976); *Omaha City Architecture* (1977). See also Penelope Chatfield, "Old Market Historic District," *National Register of Historic Places Inventory-Nomination Form,* December 1977, (in the State Historic Preservation Office of the Nebraska State Historical Society).

Chapter 5

The main themes in this chapter involve agricultural progress, the resurgence of the Union Pacific Railroad, the rise of Gurdon W. Wattles, labor troubles, the development of community economic goals, industrial advances, the impact of World War One, the role of James E. Davidson in the electric power business, and the prosperity of the 1920s. There is rich material on economic matters in Olson, *History of Nebraska*. Specific information on Omaha can be found in Wakely, *The Gate City;* Sorenson, *The Story of Omaha;* Morearty, *Memories.* Leighton, *Five Cities,* attacks Wattles's handling of the 1909 transit strike and takes a dim view of Davidson's motives. Trottman, *Union Pacific,* has a good analysis of how E. H. Harriman improved the Union Pacific's fortunes. Wattles defended his role in the transit strike in a privately printed work, *A Crime Against Labor: A Brief History of the Omaha and Council Bluffs Street Railroad Strike* (n.d.). His papers make it clear that he did not consider himself anti-union. There were strikes in Omaha before Wattles: Ronald Gephart, "Politicians, Soldiers and Strikers: The Reorganization of the Nebraska Militia and the Omaha Strike of 1882," *Nebraska History* 46, June, 1965. The Omaha Livestock Market, Inc., papers reveal the continued growth of the livestock industry. A promotional pamphlet, *Union Stock Yards Company of Omaha, Limited* (1926), has valuable data. So does the *Official Souvenir Book: Omaha Grain Exchange* (1909). The experiences of a suburban area are analyzed in Dorothy Ruth Mutz, "Benson: A Residential Suburban Community," M.A. thesis, Municipal University of Omaha, 1935. The physical expansion of Omaha is examined in a publication of the Omaha City Planning Department: Garneth Oldenkamp Peterson, *Master Plan for Historic Preservation* (1980). Victor Rosewater, "Omaha, the Transcontinental Gateway," in L. P. Powell, *Historic Towns of the Western States* (1901), painted a rosy picture of the future, as did George Craig, *Omaha's Financial, Commercial, and Manufacturing Resources Epitomized* (1912). "The Brandeis Story" is told in the *World-Herald,* April 10, 1974. The Brandeis Stores, *Down Through the Years* (1936), discusses the physical characteristics of the firm's downtown store. Optimistic predictions are made in *Omaha — Gate City of the West: The Growth of a City* (1929).

Chapter 6

Among things considered in this chapter are the character of the population, the persistence of inter-racial violence, the traditions associated with a wide open town, the imperfections of machine politics, and the search for cultural refinement. Sorenson, *The Story of Omaha,* has a section on the 1919 riot. Wakely, *The Gate City,* and Morearty, *Memories,* are of limited value for both blacks and immigrants. Neither, along with Sorenson for that matter, mentions the anti-Greek riot. The best general account of Omaha social life in the first three decades of the twentieth century is "Omaha Guide, Part 1, History of City," in the FWP Papers.

The immigrant experience, which involved South Omaha as well as Omaha proper, has been chronicled in a number of places. Special FWP reports include J. H. Norris, "Russians in Omaha," October 4, 1937; Rose Michael, "Russian Recreation in Omaha," December 10, 1936; Ray Cunningham, "Chinese in Omaha," September 14, 1936, and "Japanese of Omaha," September 14, 1936; Robert Curran, "Syrians in Omaha," December 30, 1936; Marie Donohue, "Sheeley Town," August 8, 1938. The Sons of Italy sponsored the publication of a FWP manuscript, *The Italians of Omaha* (1941). For other studies of immigrants see Rose Rosicky, *A History of Czechs in Nebraska* (1929); Jeronimus Cicenas, *Lithuanians of Omaha* (1955); T. Earl Sullenger, *The Immigrant in Omaha* (1934). See also " 'Twas a 'Melting Pot,' "

South Omaha Sun, June 10, 1971. Resentment against an ethnic group resulted in violence in 1909. Two works by John G. Bitzes cover this incident: his dissertation, "The Anti-Greek Riot of 1909–South Omaha," M.A. thesis, U. of Omaha, 1964, and his subsequent article which has the same title, *Nebraska History* 51, summer, 1970.

The *World-Herald,* the *Bee* and the *News* all afforded extensive coverage to the 1919 riot. An editorial in the *Monitor,* October 2, 1919, expressed the view of a black editor. *Omaha's Riot in Stories and Pictures* (1919) is a straight-forward account. An excellent summary in the FWP reports is D. K. Bukin, "Omaha Race Riot." A recent scholarly account is Michael L. Lawson, "Omaha, A City of Ferment: Summer of 1919," *Nebraska History* 58, fall, 1977. For background see a FWP monograph sponsored by the Omaha Urban League Community Center, *The Negroes of Nebraska* (1940).

Political reform efforts failed to change conditions in Omaha. Newspaper reaction to the commission plan is analyzed in William F. Schmidt, "Municipal Reform in Omaha from 1906 to 1914 as Seen Through the Eyes of the Omaha Press," M.A. thesis, U. of Omaha, 1963. Mayor Edward Smith's ill-fated administration is examined in Louise E. Rickard, "The Politics of Reform in Omaha, 1918-1921," *Nebraska History* 53, winter, 1972. Two recent accounts of machine government are John Kyle Davis, "The Gray Wolf: Tom Dennison of Omaha," *Nebraska History* 58, spring, 1977; Orville D. Menard, "Tom Dennison: The Rogue Who Ruled Omaha," *Omaha* 3, March, 1978. A Baptist minister and researcher, Alan Jacobsen, has theorized that Dennison played a role in the 1919 riot: *World-Herald,* February 10, 1979; *Gateway* (University of Nebraska at Omaha student newspaper), February 2, 1979. An article in the *Sun* publications on September 20, 1979, by H. W. Becker, said the 1892 death of a South Omaha mayor, Charles P. Miller, sounded like a "Tom Dennison gang frameup." Josie Washburn exposed vice practices in *The First Drink Saloon and Dance Hall* (1914). The scrapbooks in the James Dahlman Papers in the Nebraska State Historical Society shed some light on his career. See also Fred Carey, *Mayor Jim: An Epic of the West* (1930).

There is an excellent description of the Joslyn Memorial in The American Guide Series, *Nebraska.*

Chapter 7

The central concerns of this chapter are depression, war, and prosperity. Topics include William Randolph Hearst's temporary entry into Omaha, the collapse of the economy, the frustrations of the Omaha business community, the role of the New Deal, the traction strike, the impact of World War Two, the plans for postwar consolidation, the acquiring of Strategic Air Command headquarters, and the prosperity of the 1950s. Dustin, *Omaha*, has the best general survey of the period. Much valuable material can be found as well in Rawley's centennial history. Olson, *History of Nebraska*, details the economic fortunes of the Cornhusker State during what was a changing and difficult period.

A spokesman predicted great things for Omaha in "Hearst Has Faith" in Fred Carey, *Romance of Omaha* (1929). The survey of the transit strike of 1935 in Leighton, *Five Cities*, takes the side of labor. There is an account of the strike in "Omaha Guide, Part 1, History of City," in the FWP Papers. Scrapbooks in the Roy Nathan Towl Papers in the Nebraska State Historical Society contain clippings concerning the strike. For a chronology of the strike see the *Evening World-Herald*, June 21, 1935. Press reaction to events of the 1930s is analyzed in Ira Jones, "A Study of the Editorial Policy of the Omaha *Bee-News* and the Omaha *World-Herald* with Regard to Social Problems," M.A. thesis, Municipal University of Omaha, 1937. The Omaha Chamber of Commerce Industrial Bureau, *Omaha* (1936) aimed at attracting new industries. A "confidential" report, U.S. Department of Labor, Nebraska State Employment Service, Affiliated with Social Security Board, "A Survey of the Employment Situation in Omaha, Nebraska" (1941), in the Nebraska State Historical Society summarized the labor situation on the eve of World War Two.

Nebraska politicians helped the Omaha area gain wartime and postwar facilities. Richard Lowitt, *George W. Norris: The Triumph of a Progressive* (1978), has valuable material on George Norris' role in obtaining an aircraft assembly plant. See also the George Norris Papers in the Manuscript Division of the Library of Congress; the Chester Davis Papers in the joint collection of the University of Missouri Western Manuscript Collection and the Historical Society of Missouri Manuscripts, PPF880, "Davis, Hon. Chester, Member, Advisory Com. to council of Ngt. Defense, November 30, 1940," in the Franklin D. Roosevelt Library. Simmons, ed., *Bellevue*, has a section on military activities in the Bellevue vicinity. The SAC Historian's Office at Offutt Air Force

Base has some unclassified material on the move of SAC headquarters to Nebraska. Kenneth S. Wherry's role is detailed and analyzed in Harl Adams Dalstrom, "Kenneth S. Wherry," Ph.D. thesis, U. of Nebraska, 1965. The SAC commander at the time of the move to Omaha said he played no part in the decision: Curtis E. LeMay with MacKinlay Kantor, *Mission with LeMay* (1965). See also Robert L. Branyan, *Taming the Mighty Missouri: A History of the Kansas City District Corps of Engineers, 1907-1971* (1974); Marion Ridgeway, *The Missouri Basin's Pick-Sloan Plan: A Case Study in Congressional Policy Determination* (1955).

Reports produced by the Omaha City Planning Department either helped to set or explain policy: *Omaha, Nebraska, City Plan* (1945); *Housing* (1946); *Housing Plan* (1977); *Future Land Use* (1977). Dustin, *Omaha,* has good material on the rise of the insurance industry. For the story of a remarkable local enterprise see Robert C. Phipps, *The Swanson Story: When the Chicken Flew the Coup* (1976). For another side see David Harris, "Swanson Saga: End of a Dream," *New York Times Magazine,* September 9, 1979. The changing fortunes of the power industry are examined in Martin Pennock, "The Formation of the Omaha Public Power District," M.A. thesis, U. of Omaha, 1971. A valuable factual summary of statistics about Omaha in the late 1950s is Omaha Chamber of Commerce, *This is Omaha* (1958).

Chapter 8

Featured in this chapter are the realities of the Great Depression, the effect of New Deal social programs, the changes wrought by World War Two, the gradual shift of Omaha from a blue to white collar town, and the quest for political reform.

The 1930s were harsh years for the people of Omaha. Blacks experienced very hard times as illustrated by T. Earl Sullenger and J. Harvey Kerns, *The Negro in Omaha* (1931); J. Harvey Kerns, *Industrial and Business Life of Negroes in Omaha* (1932); Francis Y. Knapple, "The Negro High School Student: A Study of the Negro Students in Omaha Central High School (1935-1941)," M.A. thesis, Municipal University of Omaha, 1952. The FWP Papers contain invaluable "Life Histories": R. F. Worley, "Peter Christensen," May 1, 1941; Joseph Glarizo, "Sam Piccioni," March 28, 1941; A. E. Finch, "James Breezee," August 22, 1941; Louis B. Adams, "Wesley J. Cook," November 26, 1941. WPA and PWA final reports for Nebraska, such as "Nebraska, Division of

Women's and Professional Projects," Part 1 (1938), in the National Archives Building, NARS, Washington, D.C., are of great value. The 1940s saw a general upturn in the hopes and aspirations of Omahans. For a survey of wartime trends see Dorothy May Cathers, "Civilian War Activities in Omaha During World War II," M.A. thesis, U. of Nebraska, 1952. A 1944 report of the Omaha City Planning Commission, *Land Use and Zoning,* contains valuable data. There is interesting information on postwar social conditions in *Report of a Community Survey of Omaha, Nebraska* (1946). The Young Men's Christian Association and Young Women's Christian Association Committee for Program Planning in Omaha prepared the report. Grandiose hopes for Omaha's postwar plan are discussed in "An American City's Dream," *Life* 23, July 7, 1947. The 1950s saw the adoption of a new form of local government. This subject, which received massive newspaper coverage, is analyzed in an excellent dissertation: Harold T. Muir, "The Formation and Adoption of the 1956 Omaha Home Rule Charter, 1954-1956," M.A. thesis, U. of Nebraska at Omaha, 1969. Conflicting views of city life are presented by the Omaha Chamber of Commerce, *This is Omaha,* and by Jack Lait and Lee Mortimer, *U.S.A. Confidential* (1952). Omaha received good national publicity when it gained an award: Ben Kocivar, "The National Municipal League and *Look* Salute the All American Cities," *Look* 22, February 4, 1958. There are many excellent aerial photographs of the Omaha area in a *World-Herald* project, *Omaha from the Air: Magic Carpet Photo Series* (1947). See also J. J. Hanighen Co., *Omaha Skyline, A History: 75 Years of Building* (1961).

Chapter 9

Subjects covered in this chapter include debates over the quality of life, the changes in the economic sector, the continuation of federal involvement, the nature of the dominant groups, and the attempts to rejuvenate the older parts of town. There are few historical works on the 1960s and 1970s; so historians have to construct their own conceptual framework and act as "instant sociologists." Fortunately, there is a rich trove of newspaper materials. Excellent articles in the *World-Herald* and the *Sun* publications make it possible to build a synthesis.

Journalistic accounts about the quality of life are augmented by John P. Zipay, *The Changing Population of the Omaha SMSA 1860-1967 with Estimates for 1970* (1967); Lawrence A. Danton, *The Economic Structure of the Omaha SMSA* (1967); Keith Nollen, "An Inventory of Land Uses: Northwest Omaha," M.A. thesis, U. of Nebraska at Omaha, 1972. Of special value is the Omaha City Planning Department, *The Urban Development Policy* (1977, updated March, 1980). The role of the Eppley Foundation in improving the airport is discussed in Harl Adams Dalstrom, *Eugene C. Eppley: His Life and Legacy* (1969). South Omaha's triumphs and tragedies are summarized in Niel M. Johnson, *South Omaha: A Brief History* (1977); "South Omaha — Centennial City," *Sun* publications, April 13, 1967; "South Omaha: A Special Report," *World-Herald*, April 23, 1976, there is some interesting material in Downtown Omaha, Inc., *The Downtowner*, advertising supplement to the *World-Herald*, March 8, 1976. For material on a major restoration project see *Orpheum* (1975).

Analyzing a community power structure is a very difficult task. One of the best studies ever produced on the dominant groups in an American city is Paul Williams, "Twenty Top Omaha's Power Structure," *Sun* publications, April 7, 1966.

Chapter 10

This chapter contains material on social unrest, housing patterns, higher education, cultural trends, Boys Town's financial condition, vice matters, natural disasters, and the quality of life. Most of the story has been pieced together from the *World-Herald,* the *Sun* publications, and the *Star.*

There is valuable background information on the urban crisis in Marion Taylor, "A Survey of Employer Attitudes Toward the Employment of Qualified Negroes in White Collar Positions in Omaha," M.A. thesis, Municipal University of Omaha, 1954; Dennis Mihelich, "World War II and the Transformation of the Urban League," *Nebraska History* 60, fall, 1979. For the changing aspects of Omaha living patterns see George W. Barger, *Social Cohesion in Omaha: A Preliminary Study* (1968); Al Pagel, "Two Lifestyles in the City — the Old and the New," *Sunday World-Herald Magazine of the Midlands,* October 16, 1977.

The development of Creighton University is covered in an article in the same publication on February 12, 1978, authored by Gary Johansen. It was titled, "The School was Too Far Out." Two useful sources on the University of Nebraska at Omaha are Lillian Henderson Campen, "The Early History of the University of Omaha," M.A. thesis, U. of Omaha, 1951; Martha Helligso, "The Administrative Development of Graduate Education at the University of Omaha, Nebraska, 1891-1971, M.A. thesis, U. of Nebraska at Omaha, 1971.

"Boys Town: America's Wealthiest City," *Sun* publications, March 30, 1972, received a Pulitzer Prize. Investigative accounts on sin include "Call Girls Tell their Story," *Sun* publications, September 10, 1970; "Prostitution in Omaha: Business is Brisk," *World-Herald*, June 23, 1971. *The Omaha Tornado, May 6, 1975* (1975), covers the disaster as does a work by the Omaha City Planning Department, *Disaster Response: The 1975 Omaha Tornado* (1977). There is an excellent biography of literature on Omaha natural disasters in Dustin, *Omaha*. A new Omahan praised the city in Joseph Levine, "Omaha, I Love You," *Look* 24, July 30, 1960. Omaha is compared with other cities in Arthur M. Lewis, "The Worst in the U.S. and Omaha's Standing," *World-Herald*, January 29, 1975.

Chapter 11

This chapter treats the history of Omaha from the early 1980s to 1997. During this period, redevelopment plans conceived in the early 1970s were at least partially fulfilled. The reconfiguration of Omaha's economy toward a service orientation continued and by the mid-1990s information age enterprises were fundamental to the city's vitality. Despite a vigorous local economy marked by suburban growth, the socio-economic problems that exploded in the 1960s were largely unresolved.

The principal sources for this chapter were the many excellent feature stories in the *World-Herald* and *Sunday World-Herald*. An eight-part series, "Omaha: A Community Profile," published April 6-14, 1997, provided basic information on recent socioeconomic trends in Omaha as a whole and in its seven City Council districts. The clipping files at the W. Dale Clark Public Library were very helpful for older stories. Articles on Omaha in *The New York Times* sometimes provided a summary perspective. Material on city planning and some statistical data is from Janet Daly-Bednarek, *The Changing Image of the City: Planning for Downtown Omaha, 1945-1973* (1992). Leonard K. Eaton, *Gateway Cities & Other Essays* (1989) and Jim Schwab, "Omaha Held Hostage," *The Progressive* 53, May, 1989, treat the plight of Jobbers' Canyon. Statistical data from the Greater Omaha Chamber of Commerce showed recent economic trends, and material from the City of Omaha Planning Department indicated demographic changes and suburban expansion.

Publications of the Center for Public Affairs Research, University of Nebraska at Omaha, were also useful. Published surveys of black- and women-owned businesses, Bureau of the Census, U.S. Department of Commerce, showed some social and economic changes as did material from the National Foundation for Women Business Owners. The Historian's Office, U.S. Strategic Command, Offutt Air Force Base, provided information showing key changes at Offutt in recent years. Michael Peterson's "72nd St. a Critical Boundary for Candidates," *Nebraska Observer*, April 26, 1989, is useful for understanding Omaha's recent political geography. William Cronon, *Nature's Metropolis: Chicago and the Great West* (1991) and especially James C. Malin, *The Nebraska Question, 1852-1854* (1953) were valuable in discussing the relationship of Omaha in the 1990s to the city's nineteenth-century origins.

The author thanks Ms. Shelly Draheim of the Greater Omaha Chamber of Commerce; Ms. Karen Klein of the Planning Department, City of Omaha; Dr. Todd White and Lt. Col. Rita Clark, Historian's Office, U.S. Strategic Command, Offutt Air Force Base; S. Sgt. Dwight E. Mayhand, Historian, 55th Wing Historian's Office, Offutt Air Force Base. He also thanks the following colleagues at the University of Nebraska at Omaha for their assistance: Professor Carol J. Zoerb, University Library; Professors Bruce M. Garver and William C. Pratt, Department of History; Ms. Sharon N. Emery, International Student Advisor; Tim Fitzgerald, University Relations; and Les Valentine, University Archives. He also thanks Kay Calamé Dalstrom for her thoughtful reading of this chapter and assistance with word processing.

Recent Works

Since this book first appeared in 1982, a number of good sources of Omaha history have been published. Richard E. Bennett's *Mormons at the Missouri, 1846-1852: "And Should We Die"* (1987) puts the Mormon sojourn in the Omaha area in its broad geographical and historical context. The nineteenth- and twentieth-century evolution of what has been called the Near North Side is told in Garneth O. Peterson's historical narrative in the Omaha City Planning Department's *Patterns on the Landscape: Heritage Conservation in North Omaha* (1984). Clare V. McKanna, Jr., in *Homicide, Race, and Justice in the American West, 1880-1920* (1997), compares homicide in Douglas County with that in Las Animas County, Colorado, and Gila County, Arizona. Readers will be especially interested in the chapter, "Seeds of Destruction: The Black Experience in Omaha, Nebraska." Three other books relate important aspects of Omaha's twentieth-century development: Orville D. Menard,

Political Bossism in Mid-America: Tom Dennison's Omaha, 1900-1933 (1989); Harl A. Dalstrom, *A. V. Sorensen and the New Omaha* (1988), and Janet R. Daly-Bednarek, *The Changing Image of the City: Planning for Downtown Omaha, 1945-1973* (1992). Daly-Bednarek's book also has significant material on Omaha in the 1930s.

Two interesting and candid works on key institutions are Stephen Szmrecsanyi, *The History of the Catholic Church in Northeast Nebraska* (1983), a history of the diocese and archdiocese of Omaha, and Tommy R. Thompson, *A History of the University of Nebraska at Omaha 1908–1983* (1983). Maury Klein's two volumes, *Union Pacific: The Birth of a Railroad 1862–1893* (1987) and *Union Pacific: The Rebirth 1894–1969* (1990), tell much of the story of a company that remains vital to Omaha. John Peterson's illustrated article, "Omaha and Council Bluffs: Gateway Cities to the West," *Passenger Train Journal* 20, September, 1989, provides essential detail on rail passenger terminals, trackage, and other aspects of passenger service in the metro area from the 1960s to the Amtrack era. Richard Orr, *O&CB: Streetcars of Omaha and Council Bluffs* (1996), is exceptionally thorough in narrative and illustration. So too is Hollis Limprecht, *The Kiewit Story: Remarkable Man, Remarkable Company* (1981). The career of a famous contemporary Omahan is recounted in Andrew Kilpatrick, *Of Permanent Value: The Story of Warren Buffett* (1994) and Roger Lowenstein, *Buffett: The Making of an American Capitalist* (1995). Robert T. Reilly, *The Omaha Experience* (1990) and Eileen Wirth, *Omaha: The Omaha Experience* (1996) are extensively illustrated Greater Omaha Chamber of Commerce booster works that contain helpful material.

Leonard K. Eaton, *Gateway Cities & Other Essays* (1989) has a chapter on the Jobbers' Canyon wholesale district. Samuel Mercer, *The Old Market and Omaha* (1994), gives the perspective of someone who played a crucial part in preserving and reanimating this distinctive commercial area. William C. Pratt's booklet, *Omaha in the Making of Nebraska Labor History* (1981), is his first of many writings on organized labor in Omaha. Among his other works are two book chapters, " 'Union Maids' in Omaha Labor History, 1887-1945," in *Perspectives: Women in Nebraska History* (1984), and "Employer Offensive in Nebraska Politics, 1946-1949," in Richard Lowitt (ed.), *Politics in the Postwar American West* (1995). Louise Gilmore Donahue's booklet, *Pathways to Prosperity: A History of the Greater Omaha Chamber of Commerce* (1993) has much useful information on the work of the Chamber of Commerce and its predecessor, the Omaha Commercial Club.

The following booklets, published in 1989 and available through the Historical Society of Douglas County, cover the span of Omaha history:

Jerry E. Clark, *The Indians of Eastern Nebraska at the Time of White Settlement: An Anthropology of the Pawnee and Omaha*; Charles W. Martin, *Early Pioneer Trails and Their Impact Upon the Omaha Area*; Richard E. Bennett, *The Mormon Experiment at the Missouri*; Lawrence H. Larsen, *Frontier Omaha and Its Relationship to Other Urban Centers*; Garneth O. Peterson, *Urban Settlement and Growth in Douglas County*; Janet Daly, *Urban Visions: City Planning in Twentieth Century Omaha*, and Harl A. Dalstrom, *A. V. Sorensen and the New Omaha*.

For the extensive periodical literature of the Nebraska segment of the greater Omaha area, readers should consult Michael L. Tate, comp., *Nebraska History: An Annotated Bibliography* (1995). This indispensable volume also includes book citations, theses, dissertations, and other materials.

Of the many fine articles on Omaha which have appeared in the past decade and a half, one deserves special mention. Garneth O. Peterson's "Who's in Charge? A Framework for Examining Community Leadership in Omaha over the Past Century," *Nebraska History* 72, summer, 1991, analyzes the changing patterns of civic leadership in Omaha from the founding of the city to 1990.

Articles published after Michael Tate's bibliography was completed include Harl A. Dalstrom, "Bess Streeter Aldrich's Frontier Omaha, 1866-1868," *Heritage of the Great Plains* 28, fall/winter, 1995. R. K. DeArment, "Omaha's Cowboy Mayor," *True West* 42, March, 1995, considers the pre-Omaha years of James C. Dahlman. New works on social history include Clare V. McKanna, Jr., "Alcohol, Handguns, and Homicide in the American West: A Tale of Three Counties, 1880-1920," *The Western Historical Quarterly* 26, winter, 1995; McKanna's "Seeds of Destruction: Homicide, Race, and Justice in Omaha, 1880–1920," *Journal of American Ethnic History* 14, fall, 1994; and Dennis N. Mihelich, "The Origins of the Prince Hall Mason Master Grand Lodge of Nebraska," *Nebraska History* 76, spring, 1995. Oliver B. Pollak, "The Workman's Circle and Labor Lyceum in Omaha, 1907-1977," *Nebraska History* 76, spring, 1995; William C. Pratt, "Advancing Packinghouse Unionism in South Omaha, 1917-1920," *Journal of the West* 35, April, 1996; and Wilson J. Warren, "The Impasse of Radicalism and Race: Omaha's Meatpacking Unionism, 1945-1955," *Journal of the West* 35, April, 1996, add to the literature on labor history. The evolution of bus transit service in Omaha from 1925 to 1951 is related in G. Mac Sebree's well-illustrated two-part article, "Omaha and Council Bluffs," *Motor Coach Age* 47, January-March and October-December, 1996. For the World War II era, see Douglas R. Hartman, "Lawrence W. Youngman: War Correspondent for the *Omaha World-Herald*," *Nebraska History* 76, summer/fall, 1995.

Two recent University of Nebraska at Omaha theses contribute to local historical literature: Michelle C. Gullett, " 'If Even a Few Souls are Reclaimed, the Labor is not Lost': William Hamilton's Life among the Iowa and Omaha Indians, 1837-1891" (1994), has a chapter on Hamilton's missionary work in Bellevue from 1853 to 1867, and Deborah C. O'Donnell, "The League of Women Voters of Greater Omaha 1920-1995" (1996), surveys the history of an important organization.

Index

City Waterworks Company, 104-5
Civil Rights Act of 1964, 271, 272
Civil War, 2
Civil Works Administration, 199
Claim House, 35
Clancy, William, 38
Clark, William, 5
Cochran, Robert, 203, 204, 230
Coleman, John, 259
Colorado, 15, 18, 19
Colorado Springs, Colorado, 212
Columbia, Nebraska, 27
Commercial Club, 116
Compromise of 1820, 8
ConAgra, 302, 303-5
Congregationalists, 51, 53
Congress of Industrial Organizations, 204
Continental Can Company, 214
Cooper, Peter, 51
Council, Brenda, 316
Council Bluffs, Iowa
    mentioned, 7, 8, 19, 27, 37, 111, 318
    & metropolitan area, 127, 243
    & Mormons, 6
    & steamboats, 15, 16, 19
Council Bluffs and Nebraska Ferry
    Company
    & early Omaha, 10-11, 12, 13, 41
    & founded, 7
    mentioned, 19, 53
Council Bluffs & Omaha Electric Line,
    107
Cousins, Phoebe, 101
Cozzen's House Hotel, 27
Credit Foncier of America, 27
Credit Mobilier of America, 28, 29, 30
Creighton, Edward
    mentioned, 64, 72, 140, 193
    & telegraph, 21, 32
Creighton, James, 21, 99
Creighton, John, 21, 73, 114, 131-32
Creighton, Joseph, 21
Creighton, Mary, 114
Creighton University
    & basketball team, 283
    & blacks, report on, 272
    & description of, 279
    & endowment, 287
    & expansion, 266
    & founded, 114

mentioned, 132, 261
Crime
    early, 45, 46, 47, 48
Criss, Dr. C. C., 214
Criss, Mabel L., 214
Croatians, 162
Crystal Saloon, 91, 92, 94
Cudahy Packing Company, 77, 142, 250
Cuming, Thomas B.
    & acting governor, 12
    & background, 12
    mentioned, 19, 32, 42
    & railroads, 14
Cunningham, Robert, 261, 262, 288
Curry, Dick, 99
Czechoslovakians, 157

Dahlman, James C.
    & background, 177, 179
    & machine, 179-80, 182-83
    & mayor, 176-77
    mentioned, 227, 230, 237, 256
Daily News, 164
Dakota City, Nebraska, 250
Daley, John, 46
Daly, Leo A., 258, 269
Danbaum, Benjamin, 202
Danish Brotherhood, 116, 160
Dargaczewski, "Long Hip," 161
Daub, Hal, 317
Daughters of the American Revolution,
    116
Davidson, Fleming, 38
Davidson, James E.
    & background, 149
    mentioned, 152, 180, 193
    & Nebraska Power, 149-50, 209, 221
Davis, Chester C., 207
Davis, John, 39
Davis, John F., 258
Davis, Thomas, 38
Delaware River, 3, 4
Denmark, 122, 157
Dennison, Thomas
    & background, 180
    & machine, 181-83, 230
    mentioned, 227, 237, 256
Denver, Colorado, 62
Detroit, Michigan, 4
Dickey, J. J., 109

Glenn L. Martin-Nebraska Co., 207-8, 211
Glenwood, Iowa, 14
Golden Observer, 1
Goo's Hotel, 120
Gordon, A. W., 258
Gould, Jay
    & Missouri River Bridge, 65
    mentioned, 131, 148
    & Union Pacific, 74, 129
Government
    early, 54, 56
Grand Army of the Republic, 116
Grand Central Hotel, 109-10
Grange, 81
Grant, Ulysses S., 26
Grasshopper Sam, 96
Great Depression
    & farm prices, 196
    mentioned, 2, 199, 217
    & Omaha, 197-99, 204, 221-22
Great Lakes, 4
Great Plains, 3
"Great Platte River Route," 15
Greeks
    mentioned, 158
    & Omaha, 163
    & riot, 164-66

Hamilton, Charles W., 38
Hamilton, Peter, 194
Hannibal & St. Joseph Railroad, 15, 23
Hanscom, Andrew J., 73, 118
Hanscom Park, 118
Harper, Charles M., 303, 304
Harpers, 292
Harriman, E. H.
    mentioned, 131, 307
    & Union Pacific, 129-30
Hawes, Patrick O., 91
Hearst, William Randolph, 194
Heartland of America Park, 302
Henry Doorly Zoo, 284, 317
Herald, 99, 101
Herndon House, 19, 31, 56
Hibernians, 116
Higgins Packing Company, 142
Hilton Hotel, 266, 269, 288
Hispanics, 308, 311
Hitchcock, Gilbert M.
    & background, 101

& *World-Herald*, 98, 174
Hitchcock, Phineas, 101
Hoffman, Millard, 168, 169, 172
Hoffman Brothers, 142
Hogan, Mae, 183
Holland, Kenneth C., 258
Home of the Good Shepherd, 113
Homestead Act of 1862, 40
Hoover, Herbert, 199
Hopkins, Harry, 201
Horbach, John A., 38
Hosford, Willard D. Jr., 258
Housing, 278, 309-10, 311-13
Houston Natural Gas, 303
Human Relations Board, 273, 274, 275
Hungarians, 157, 162
*Hunt's Merchants' Magazine and
    Commercial Review*, 4-5
H. Z. Vending Co., 261

Ilher, John S., 46-47
Illinois Central Railroad, 40, 130, 131
Independence, Missouri, 6
Independent Order of Good Templars, 116
Independent Order of the Vikings, 160
Indians, 5, 6, 122, 308
Insull, Samuel, 148
Insurance industry, 214-15, 251-52, 307
InterNorth, 302-3
Interstate Highway Act of 1956, 211, 255
Interstate & Street Railway Co., 107
Iowa, 2, 7, 8, 13
Irish, 122, 123, 157, 160-61
Italians, 122, 157, 161-62
Izard, Mark W., 13, 35

Jacksonian Club, 97
Jacobs, Morris E., 258
Jacobson, A. F., 258
Jeffers, William M., 221
Jefferson City, Missouri, 4
Jewish Community Center, 161
Jews, 115, 158, 161
J. J. Brown Block, 120
J. L. Brandeis & Sons, 258, 266, 267
Jobbers' Canyon, 304
John Deere Plow Co., 258
Johnson, Andrew, 29
Johnson, Frank B., 181
Johnson, Lyndon, 252, 255

receipts, 142, 251
South Omaha, 77
Palladium, 13
Panic of 1837, 4
Panic of 1857, 18, 19, 37
Panic of 1873, 61, 66
Panic of 1893, 61, 86, 118, 199
Parks, 118
Patrick, Edwin, 39
Patrons of Husbandry, 81
Pattison, J. W., 9-10, 32
Pawnee Indians, 6
Paxton, William A.
  background, 72-73
  & banking, 79
  mentioned, 131, 140, 193
  & stockyards, 74
Paxton & Vierling Iron Works, 142
Peter Cooper Club, 98
Peter Kiewit Sons Co., 208, 258, 269, 305
Philadelphia, Pennsylvania, 4
Piccinoni, Sam, 223-24
Pick, Lewis A., 211
Pick-Sloan, 211
Pierce, Franklin, 8, 12
Pike's Peak Gold Rush, 18-19
Pinkett, H. J., 166, 169
Pittsburgh, Pennsylvania, 4
Platt-Deutschen Verein, 159
Platte River, 5, 6, 16
Platte River Valley, 2, 6
Platte Valley, 16
Plattsmouth, Nebraska, 12, 14, 18
Pokrok Zapadu, 159
Poles, 157, 161
Polish Citizens' Club, 161
Polish Roman Catholic Union, 161
Polish Union of the United States, 161
Polish Welfare Club, 161
Poppleton, Andrew J., 25, 73
Population, *see* Census figures
Populists, 82, 98, 179
Portland, Oregon, 62
Prairie Music, 1
Preemption Act of 1841, 40
Presbyterians, 51, 53, 114
Promontory Point, Utah, 31
Prostitution, 94-95, 183-84, 287-88
Public transportation, 106-8, 314
Public Works Administration, 199, 206

Pulaski Club, 161
Pulcar, Joseph, 164
Pulitzer Prize, 287

Quality Environment Council, 245

Railroads
  mentioned, 23, 31, 79
  strategy, 63-64
  see also Union Pacific
Rankin, Marshall, B. P., 43
Rapid City, South Dakota, 63
Rawley, Walter H. Jr., 217
Reagan, Ronald, 252, 270
Real Estate Owners' Association, 116
Red Cloud, 179
Red Cross, 231
Religion
  census of 1936, 233
  early Omaha, 51, 53
Republican, 99
Rescue Home Association, 113
Reynolds, A. W., 244
Ricketts, M. O., 167
Ringer, J. Dean, 176
Riots
  black, 273-74, 275
  "Court House" 1919, 168, 169-72
  Greek, 165-66
  traction, 203
Rising Sun, Wisconsin, 3
Riverfront Development Foundation, 262,
  263
Riverfront Development Program, 262,
  263, 297-302
Riverside Park, 118
Rockefeller, William, 132
Rockwell, Norman, 283
Roman Catholics, 51, 114, 115, 161, 162,
  163
Romanians, 162
Rooney, Mickey, 286
Roosevelt, Franklin D., 199, 200, 207,
  227, 271
Roosevelt, Theodore, 179
Rose Blumkin Performing Arts Center,
  317-18
Rosenblatt, John A., 238
Rosewater, Andrew, 105, 106, 118

Utah, 18

Van Buren, Martin, 40
Vandenberg, Hoyt S., 212
Vanderford, Paul, 82
Variety Bazaar, 94
Veterans Administration, 211
Veys, Al, 261, 262, 309, 315
Veys Foodland, 262
Vietnam War, 254
Visiting Nurse Association of Omaha, 113
Vogt, Phil, 244
Vondicka, U. L., 159

Wadman, Robert, 315
Wagner Labor Relations Act of 1935, 204
Walker, Richard W., 258
Wallace, George, 275-76
Waring, George Jr., 105
Water, see City Waterworks Company
Waterworks, 104
Wattle, Gurdon W.
  background, 86
  civil leader, 132, 134, 140
  & grain, 137, 138, 139
  mentioned, 142, 180, 193, 206, 256
  traction problems, 107, 136, 201, 209
  & Trans-Mississippi, 87
Weaver, James B., 81
Werner Enterprises, 307
Western Art Association, 116
Western Engineer, 15
Western Heritage Museum, 284, 286, 317
Western Newspaper Union, 187
Western Pacific Railroad, 307
Western Stage Line, 19
Westin Aquila Hotel, 305
Wherry, Kenneth, 211, 212, 213
Wherry Housing Law, 213
Whitted, Robert B., 38
Williams, John, 168, 174
Williams, Paul, 256-58
Willow Springs Distilling Company, 144
Wilson, Anna, 95
Wilson, Woodrow, 174

Wilson Packing Co., 250
Winter Quarters, Nebraska, 6, 7, 15
Withnell, John, 39
Woman's Christian Temperance Union,
  116
Women
  & business, 311
  & politics, 315, 317
Wood, General Leonard, 172
Woodman Linseed Oil Works, 79
Woodmen of the World, 116, 214, 252
Woodmen of the World Tower, 266, 269,
  292
Woodward, Kenneth, 292
Works Progress Administration
  Federal Writers Project, 222-24, 227
  & Omaha, 199, 206, 221, 225, 230,
  279, 284
  & Tri-County Power, 207
WorldCom, 305
World-Herald
  & city growth, 247
  & construction, 217
  founded, 101
  mentioned, 200, 258, 305
  & Morrison, 274
  & riots, 165, 166, 172, 174
  & Wallace, 276
World War One, 145
World War Two, 2, 206-8, 231
Wyeth, Jamie, 283
Wyoming Stockman's Association, 179

Yates, Henry W., 120
Young, Brigham, 6, 21
Young Men's Christian Association, 113,
  231-32
Young Women's Christian Association,
  113, 231-32

Zelma, Indiana, 3
Zero Population Growth, 245
Zorinsky, Edward
  mayor, 246, 247, 248, 261-62
  & Western Heritage Museum, 284, 286